enchantment of the mind
manmohan
desai's films

Other Lotus Titles:

Aitzaz Ahsan	*The Indus Saga: The Making of Pakistan*
Alam Srinivas	*Storms in the Sea Wind: Ambani vs Ambani*
Chaman Nahal	*Silent Life: Memoirs of a Writer*
Duff Hart-Davis	*Honorary Tiger: The Life of Billy Arjan Singh*
Ed. by: Namita Bhandare	*India and the World: A Blueprint for Partnership and Growth*
Frank Simoes	*Frank Unedited*
Frank Simoes	*Frank Simoes' Goa*
M.J. Akbar	*India: The Siege Within*
M.J. Akbar	*Kashmir: Behind the Vale*
M.J. Akbar	*Nehru: The Making of India*
M.J. Akbar	*Riot after Riot*
M.J. Akbar	*The Shade of Swords*
M.J. Akbar	*Byline*
Meghnad Desai	*Nehru's Hero Dilip Kumar: In the Life of India*
Nayantara Sahgal (ed.)	*Before Freedom: Nehru's Letters to His Sister*
Rohan Gunaratna	*Inside Al Qaeda*
Maj. Gen. Ian Cardozo	*Param Vir: Our Heroes in Battle*
Maj. R.P. Singh, Kanwar Rajpal Singh	*Sawai Man Singh II of Jaipur: Life and Legend*
Mushirul Hasan	*India Partitioned. 2 Vols*
Mushirul Hasan	*John Company to the Republic*
Mushirul Hasan	*Knowledge Power and Politics*
Rachel Dwyer	*Yash Chopra: Fifty Years of Indian Cinema*
Satish Jacob	*From Hotel Palestine Baghdad*
Veena Sharma	*Kailash Mansarovar: A Sacred Journey*
Verghese Kurien as Told to Gouri Salvi	*I Too Had a Dream*

Forthcoming Titles:

Bhawana Somayya	*Hema Malini: An Authorised Biography*
Neesha Mirchandani	*Freedom Song: The Life of Baba Amte*

enchantment of the mind
manmohan
desai's films

Connie Haham
Foreword by **Amitabh Bachchan**

LOTUS COLLECTION
ROLI BOOKS

Lotus Collection

© Connie Haham 2006
All rights reserved. No part of this publication may be reproduced or transmitted, in any form or by any means, without the prior permission of the publisher.

This edition first published in 2006
The Lotus Collection
An imprint of
Roli Books Pvt. Ltd.
M-75, G.K. II Market
New Delhi 110 048
Phones: ++91 (011) 2921 2271, 2921 2782
2921 0886, Fax: ++91 (011) 2921 7185
E-mail: roli@vsnl.com; Website: rolibooks.com
Also at
Bangalore, Mumbai, Varanasi and Jaipur

Cover: Arati Subramanyam
Layout: Kumar Raman

ISBN: 81-7436-431-5

...ion by Roli Books Pvt. Ltd. and printed at Syndicate Binders, Noida - 201 305

contents

Foreword	vii
Acknowledgments	xii
Preface	xiii

manmohan desai
    The Filmmaker, The Man   3

two films in close-up
    Amar Akbar Anthony   29
    Coolie   45

a wide angle on manmohan desai's work
    Kaleidoscope   65
    Kinetics   71
    Technical Choices   76
    The Players   87
    The Child   96
    Comedy   105
    Serious Undertones   114
    Reality   143
    Women   157
    The Manmohan Desai Legacy   177

Endnotes	182
Filmography	186
Bibliography	201

foreword

Clearly, the re-assessment and insightful commentary on Manmohan Desai was long overdue. After all, his films stemmed from a concern with the way people live together and how this co-existence could perhaps even come close to a state of utopia. At the heart of Manmohan Desai's immense oeuvre was an affirmation and celebration of struggle.

Manji, as he was called by those who loved and admired him, would perhaps balk at any cerebral analysis or research about his films. Without knowing it—like all great masters—effortlessly he had posited significant sub-texts into his hyper-fantasies, which to the superficial eye seemed like fleeting, will-o'-the-wisp entertainers.

Somewhere within, he was quite prescient about the fact that his films, as a collective whole, would be ultimately accorded their just estimation by the critics, thinkers and academicians. 'Laugh at me today,' he would tell his detractors good-naturedly, 'but mark my words, you'll appreciate my work some day, even if it's too late.'

It's never too late. Indeed it's a matter of personal pride for me that at long last, Manmohan Desai has been given his richly deserved stature in the pantheon of film greats.

In film after film, he had set his own rules of right conduct, a fierce sense of loyalty towards fellow-beings and above all, a deep veneration of the mother figure. At a time, around the 1970s, when families all over the world were splintering and it had become fashionable for young people to go independent, he insisted that parents came above God and of course, above self. Hurt them and you hurt yourself, was his simple, oft-repeated credo which continues to echo in the techno-savvy cinema of today.

Needless to say, Manji has been frequently imitated but never quite equalled. Not by a long shot. Because part of the distinctive drive and brio of his work came from his instinctive belief that films are a temporal as well as a spatial medium. He loved flamboyant colour, costume, and décor, but he never allowed these elements to freeze into static compositions. A genius of changing patterns and complex movements, he filled his pictures with swooping crane shots, voluptuous displays of story telling, dance-music-action, superbly colloquial dialogue and spontaneously orchestrated background detailing.

Stylistically and thematically, Manmohan Desai's films might be described as 'fantasticated' expressions of romantic idealism. In fact, love, honour, separation, vindication and reunion were his abiding obsessions. While recounting those deceptively believe-it-or-not stories, he retained that key element of wonderment. He was akin to a child who had lost himself in a fairground, had clambered onto a Ferris wheel and could have enjoyed the ride till kingdom come. He never betrayed the slightest sign of exhaustion; he continued to be an irrepressible *ranconteur* even when a chronic backache confined him to a hardboard chair.

The diverse personalities of the dramatic director and the extravagant producer coalesced in Manji. His films generally took place in scenic outdoor locations or in studio-manufactured settings, where the boundaries between fantasy and everyday life could be transgressed.

Maybe it was the shortsightedness of the film commentators of the time that drew the simplistic comment that his work was absurd, far-fetched, incredible and unreal. Compared to the inter-planetary adventures of Steven Spielberg and George Lucas, Manmohan Desai's foreverland was as familiar and as authentic as the people living next door. 'See, people praise Spielberg's imagination but have problems with mine,' he would declare with bemusement.

Rationalists quibbled but audiences adored him. They wanted more. The criticism that Manji belted out films which were so fast, furious and funky that the viewers were not allowed any time to think, just doesn't hold any water today. The fact is that several of his films—*Sachaa Jhutha, Aa Gale Lag Jaa, Amar Akbar Anthony, Naseeb* and *Coolie* to name a few—have achieved cult status, constantly inviting thought, discussion, and most hearteningly, hosannas of approval.

Any list of films which have advocated secularism is now topped by *Amar Akbar Anthony*. When it was released, its full-throttle message of communal harmony wasn't perceived, but it is acknowledged unconditionally today. True to his nature, Manmohan Desai never spoke about his films' agenda because he didn't have to.

Stories came to him naturally, inspired infallibly by the conditions and people around him. Anthony was a drunken lout he had encountered oftentimes in the back alleys of Khetwadi, a cramped city area where Manmohan Desai felt completely at home. No wonder, he retreated back to the congestion and the crowds after shifting for a short while to the upscale Malabar Hill.

To know Manmohan Desai was to know a man of compassion. Despite the tremendous success of his films, his feet never left the ground. His screenplays often germinated from major and minor incidents, which he may have read in the newspapers or heard about from his neighbourhood gully cricket pals. He belonged to an era when the director was an *auteur*, imprinting a firm signature on every frame of his films. And his signature was of a spry wizard who coaxed the audience towards a wild and improbable realm, and yet remained strongly rooted in the soil. A paradox yes, but a splendid, unparalleled one.

The story ideas of *Amar Akbar Anthony* and *Coolie* were inspired by real life. If they seemed like fantasies, it was because his USP was to make the tough reality palatable, underscored by optimism. His valorous protagonists did not die in his films; they lived even after they had been riddled with bullets. The most obvious example of this was the recovery of the eponymous Coolie, attacked by gunfire at the Haji Ali durgah. Miraculously, in real life too, I survived a serious physical injury on the sets of the same film. His concern and prayers were always with me, as they were indeed with all the actors and technical crew whom he treated as an extended family.

Whether it was at a music sitting, a script brainstorm or a shooting schedule, Manji was the livewire. His enthusiasm and self-belief were immediately infectious. Nothing was impossible for him to conceive and execute, from a helicopter flight over the London skyline, a shootout in a revolving restaurant or a chase atop a speeding train. He encouraged actors to delve deeper into themselves, and discover facets they didn't know existed.

From my personal experience, I can say the drunken act, which I came to be associated with, was tossed off by him—in the snap of a finger just as the camera was about to roll. The soliloquy addressed to my mirror image is remembered to date for the hilarity that Manji invested in a sequence that everyone thought was unimaginable.

From his first film on, the black-and-white *Chhalia*, featuring the stalwarts Raj Kapoor and Nutan, it was evident that the young man in his 20s then, would redefine Hindi cinema. He did just that, unfazed by the fluctuating trends and fads right till *Gungaa Jamunaa Saraswathi*. Eventually he handed over the reins to his son Ketan, but there were still many more films that were ticking in his heart and mind. Everyone who knew him was convinced that he would be back in action, with renewed vigour.

Manji was full of surprises. He suddenly upped and decided to go, he left just as a fist disappears when we open our palm. He had the last laugh.

A study of his incalculable cinema was pending for decades. I am deeply grateful for the painstaking years that Connie Haham has spent on the book. Her dedication, understanding and appreciation of Manmohan Desai are palpable in every page and word.

The author has been one of the earliest and unwavering supporters of popular Indian cinema. With this book, she has contributed immeasurably in preserving the memory of the great director and the great man. A humanist who never said he was one.

Thank you Connie. On behalf of Manmohan Desai, myself and the undiminished legion of admirers of the Manji of real miracles.

Amitabh Bachchan

acknowledgments

My thanks to Nasreen Munni Kabir for encouraging me to undertake this project, to *Filmfare* magazine for access to their archives, to critic Louis Marcorelles of *Le Monde* for his kind and repeated encouragement, to film critic Michel Ciment whose intellectual integrity and thoroughness during weekly radio debates have inspired me, to my husband and children for making the major adjustments necessary to allow me to spend a month researching in Bombay and also to Urvashi Butalia, P.K. Nair, Bikram Singh, Gul Anand, Edward H. Johnson, Prakash Pange, Uday Row Kavi and Rao Chelikani, and Johnana Clark, Helene Meyers, Keith Walters, Philip Lutgendorf, Henri Micciollo, Dipa Chaudhuri, and to all those who were good enough to grant me interviews.

preface

1 March 2004 marked the tenth death anniversary of Manmohan Desai. A fall from the terrace of his Khetwadi home brought the 57-year-old filmmaker's life to an end in the spring of 1994. The suspected suicide came as a shock both to those nearest to him and to the film world as a whole, as testified in countless articles and tributes in the Indian and international press in the month following his death. The articles that appeared spanned the gamut of reactions: praise for Desai as a man and as a filmmaker, heartfelt remembrances from those who had worked with him, indignation and disbelief over the circumstances of his death, and speculation over possible motives for suicide—depression over severe backaches being most frequently offered as an explanation.

At that time, I could not help feeling a personal sadness over his death. I had, after all, spent the better part of four years studying Manmohan Desai's work before completing an initial version of this book in 1987. It was, therefore, consoling to have immediate and direct evidence of Desai's work living on beyond his death, as happened one day in 1994 when I walked into an Indian carry-out restaurant in Paris and saw a colourful dance scene from *Dharam-Veer* playing on the conspicuously placed

VCR. Those waiting in line stood transfixed before the screen, their faces radiating joy. Curious to know if Desai's work had crossed the generations, I asked a young man in his twenties if he knew who had directed the film. 'Manmohan Desai,' came the answer without hesitation. Now, films, we know, come and go. Only the best remain in the public memory. Just as in the West each new generation has rediscovered *Casablanca, It's A Wonderful Life,* or *The Wizard Of Oz,* so in India, there are examples—*Shree 420, Mother India, Mughal-e-Azam* and *Sholay,* among others—that have come to be classics. Some of Manmohan Desai's films have joined that select group of films that never die, that remain etched on so many individual psyches that they become a part of a shared collective memory.

This book covers Manmohan Desai's filmmaking from 1960 to 1988, but with special emphasis on what might be called the 'Desai years,' a time when Manmohan Desai was a major trendsetter and the biggest moneymaker in the film industry, a time when younger directors measured their own success against the Desai standard. In a fit of fevered activity between 1975 and 1985, Desai made nine films, all very successful, with *Coolie* and *Amar Akbar Anthony* reaching Platinum Jubilees, *i.e.,* 75 weeks' continued showing. Following the release of *Gangaa Jamunaa Saraswathi* in 1988, Desai left active directing. He continued his involvement with the film industry more indirectly through his son Ketan's *Allahrakha* (1986), *Toofan* (1989) and *Anmol* (1993). But by that time, the 'Desai years' were over; unfortunately, so too was Manmohan Desai's life one year later.

That an American teacher of English in Paris would write a book on Manmohan Desai's cinema probably raises questions. In partial explanation and as an introduction, let me relate my discovery of Hindi popular cinema.

Generally speaking, I enjoy coming in contact with different cultures. I am also a fervent movie-goer. Living in Paris has allowed me to combine these two interests quite conveniently.

Here, I have been able to roam new worlds from the comfort of motion picture theatre seats. With a selection of over 300 films per week, Paris offers journeys through time and space for relatively modest sums—with the added benefit of freedom from jet lag. During the 1970s I saw films from China, Senegal, Mexico, the U.S.S.R., Japan, Poland, Italy, Iran, and many countries more. Yet I remained dissatisfied ... .

Among those who are attracted to cultures other than their own, it is common to find individual preferences in favour of one country over others. An affinity can spark curiosity or curiosity can reveal an affinity. Which comes first is often difficult to say. In my case, it is clear that India always interested me. Reading fiction and non-fiction had opened the doors to the country. I was disappointed then that Paris, even with its abundance of films, offered no cinematic trips there ... or so I thought.

In 1979 in one of the theatres in town, the first International Third World Film Festival was organized with an impressive selection of Indian films on the programme. I went off in high hopes of seeing what Indian cinema was about. I had only an inkling. In the Algerian film *Omar Gatlato* (by Merzak Allouache, 1976) the hero Omar watches *Mangala El Bedouina* (what I later learned was *Aan*, Mehboob Khan, 1952), and for several seconds we watch the film along with him. I wondered why the Algerians were permitted to see these delightful and colour-filled films while we in Paris—by many standards the film capital of the world—were not. Disappointingly, the Indian films did not arrive; African films were shown instead. However, the festival left me not only with images of the red soil of Burkina Faso but also with a teasing and intriguing printed list of the programmed Indian films. Synopses of *Mother India*, *Pyaasa*, *Do Ankhen Barah Haath* and others whetted my appetite. India obviously had a long cinematic heritage and boasted a wealth of films. It seemed all the stranger that we in Paris did not see them. At that point I could not have guessed that Indian films had already been playing regularly in town for some time.

There was no way to know about the Avron Palace or the Delta unless one happened to pass by or to learn about them through the immigrant communities' grapevines. These two cinemas never had their films listed in the weekly film line-up magazines. One week, though, an exception was made. The name *Amar Akbar Anthony* appeared on the same footing as the new French, American, Japanese and Italian films released that week. Though I was eager to see the film, I could not help feeling a bit uneasy as I imagined possibly finding myself the only woman in the midst of an all-male audience at the Avron Palace. Pushing these doubts aside, I gave rein to my curiosity.

The exact time of each show was not listed in the cinema guide. I tried to gauge my arrival to coincide with the second Sunday showing. Of course, since I was using European time logic, I miscalculated. My initial error was to suppose that the first show would actually begin as announced, at 2:30 p.m. In fact, I later learned, a 2:30 show could begin any time between 2:30 and 3:15. My second mistake was to suppose the film would be two hours long. In reality, it lasted almost three hours. Finally, I did not take into consideration the intermission time, as I had never seen a film with a twenty-minute break that allowed the audience to stretch their legs and eat *samosas*. The sum of my faulty assumptions led me to arrive before the intermission of the first show.

I need not have worried about the proportion of men to women in the audience. Entire families filled the screening room. The seats were wooden. I managed to find one of the two vacant ones on the front row, and for the next few hours, I more or less stopped breathing. In spite of some 15 'No Smoking' signs posted around the hall in French and in English, cigarette smoke enveloped the audience in a thick haze. Normally, I would find any sort of enjoyment impossible under such conditions. A part of me (my lungs) wanted to head immediately for fresh air, but another part of me was instantly enthralled. My lungs lost.

I had not the slightest idea what was happening in the story. The characters were many and confusing. I thought the one called Salma was several different women because in one scene she was singing and dancing, in another scene, working as a doctor, in another, being chased into the house by her tyrannical father, in another, wearing a black robe and veil, in another, working as a seamstress with her husband. There was a rich man who became poor and a poor man who became rich. There was a mother who started out with tuberculosis and then spent much of the film blind until a miracle restored her eyesight. The miracle took place in front of a statue to which the Muslim Akbar was singing, something that I found unthinkable, given my previous exposure to Islam through the Arab world. The one called Anthony was unmistakable even in all his disguises, but I could not understand how he sometimes could be so tough and sometimes so silly, even stupid. He seemed to be involved in all sorts of illicit doings, and yet on Sunday he was all dressed up, playing the organ at church. I think that following the story would have been impossible in any circumstances, but my confusion was confounded because I saw the second half of the film first and, likewise, because the French subtitles were not at all synchronized. I could never be sure if what I was reading was what was being said, what had just been said, or what was about to be said.

I would not have been capable of retelling the story after I left; nor did I understand why the characters on screen had acted and reacted as they did. However, my perplexity did not dampen my spirits. On the contrary, it further kindled my interest. And the song, dance, colour, and comedy enchanted me, even left me bubbling for days. I felt I had reentered the magic world that cinema had represented for me as a child when I had wholeheartedly participated in each film, leaving myself behind for a few hours in order to live fully with the characters on the screen. I knew that I had to see more such films, both for the pleasure of the viewing and also to satisfy my curiosity about the logic of the genre.

As I tried to grasp what I had seen, naturally enough, I made analogies with what I already knew. Thus, *Amar Akbar Anthony* seemed to be a mixture of Shakespearean comedy with unlikely chance meetings and situational turnarounds, of Elvis Presley fight-sing-and-dance films, of Yiddish stories with touching mother-son scenes, of cowboy or gangster bad-guy sequences, of Tarzan-style rope swinging to save those in danger, and of a Three-Musketeers spirit of camaraderie—the whole spiced with what I supposed to be a very Indian view of mystical healing and religious tolerance.

Seeing *Amar Akbar Anthony* proved a lucky encounter. I could have happened upon some violent, plotless, badly acted film and never wanted to see another Indian film again. Thanks to *Amar Akbar Anthony*, I was back at the Avron Palace the following week to see *Trishul*. Fascination flamed. And I decided, as I later learned millions of others around the world had done, that the actor who had played Anthony in *Amar Akbar Anthony* and Vijay in *Trishul* was absolutely electrifying. Studying the film posters, I deduced his name to be Amitabh Bachchan.

I began to see one or two films every week. Some films I saw again and again, each time they were programmed. Gradually, the stories that had seemed so exotic that I had had trouble following them began to make sense. I could guess in advance the reactions the characters were likely to have. The element of repetition from scenario to scenario made the stories more understandable but also removed some of the initial pleasure of the discovery. It became clear that quality was uneven in Indian cinema. I became more discerning, my tastes more defined in actors, directors and scriptwriters. I reached a point at which I would not see just any film that was playing. But I tried never to miss an Amitabh Bachchan starrer, a film with Raakhee, a film scripted by Salim-Javed, or any film made by Ramesh Sippy, Yash Chopra, or Prakash Mehra. A visit to London brought me in contact with a slightly more highbrow Hindi cinema. Seeing *Junoon* was a new and passionate experience. Afterwards, I made a point never to miss a Shyam Benegal film at film festivals I attended. The uncertainty of the subtitling led me to study Hindi. Little by little, on video and at the theatre, I became acquainted with classics such as *Diamond Queen, Mother India, Shree 420, Awaara, Gunga Jamuna, Pyaasa*, and more. I found them all interesting. But Desai's films, I slowly realized, held a very special attraction.

Initially, Manmohan Desai's name was not a drawing card for me. After all, I had seen only his *Amar Akbar Anthony*. A few months later I watched *Dharam-Veer*, unaware of who had directed it. The period, the costumes, and the style were unlike anything I had seen to date. Throughout the viewing, I felt the story was being told on two levels at once—in dead earnest and with tongue-in-cheek. I laughed and enjoyed the film, but I also felt a bit puzzled, as though a key necessary for understanding was just beyond my reach. Studying the publicity poster outside after the show, my glance fell on Desai's name and the key clicked in the lock. Of course, I thought, here again was that same speed, that same colour and liveliness, that same marvellous sense of humour, and that same theme of fate first separating and then reuniting a family. Though *Dharam-Veer* seemed unique, it nevertheless carried marks of the guiding hand responsible for *Amar Akbar Anthony*. Manmohan Desai's name went on my list of directors to watch for. Still, I thought, his films were not worthy of serious consideration. They were too much fun.

One day *Sholay* was billed with *Amar Akbar Anthony* in a double feature. I preferred to see *Sholay*: first, because I had already seen *Amar Akbar Anthony* three times while I had only seen *Sholay* twice, and second, because *Sholay*, I felt sure, was a more estimable film. The schedule at the Avron Palace was extremely flexible. What was programmed for 2:30 often ran at 6:00 and vice versa. So it is that I saw *Amar Akbar Anthony* by chance for the fourth time and missed *Sholay*. My reaction at the beginning of the film was both disappointment and a bit of scorn. After all, *Amar Akbar Anthony* was nonsense. No matter that I had shaken with laughter the first three times I had seen it. *Sholay*, on the other hand, was dramatic and thus important. We cry at the end when Jai dies. Obviously, sorrow weighs heavier in the balance than mirth.

It was not until several months later at the end of my fifth viewing of *Amar Akbar Anthony*, when I was still laughing, still having my fancy tickled and still seeing details I had missed in earlier viewings, that I realized what some geniuses of the medium had already learned: comedy well done has a nobility of its own. A film with a serious content may actually take less effort to make into a success because of the basic bias of the public who enjoy a good comedy but who refuse to respect it as highly as a good drama.

By now, I have seen *Amar Akbar Anthony* more than twenty times and listened to its sound track at least fifty times. The initial joy remains. It is this joyful response that has led me to explore Manmohan Desai's work ever more closely, to view all of his films, to travel to India's Hollywood—Bombay as it was still called in 1984—in order to interview the director himself and to see him at work. Finally, it was the continued enthusiasm I felt over my discoveries that prompted me to write this book.

Paris, 2005

manmohan desai

the filmmaker, the man

khetwadi

Manmohan Desai was born to Kalavati and Kikubhai Desai on 26 February 1937, the third child in the family. Though his roots were Gujarati, Desai's home was always Bombay, a city that he loved and that he often portrayed on screen. He was four years old when he began living in his much-loved Khetwadi neighbourhood.

In 1984, neither Khetwadi district nor Manmohan Desai's street was marked on the map of Bombay. The tourist bureau had never heard of it. In most parts of the city the taxi drivers, too, gave a blank look when shown the address of MKD Films and suggested trying another driver. But Khetwadi was not inconveniently located, hidden or inaccessible. Only a short walk away was the bustling Grant Road, well-known to the movie-going public for the many theatres that lined it. On the sidewalks, here more than elsewhere, vendors hawked film-related wares: picture postcards of film stars, booklets of film songs and dialogues, and even box loads of photos taken on film sets. Khetwadi was on the back streets, protected from this hustle-bustle. On Dr. Bhajekar Street was a large building marked Jeevan Complex. In 1984 it was still in very mediocre condition. Later it was entirely remodelled so as to exude the air of wealth that one would expect from the office and lodgings of a successful film producer. Even in 1984, the already refashioned two-room ground-floor office with its marble floors and walls provided a sharp contrast with the surrounding neighbourhood. Yet the air conditioning and the inner luxury did not create a fortress effect. Desai was not cut off from the outside. Indeed, he was constantly glancing through his windows at the street beyond, taking note and gathering inspiration. His street looked not unlike Kishanlal's in *Amar Akbar Anthony*. 'Khetwadi may not be the centre of the world,' he said, 'but from here I can see the joys and sorrows of the middle class; mainly Gujaratis and Maharashtrians live here.'

The word 'office', for many people, brings to mind desks, chairs, maybe bookshelves, file cabinets, and typewriters or computers. Desai's office was nothing of the sort. A door opened from the hallway into a medium-sized white room. The workspace was a huge semi-circular couch-bed covered with a white sheet and elevated on a platform, with cushions against three walls. Desai was attached not only to the neighbourhood, but also to that room.

> Right from the time I was nobody, I used to sit here and make scripts. My wife Jeevanprabha used to bring some snacks for me to eat. Since that time I've been working on all my scripts here. This room is very lucky. Many hit songs were made here as well as the scripts for *Vaada*, *Aa Gale Lag Jaa*, and *Roti*. For my son Ketan's script we are stuck at a certain stage, so I said, 'From Monday we're sitting here, from morning to evening.' Writers now tend to want to stay in five-star hotels while they work on scripts. I say, 'Okay, but when you get stuck, you come back here.' This is where I lived as a boy.

Not only purely creative work went on in his 'lucky room'. Business had to be discussed with financiers. Reports on earnings needed to be heard, practical problems solved, many and sundry questions answered. During the remodelling of Jeevan Complex, Desai was called upon several times each hour to make decisions about the quality and colour of the tiles and fabrics to be used. Quickly and assuredly, he chose simple colours and careful harmonies.

At lunchtime, a tray was wheeled out; work slowed but did not stop; discussion continued between Desai and his assistants about matters at hand. With lunch over, however, work came to a halt. It was naptime.

> After lunch I must have an hour's nap. I can go to the next room and take my nap. That's a dirty habit I have. Even when we're shooting, I have a quick lunch and for forty-five minutes I have my nap. By the time I give my shot to the cameraman, I say, 'Look, don't get ready for half an hour. Take half an hour for lighting the shot so I can finish my nap.' I must have my nap because otherwise I feel disgusted after five o'clock in the evening. I don't go to sleep. I close my eyes, have my forty winks, and I feel very fresh after that. Then if they make me work up to 9:00 p.m., I don't say a word.... That's how I function. Let me shut my eyes for half an hour. Then I'm a king again. Otherwise, I'm very irritated, very jittery, dull.

From the ground floor one could take an elevator upstairs, the two-floor walk up being sometimes impossible for Manmohan Desai who had, more than once, injured his legs or his back while playing cricket. Secretaries and clerks were busy at desks. Typewriters and file cabinets created the atmosphere of a more traditional office. This was the paperwork area. Agendas were studied. Information was stored. Desai seemed more comfortable in his 'lucky room' downstairs.

Nighttime came and work went on. It was January 1984. Downstairs, a music session was about to begin in preparation for the MKD production *Allahrakha*, the first directorial venture for Desai's son Ketan. Music director Anu Malik was on the harmonium. Two other musicians backed him up, one on the drum, one on the strings. Manji (as Manmohan Desai was affectionately known), Ketan, Anu Malik, and the man who supervised the tape recorder filled up the semi-circular couch-bed. Anu Malik introduced a tune and several lines that he had been preparing. He sang with a big smile and the kind of bubbling energy that appealed to Desai. Desai himself was lying down; his back was bothering him again. He wore casual Indian dress, shoes off, rings on his fingers, a twinkle in his eye. Doctor's orders were soon forgotten. The enthusiasm and the energy conveyed through the tune soon brought him to sitting position. He began clapping, singing along, gesturing *qawwali*-style with his hands and arms, and predicting the song would be a smashing success. One by one, the participants added a word, a line or a musical swirl. Desai added his own and okayed others. The volume mounted. Hyperbole was in the air. 'Super!' 'Great!' 'Terrific!' 'I'll pay anything to have this film made! People will be standing in line just to see this song!' The overstatement and the passion that characterized Desai's films were to be found in their making.

Desai had no doubt given an outline of the story situation to Anu Malik in their last meeting. He now explained the setting in greater detail. Ketan added a suggestion to further build up the scene. The words and the music were inseparable. At the starting point was the cliché, but as the group played with the sounds, intricacies were added; variations and elaborations soon brought originality and individuality. Several more lines to the song were developed. A look from the harmonium player or from Desai gave the strings or the drum permission to stand out for a few moments. '*Ah, ah, wah, wah!*' (Bravo!) The whole room was in movement. Another verse took form. Then it was back to the chorus, '*Kasam na dena, o-o-o! Kasam na lena, o-o-o! Kasam denewale kasam tor dete hain.*' Everyone seemed to savour the sounds and to delight in rolling them about in their mouths.

During a tea break Desai elaborated his theories on film music:

> I must always like a song. But for a good song, there's always a situation. The situation comes before the scene and doesn't force the scene. Naushad, before 1960, made the greatest music ever, the simplest possible tunes. I want a song for children, a song my granddaughter Pooja will sing. I want to make a song so strong, so appealing that people will forget themselves and start throwing money. I want simple words so that even those who don't speak Hindi will understand. I am inspired by Raj Kapoor's films, his style of music. I like accordion music. I like his style of tunes, simple. I believe a tune should be so simple that even a man who doesn't know how to sing can hum a tune. That's a hit song.... That's his forte. I wish I had learnt the piano because if I had, I could have composed the music for all my songs. Anu Malik is working on *Mard*, a very bright boy. He's like a man charged, and I get the best out of him.

Then Desai gave his down-to-earth translation of the chorus that had just been created, 'Promises are bullshit. Don't take them. Don't make them.' Tea was over. Work began anew. Desai introduced another situation he had imagined for his film. Anu Malik offered several possible tunes. A tune could spark a word; a word could trigger a tune. The enthusiasm and the volume quickly mounted again. Vibrations were bouncing off the marble and the mirrors on the walls. Desai neighed like a horse or added other sound effects that provoked images of the scene taking shape.

Finally, it was late. Everyone was anxious to return home. Principally, the group had been working on two songs during the evening. Neither was completely finished. The tape recorder would act as a memory and give the starting point during the next music session.

beginnings

Manmohan: his name literally meant 'mind charmer'—'*Man*': mind; '*Mohan*': enchantment, charm. It was a fitting name considering the enchanting fantasy that he brought to the screen. Manmohan Desai himself saw his name in a different light and found it appropriate for other reasons:

> Manmohan is one of the names of Krishna. My father and mother must have given me the name because they knew I'd turn out a womanizer; they gave me the correct name. Once I told my wife that if I womanize, it's not my fault. My father gave me the name Manmohan, that Charlie who had one thousand *gopis*—women—around him. So if I have a couple... . She said, 'That's no excuse!'

While at one moment Desai was ready to use his namesake's activities as a rationalization for his own behaviour, at other moments he vehemently lashed out against the lord he considered to be unworthy of worship:

> Krishna! He's no god! He left Rukmani for Radha. Why glorify a man who has a mistress, who was a womanizer with all those *gopis!* And he won the whole Mahabharata war by cheating, by deceit, treachery. I have no respect for Krishna. He makes my blood boil. I've talked to pundits, but they can't answer my questions about Krishna!

Manmohan Desai was as energetic talking as filmmaking. His boisterous enthusiasm whipped contagiously through the room as he added rhythm and emphasis to his speech by raising his arms, beating the air and slapping the back of one hand against the palm of the other. Finally, he punctuated his sentences with a nervous tick, drawing his forefinger assertively under his nose to the accompaniment of a loud sniff. He spoke at such a rapid clip that it was often difficult to catch each word, but when he decelerated, his intonation became eloquently lilting. His voice was that of a much younger man, and in 1984 at 46, when he broke into song, one could easily have divided his age in half. By his own admission, he was no diplomat. His rage at his pet peeves was unapologetic, uncompromising, and easily provoked. Lord Krishna, school, and art films were a few of the subjects that sparked his fury. If he was not one to mince words, neither was he one to economize them. He often repeated himself to embellish a story or to drive home a point.

This is Manmohan Desai's story as he told it:[1]

My father was a film producer. He made films between 1931 and 1941. He made about 32 films, mostly stunt films.[2] We had our own studios, but he died at the age of 39, due to a ruptured appendix. The irony was that there was no penicillin, but penicillin was discovered one month after he died. We had a very big bungalow in Versova, with a fleet of cars and servants. My mother, my brother who died (Subhash) and my sister and I came here (to his office in Khetwadi). I was about three or four. We came back to just nothing. My father had two or three films on the set. He died suddenly with heavy liabilities, debts. So my mother said, 'No, I don't want to live with debts.' She sold the bungalow, sold the cars, everything. We paid off the debts and we stayed in these four rooms here on a meagre Rs. 500. She fought like a tigress while we were growing up. She didn't sell the studio. She said, 'That's my monthly income; I must have some money coming in.'

Then in 1955 when my brother was an assistant production manager at Homi Wadia's, he decided to become a full-fledged producer of mythological films like *Sati Naag Kanya* and *Janam Janam Ke Phere*. Then he made a historical film with Babubhai Mistry, *Samrat Chandragupta* (starring Bharat Bhushan and Nirupa Roy). I was in school. Instead of playing cricket as school captain, I was chasing girls, so I failed in the second year there. My brother gave me a chance as an assistant director under Babubhai Mistry, my guru. I learned under him. He was a master special effects man, and is even now. But to do special effects, you have to have patience. I didn't have patience then. I didn't learn special effects; the technique is slow and tiring. A pity, because it would have helped me now. But I did learn direction. I learned the importance of being precise, how a director must prepare his scene to the last detail and then go on the set. I assisted him in *Samrat Chandragupta* and *Bedard Zamana Kya Jane* in 1957.

In 1959 I got married. My wife (Jeevanprabha Gandhi) lived just across the street. It was a love marriage. She used to smile at me from the window. She was Marathi. My family was Gujarati.

So my brother said, 'I'll give you a chance as a director. Who do you want in your film?'

I said, 'I'm a great fan of Raj Kapoor and Nutan.' ...I was only 22.

Raj Kapoor said, 'Okay, he's your brother. Fine, but can he direct? I'll see him for a couple of days, and if not, Mr. Desai, we'll change the director.' Fortunately, my brother didn't tell me I was under trial. I would have been nervous. Instead, I shot with great confidence. I still like the title song *Chhalia*, a very lovely song. After I shot it, Raj Kapoor was so pleased. He said, 'Oh, you're on!' That film was made in 1960 and was very well acclaimed by the press. That's the only film of mine that has been acclaimed by the press. It did fairly well, but it got crushed under *Mughal-e-Azam* which was released at the same time.

The next film was my brother's *Bluff Master* with Shammi Kapoor and Saira Banu. My brother became too ambitious. He announced three or four big projects with Dilip Kumar and others. *Bluff Master* was delayed because of all sorts of problems, artistes and so on. My brother had to compromise and release an almost unfinished film. It had some good sequences though. The *'Govinda ala re'* dance is remembered to this day. I shot it on the streets here in Khetwadi. The police as well as the local *'dadas'* (dons) helped me to control the mobs who all wanted to touch Shammi Kapoor. But it didn't click. Once the film failed, my brother failed too. He was insolvent. Here they say nothing succeeds like success. That was in 1963. I had no work. I would sit at the window waiting for some producer who would come and sign me. I wouldn't go knocking at doors. I had too much self-respect. Someone asked me to direct a Dara Singh mythological. But my wife said, 'No, we'll wait. Someone else will come.'

A producer would ring me up and say he was coming. Then he wouldn't show up. So two years went past without any work. It's a tribute to my wife how she managed to run the house with our little savings. Whatever little ornaments we had were sold. But Sunday at

6:30 p.m., I had to see an English film, even at that time. So she would go to the theatre and get tickets for me on Tuesday. Then we would go together by bus to see that film on Sunday. She struggled. She ran the house beautifully. She never made me feel that I had no work and we were broke. Somehow, she managed to get two square meals on the table.

Then Shammi Kapoor offered me a film called *Budtameez*. We had worked together in *Bluff Master*, and I liked him and he liked me. I was told to finish doing the film that someone else had started, that it was about thirty days' work and I would get Rs. 500 per day. When I saw the incomplete film, I didn't like it, so I reshot the whole film without taking any additional money from the producers.

For four or five years I had no work, except for three days' shooting in maybe two months. That was when I wrote the script for *Raaj Kumar*. Then Ramanand Saagar came to (work on) the film, changed the script, and wanted his name put on it. But I got the money. *Budtameez* did fairly well. There was a comic in that film. Mr. Kamal Mehra, who liked my work as a director, and produced the film *Kismat*. I still like that film very much. I put a lot of hard work into it. I feel it has the best action climax ever in any Indian film. The climax involved boats, helicopters. We were working waist-deep in slush, among snakes and one day I thought we were all going to drown. We had come to a place off-shore where we were knee-deep in water. Suddenly, the tide started coming in, first up to our waists, then up to our necks. Babita's father was there cursing, 'You're going to kill my daughter!' There was only one boat, so only two or three people could leave at once. Fortunately, the water didn't rise any more, and we were able to get out okay. It was an exciting fight scene on the water, and it was exciting to shoot it.

That film did fairly well, and I got *Sachaa Jhutha*, thanks to Kalyanji Anandji who were with me in *Chhalia*. My brother gave them breaks. My brother gave lots of people breaks. He made them music directors. He made me a director, Babubhai Mistry a director. So Kalyanji liked my story idea, and he recommended me to the producers. I wrote the whole script right here with my wife.

Sometimes, if I was stuck, we would take the bus to Malabar and sit under the trees. From 11.00 a.m. to 5.00 p.m., I would sit there. My son was small. He would play. I would sit alone or with an assistant just to toss ideas. I didn't have a writer then. Those were struggling days. I gave the dialogue writing to Prayag Raj. That was for *Sachaa Jhutha*. It was made fast and became a big hit. I did some novel things in it like presenting a dog in a courtroom scene. There was the character of the sister too. A whole song, partly happy, partly sad was dedicated to her. When the hero sings *'Meri pyari beheniya'* all the brothers and sisters in the audiences must have laughed and wept. Rajesh Khanna had a double role in the film. He was just becoming a big star in those days and I gave people two Rajesh Khannas for the price of one.

I didn't work hard enough on my next release *Shararat*. I couldn't develop the situation of a village girl impersonating a city girl well enough. Mumtaz was also just about okay in the role. The film flopped so fast that no one realized it had come and gone. Then came the Nadiadwalas. They had seen the climax of *Kismat*. They were fascinated by that climax. In 1971, I was signed up for *Bhai Ho To Aisa*. Both the film and I went up like rockets. My original teacher Babubhai Mistry helped me to picturize all those tricky scenes with cobras. The film also had an interesting plot dealing with two brothers.

Then another Nadiadwala brother signed me for his film *Raampur Ka Lakshman*. The lost-and-found stuff was there again. It was a hit. The film had catchy music. Shatrughan Sinha had a powerful role. Daboo (Randhir Kapoor) was also very young and fresh then. I used to insist that he should act like his father did in *Shree 420*. That's because I admire the way Raj Kapoor used to look and act. If it was possible, I'd try to make everyone, all character actors, even Manmohan Krishna, act like Raj. For the Nadiadwalas, I did *Bhai Ho To Aisa, Raampur Ka Lakshman, Aa Gale Lag Jaa. Parvarish* was the last one.

I made *Dharam-Veer* on the biggest scale ever. It also turned out to be my biggest hit though it was slaughtered by the censors during the Emergency. I know a certain section of the industry was behind this, but who cares; they couldn't stop its success. Dharmendra's father was so pleased when he saw it that he said, *'Maine mere bete ko khilaya, pilaya, bada kiya, issi film ke lie.'* (I fed and raised my son just for this film.)

I directed *Chacha Bhatija* from Salim-Javed's script because Dharmendra asked me to. I had plenty of problems with these so-called storywriters. I like to be left alone, but they always wanted to poke their noses in. The film's strongest point was its exciting climax.

Desai rejected the notion that his success was related to the general upswing in the film industry in the seventies. Continuing to look to the past, he explained his theory of the importance of destiny:

From 1970 everything has gone my way. But in 1967 I wrote a film called *Vaada*. I still feel it was the best script ever—based on *Fanny*. It was with Shashi Kapoor, Saira Banu and Jeetendra. But the producer didn't have money, so after eight reels the film was shelved. Had that film been made in 1967 when I started, I could have struck limelight then, but you can't fight destiny. Eight reels of my best script of my life were blocked. Now it's too late. After that, many other films based on that idea came along: boy (Shashi Kapoor) and girl (Saira Banu) are in love; they get married secretly. The girl's father doesn't approve. The boy is swept away in a river, an accident. Then he goes on the other side of the border to Pakistan. He doesn't think he'll ever come back. The wife thinks he's dead. She bears his child. She doesn't know what to tell people. Another man (Jeetendra) who wanted to marry her earlier offers to marry her now, 'I'll give the boy my name. You stay in my house as my wife. I won't even touch you.' Jeetendra raises the boy till he is seven or eight years old. Shashi escapes from Pakistan, returns to find she has married. He wants to get out of her life. The wife doesn't know what to do. Jeetendra and Shashi are in the army. Jeetendra comes to know about Shashi and Saira. So Jeetendra says before he gives his life, 'Go, your wife is waiting.' The last scene is a cortege. Saira and Shashi are standing watching as the body of Jeetendra is taken away. The little boy is there. He gives a salute.

Beautiful triangle. If that had been made then, I would have been a success then, but nothing happens before its time.

...I had a very tough time between 1960 and 1970, the ten worst years of my life. That's when my wife stood by me like a rock. A great lady she was. I couldn't have asked for a better wife than that.... . She said, 'Don't give up films.' And I used to think up ideas in the night. I couldn't get to sleep. I'd wake up my wife. I'd wake up my son. 'Please, look, I made up this idea. Here's a plot.' She would hear me for two hours. She would say, 'Now it's late, Manmohan. Go to sleep. Okay? We'll hear it in the morning.' I am what I am because of her. She prayed for me. She stood by me. Very possessive. Naturally, since we had a love marriage, I wasn't supposed to monkey around after marriage. But I did. She didn't like that. But she looked after me and my home. She was very loyal to me, very faithful, looked after every need of mine.

Now I realize... . There's a saying: you know a person's worth when he's not there. Why a person? Any object, for that matter. You only know when it's not there. Now I think she might have been my spinal cord, my backbone. I never had to bother in my house whether anything was there or not. So I miss her. Now my spinal cord is my son... I suppose all filmmakers are womanizers in a way. Anyway, I don't like to be a hypocrite and say I'm a person of virtue. No. But just one vice! Others have plenty. I used to say to my wife, 'Look, in the film world, people drink, smoke; they gamble; they go to the races. I don't do all that. I only womanize.'

She said, 'That's no excuse.'

But my weakness is like my father's. My brother died in August, 1983. He was elder than me by six years: cirrhosis of the liver. So I always told him, 'We have divided the vices in our family.' He never womanized. He only drank—cards, races, smoking—no womanizing. I suppose any man who thinks, who works mentally, he needs a diversion. Alcohol is not a good diversion. I feel alcohol benumbs your nerves in the long run. So I don't take refuge in alcohol, nor in gambling. I don't like to lose. I'm a bad loser. So I said, my only refuge is womanizing. But I used to get in trouble with my wife.

Desai continued to remember the past and to describe his working habits during the seventies when he was full of pent-up energy:

> Up until 1976 I could shoot at 6:00 in the morning. In the evening I'd go to my room. My wife used to be there. I'd have my bath. I'd sit, talk with her. Early dinner and try to be in bed by 9:00 p.m. so I could get up at 5:00 or 6:00 in the morning and be there at 7:00. But now I can't get up in the morning like I used to.
>
> And I used to direct more films at a time. When I made *Amar Akbar Anthony*, I had *Parvarish* on set, *Dharam-Veer*, *Chacha Bhatija*, *Suhaag*—five films on set I had, and all five clicked. But after my wife died in April, 1979, I lost interest in work outside. Now that my son wants to direct, I'm going to start a second film in March (*Allahrakha*; the other being *Mard*). Otherwise, I'm not taking work from outside, working for another producer. At that time I had to prove some things to my wife, 'Look, I'm somebody.' Now I don't have to prove anything to anybody. I don't feel like doing more. I'll work on my scripts, work on my music. My needs are not more in life. I want to make one film a year. That's it. At that time I used to do scripts, shoot, do editing. I had five films on the floor. I don't know how I did it. My greatest period was 1974, '75, '77. Even if I had fever, I would work on the set. I was shooting almost every day. In the studios there are two stages, one set for one film, the other set for the other film. When the shot was ready, I'd go. I used to run from one stage to the other with my assistants. They (the films) all clicked. That was a great period in my life. My mind was so alert. I was shooting two films simultaneously.
>
> They were all laughing, saying, 'How can you do this?'
>
> I said, 'Look, I'll do it.' What I didn't do between 1960 and 1970, I made up for, I think, between 1970 and 1979.

Speaking of the period after his wife died, he said:

> I didn't give up films, but I lost the incentive. I lost that killer instinct. It's only my son Ketan, who kept me going. And he told me, I

remember, the very night my wife died, 'Dad, the interval of your life is over. You're an expert scripter. Your second half has always been good. Now the second half in your life begins. You will fight back. You're not going to quit films. You're not going to lose that killer instinct.' He goaded me into working. I went on making films, only due to him. He's everything now to me. He's my inspiration. He's my love. All my life is only Ketan and nothing else

Asked about his position as a movie mogul and his attitudes towards the film industry organizations, he said:

They don't call me to the council meetings because I can't stand the groupism there. They talk crap. They want to kill the small producers. Everybody has a right to make a film. Who's fighting for the film industry? No one. Each one cares for himself and nobody else. If you want to be the leaders of the film party, then it's your duty to look after every single producer, whether he's small or big. They have a caucus there. I can't stand that caucus. I refuse to go there.

'You people backbite about me, try to pull me down, use your influence in Delhi to ruin my films. Beat me at the box office,' I said. 'That's where it counts.' So far they can't touch my record (my films). So that's what hurts them most.

'The man doesn't join our group. He doesn't join our clan, doesn't join our parties; he keeps on churning out films.' Now they're saying, 'We don't understand why *Coolie* is running like this.' Keep on thinking why. Sit at home. Take a textbook, and sit down and find out why. Study. Go. I'm here. I'm in my house. I'm working. I'm scripting, or I'm scripting or making songs. No sense going with these chaps. They backbite, drink at parties, abuse each other. Why waste my time there? They're not going to help anyone else. So I said, 'Okay, I'll help myself. Forget it. Instead of wasting time on boozing and races and all that, I'd rather spend time working.'[3]

My only love is cricket. That's how I fractured my leg six months back. I got out of that and now this disc problem. My whole frustration is that I can't play cricket in the evening!!

Desai went on to talk more specifically about the importance of the box office:

> I always say the box office speaks the loudest. Why are Spielberg and Lucas known as the box office kings? Why? They have got three super-duper hits behind them. Why does nobody talk about Ingmar Bergman? Maybe you critics talk about him. Who's interested in seeing *Alexander And Fanny?* I'm not! I'll see Spielberg because I'll get to learn something: how they rake in at the box office. And believe me, it's no joke making a box office record. There are 300 Hindi films being made in the country every year. Only three or four are going to click. We've always been amongst them. All aim at the box office. Why can't they all do it? To beat the box office is not a joke.
>
> I've been working on the script of *Mard* for the last one year. Four more days and I'll be absolutely through with it. I've been revising it again and again; changing it again and again. You have to think all the time in terms of box office. I can't make these art films. They put me to sleep. I would like to beat the box office collections of my films. I'm not interested in any other films. I'm competing against myself. Now to beat *Coolie* I have a problem. My budgets are high. The prices at which I sell a film are higher than anybody else's in India. So I have to give them [the distributors] that worth. They distribute one of my films on my faith. They pay me whatever I want because they know the money's going to go in the film. They say, 'He'll do his best to make a good successful box office film.' So I owe it to them. Hence, I will think of more items, better items; items with emotion linked together should run. So I've got to compete with myself now because, to be very frank, I've got 12 jubilees in a row. 'How long' is the question. Some day the law of averages will catch up with me. Before that, I want to make as many as I can.

Later he reiterated:

> I would like to go as the champion box office maker of all times.... Awards? You take them when you're going downhill. Not now. When

you're zooming up, you don't need awards. It's the people, *people* whose love is ultimately going to matter.

Continuing on the subject of money, he explained his point of view:

> I would like to have lots and lots and lots of money because I know when I had no money what it was like. In 1962 and 1963 when my son was young, my wife was down with pleurisy. I was making *Bluff Master*. I had no other assignment. I swear upon God, I didn't have money to treat her. I remember how I scrounged for money, how Mr. Shammi Kapoor who is now my son's father-in-law—we have been friends since then—came to know of my plight. He gave me Rs. 2000, and I felt very embarrassed. I paid him back within 25 days. I didn't want to take it. He put it in my pocket, you know. He's the only hero (leading man) who I've been obliged to. At that time, I had no money to treat her for pleurisy. So I've seen what it is not to have money. I value it. That's why I don't play cards, gamble or go to the races. I know what it is not to have it. I want to have so much money that finally when I kick the bucket, my son doesn't have to stretch his hands to anybody for help. I've seen those days and I don't intend to forget them. And in our film trade it's up and down. There are no pensions. We live from day to day. In our good period we have to make tons of money and we should be able to save money for a rainy day because the rainy day is bound to come to practically everybody in the film industry sooner or later.
>
> If my son squanders the money I've made, that's his stupidity and bad luck. Money can't give you happiness, but money can bring you everything else, everything but happiness. Without money you can't do anything in this world. Suppose I fall sick and need to go abroad for treatment. I can't get treatment here, so that is why I want money. I need money. You go in a crowd of 200 people. Without money nobody speaks to you; with money you're a big man.

Coupled with Manmohan Desai's belief in the power of money and his desire to make as much of it as possible was a recurring

concern for the simple folk who made up the bulk of his viewing public.

> I don't make my films for critics. I make them for those people who are willing to stand hours in the sun and rain to buy a ticket. If they are unhappy with my film, I am unhappy too, and I would like to apologize to them.

Manmohan Desai was constantly planning new films, some of which were actually made. At one point he wanted to make a multilingual film called *Junction Rani* in six languages. *Love Birds* was another idea that Desai referred to as 'a beautiful satire.' He also had a dream of shooting abroad:

> The film I have in mind—an English language film—would be a love story with one Indian hero. The rest would be foreigners. I'm bloody sure it would be a tremendous success. We know more about emotions than they do. It would click internationally.
>
> If I'm destined, maybe somebody will come knock on my door and say, 'We want you to direct a film abroad.'

in the eyes of others

Let us now shift our point of view and look at Manmohan Desai not through his eyes but rather through the eyes of some of those who knew him, who worked with him or who simply expressed an opinion concerning his films.

In the fall of 1985, Shashi Kapoor, who acted in *Aa Gale Lag Jaa* and in *Suhaag*, offered some interesting observations about the director and related some of his experiences on set with Manmohan Desai:

> He's a *samdhi*, a relative by marriage. My niece (Shammi Kapoor's daughter) is married to Manmohan Desai's son. And he is a friend.
>
> Manmohan Desai was accepted immediately as a director. He just

started directing and he knew how to at a very young age, like my brother (Raj Kapoor). He is involved with the audience's point of view, not with a literary or aesthetic point of view. He leaves behind logic, sensibility and, to a certain extent, art quality. I believe that cinema is basically for entertainment. It is not something to be exhibited somewhere. Now, sometimes Manmohan may violate the public's sensibilities—I don't agree with illogic and such. But they work.

He is ruthless in trying to get what he wants. For instance, he is the only director who dared to tell off Salim and Javed. When he didn't like parts of their script, he changed the script. He also had some British stunt directors working for him. He wouldn't take any rubbish from them, got angry and sent them home.

I appreciate his clarity, his vision, even if I don't agree with him at certain points. He orchestrates a whole film his own way. His contribution to a film is 100%.

He has a childlike spirit, and he is a bit voyeuristic. He likes to watch a fight, for instance, not to fight himself, just to watch, a quality that is probably commendable in a film director. I attribute his success to this madness of his, this obsession almost to the point of madness.

He likes his artistes to take risks. I have done the most dangerous stunts in my long career of forty years and 250 films while working with him. In *Aa Gale Lag Jaa* in the final fight there is a fire. I was on skates and there was to be a fight with a knife. At first he wanted me to use a real knife. I said no, and he called me a 'scaredy'. But I was on skates, and we could have lost our balance. So I threw the knife at him. He ducked, and then he started yelling and cursing, 'You could have killed me!'

'Yes,' I said, 'that's just what I mean. That's why I don't want to use a real knife.'

Then in that same sequence, there was a shot where I was supposed to hit the window. Manmohan Desai wanted me to do it myself without a double. I said no, absolutely not. And the double who did that shot for me got a big slash on his head as he went through the window. He needed sixty stitches. I said, 'You see, that's the stunt you wanted me to do!'

THE FILMMAKER, THE MAN

In *Suhaag* he wanted a real shot without doubles of the motorbike and the helicopter. Amitabh and I arrive on a motorbike and we have to grab a rope ladder that is hanging down. We were in Singapore. It wasn't possible to get permission from the government at that time to use a helicopter. It was during the Janata government. He finally convinced me to do the shot myself, but I said, 'Just *one* take!' Well, we caught the rope and got off the ground. I was okay at first, and then my hands started getting sweaty, and I almost let go. We were about 100 feet off the ground, and we had to be at a certain angle for the shot, so we couldn't come down immediately. I thought I was going to die for sure. When I got down, I told him I was never going to do another action shot, and I was *never* going to do another *film* for him. I told my wife that night that she was lucky to have me alive. But he has a childlike excitement. He's a crazy man.

I think *Aa Gale Lag Jaa* was his best film, not because I was in it, but it's just his best.

I think he's scared now. He says he wants to be in the background now, to let his son take over. He doesn't want to compete with his son. He will be just a reference. But I don't think that's it. I think he just can't see himself flopping after so much success. So he gives the credit for directing to someone else.

His working style has changed somewhat recently. He uses the video now to prepare scenes. Everything is pre-rehearsed. He uses his assistants to go over scenes, checks them with the video and then has the actors do the shots just as they were planned. I don't like that. I don't think there is enough contribution from actors when he works that way.

Amitabh Bachchan, speaking in January 1984, had these comments to make about the filmmaker:

He is a very committed director. He has a tremendous planning sense. He knows exactly what he wants months before he's actually in front of the sets. He has done his homework right up to the last detail, including sometimes weather problems, problems of the artistes arriving late on the sets and what he would do if such a probability were to arise. I mean, it's amazing the amount of detail he goes into, and sometimes I've noticed that as a result of his work on so-called immaterial details we have been able to carry out a schedule because, in fact, we did face those problems.

There's very little that the artistes can invent at that time because he doesn't leave room for invention. He's done it all himself. And then when he is describing a particular sequence, for example, you may tend to laugh at it, you know, on hearing it for the first time. You may be very hesitant to do it when you're asked to. But when the results come, you stop arguing with him. I argued with him the first day that I worked, the first day of *Parvarish*'s shooting. He wanted me to do something in a particular way and I disagreed with him, but he insisted, and since it was my first day, I didn't want to get into any hassle with the director. Finally, I agreed. After that, I stopped arguing. I don't ever question what he asks me to do. I may feel silly; I may feel a little awkward at times doing things that he wants me to do. But I realize that if he wants me to do it, he's probably gone into it himself very deeply and has thought about the overall impact it's going to have. And I've never really argued with him. Instead, I've tried to help him by putting in as much of myself as I can into an awkward situation. And we've come out in the green so far. We haven't misfired. It's his conviction that pushes you into doing things like that.

I find now that with his technique the more serious-minded people are standing back and laughing at it all. But sometimes when you stand back and laugh at something you are actually enjoying it. You may not be ridiculing it; you're actually enjoying it. You may be seeing something stupid on the screen, but in fact you like it. So what has happened is you've got the intelligent viewer sitting in the hall, laughing at the stupidity of it and enjoying it and you have the masses, the uneducated masses who are there enjoying the stupidity, not knowing that it's stupidity, but actually believing it, and it's first degree. That's the only explainable reason for the tremendous success that his films enjoy.

Shyam Benegal, New Cinema director who has gained recognition worldwide, was generous in his praise of Manmohan Desai:

I enjoy Manmohan Desai's films. I would never miss one. Manmohan Desai is definitely the best of the big mainstream directors. *Amar Akbar Anthony* is my favourite.

I respect Manmohan Desai for his honesty, for never having claimed to be anything but an entertainer. In this respect, he is a success. Manmohan Desai's films are great fun. He has taken a stereotype and changed it into an archetype. He has created a new mythology. It's very clever, too, the way he can use the same material over and over again, refining it each time.

I think Manmohan Desai is totally uninterested in social messages; everything happens by miracle on screen. People leave the cinema without taking any messages, but they have been entertained.

Director Mahesh Bhatt called *Amar Akbar Anthony* a landmark film and Desai one of the 'blithe spirits of cinema—a superb artist.'[4]

Director Mrinal Sen, whose 1969 *Bhuvan Shome* is considered by many to have been the starting point of the new cinema movement, gave a veiled compliment to Manmohan Desai when he said, 'I enjoy *Coolie*. I don't react to it.'

Firoze Rangoonwala, film historian, said, 'The power of Manmohan Desai's cinema lies in its capacity to build myths. The popular song 'Govinda aala re' in *Bluff Master* is a ritual folk song in Maharashtra, but it was changed in the film by music directors Kalyanji Anandji, under the instruction of Desai. Since then the song is sung in Maharashtra the way it was sung in the film.'[5]

Closer to home, and still in a positive vein, Ekram Kashmiri, Manmohan Desai's production manager, had this to say of Manmohan Desai, 'He loves the poor. He wants to see them come up.'

Manmohan Desai, of course, had many detractors; he was the *bête noire* of some. New Wave director M.S. Sathyu, who caught the attention of the Indian and foreign critics alike with his *Garam Hawa* (1974), voiced his criticism in these terms:

> If Manmohan Desai and Prakash Mehra make their kind of film, they only want to make more and more money.... Desai's films are devoid of any kind of sensibility. As he himself admits, there's no logic in his films. He just plays with the weaknesses of people.[6]

Film critic Chidananda Das Gupta likewise took a harsh stance:

> To me they (Desai's films) are not fun. I am perhaps overly concerned with questions of value in a country divided between tradition and modernity where new cultural orientations are of immense importance if we are not to end up being brutal and mindlessly hedonist under the impact of mass production and runaway consumerism.... I don't want India to get to the point where whatever sells most becomes thereby holy.

The language used by *Filmfare* readers to describe Desai's films is worth noting. Because of his box-office success, Desai served as something of a lightning rod for Hindi popular cinema as a whole. Many berated his films in such terms as 'stale brew.' *Desh Premee* was accused of being 'packed with crass inanities.' Or again, 'Desai and his tribe churn out cheap and senseless entertainers.'

the director's directors

Let us turn once again to Manmohan Desai, this time as he expressed his tastes as a spectator. Learning what Desai liked was not difficult, for if Desai was often intransigent in his condemnation of those whose style he loathed, he was equally enthusiastic in his praise of those whose work he appreciated.

He showed humility before past masters:

> Watching *Mother India*, I said to myself, 'What are you doing making films?' Mehboob Khan was a genius. He was an illiterate man from a village. For many years he couldn't read or write English. He couldn't

even sign his name. *Andaz* and *Mother India*: they're landmarks. I consider Mehboob Khan, Raj Kapoor, Bimal Roy and Guru Dutt are in a different league altogether.

V. Shantaram is a brilliant craftsman, the best technician we've got. See *Do Ankhen Barah Haath*. He's a brilliant editor, has good photography, but the performances of his artistes are very stilted. That's why I say he is a craftsman more than a director.

I consider one Marathi actor Dada Khondke another genius. He has got seven Golden Jubilees lined up in a row, super hits from Marathi cinema. He is an ugly man who has become a household name in Maharashtra. He's a producer, a director, an actor, everything. He's my friend, and I'm his friend. He's just made a Hindi film [in January 1984]—*Mere Beech Mein*. He made it a little vulgar. Every dialogue has a double meaning. But whatever it is, I've seen his work. I'm a fan of his. I think there are two geniuses we have here, Raj Kapoor and Dada Khondke. This ugly man became a superstar. As a village bumpkin I think he's the world's number one actor. He wears short pants, big and baggy—and shirts—big and baggy. What a natural! I don't know much of the Marathi language—though I was married to a Maharashtrian—but when I see his films I think he knows the right emotions, the right comedy, the right drama, the right music. He used to say, 'I'll make a Hindi film if Manmohan Desai directs for me.' When he was awarded a silver disc for his film music, the third Marathi film to have a silver disc, he said, 'I'll take it only if Manmohan Desai presents it to me on the stage.' I arranged to attend. I presented it and I touched his feet and said, 'Dada Khondke is a genius.'

Desai reserved his greatest praise for Raj Kapoor:

There are two schools of cinema in India, Raj Kapoor's and Guru Dutt's. Guru Dutt got a trolley and moved around a singing person. Raj Kapoor has built scenes around songs. I follow Raj Kapoor.

He spoke of directors abroad whose work he appreciated:

> There are so many—Wilder, of course. I consider Billy Wilder my god for scripting. I would like to touch his feet... .
>
> And Spielberg—*E.T.!* What emotions this man has taught us in one sweep! What a friendship angle between an ugly looking character and children! And that film depicts that human beings are villains. They make you hate the villain in the second half... . Like a human being he had a heart in him. All he wants to do is go home. What sentiments! What a friendship angle he brought! The scene on the table: his [Elliot's] heart beats along with *E.T.*'s.
>
> There's a fine Italian director whom I like the best in action filmmaking: Sergio Leone—*A Fistful of Dollars, For a Few Dollars More, The Good The Bad and the Ugly*... . I think he made the best Westerns of them all. Each one was a gem by itself—brilliant camera work and brilliant editing.

Because of the frequent strong stances he took against Indian art cinema, Manmohan Desai was regularly questioned and questioned again on the subject. Actually, his views were not invariably negative as was clear when when he spoke to Nikhil Lakshman of *The Illustrated Weekly Of India*.[7]

> I saw only one film, *Garam Hawa* (by M.S. Sathyu). I was thrilled by it. It was brilliant. It moved me. I was not bored to death.
>
> Ray's films I've seen. Okay. But not my style. One thing about the man is he gets superb performances from his artistes. He has his own class.

Later, talking to Alpana Chowdhury for *Filmfare*, he rated Satyajit Ray even higher, 'If any one person has the right to criticize anybody else's work, it is Satyajit Ray. Nobody else in India.'[8]

Let us now turn our attention to Manmohan Desai's *oeuvre*. Of the 20 films Manmohan Desai directed between 1960 and 1988, many might merit individual in-depth examinations. I have, however, limited full-chapter studies to two pivotal films in Desai's career—*Amar Akbar Anthony* and *Coolie*.

**two films
in close-up**

amar akbar anthony

becoming a producer

Amar Akbar Anthony was a turning point for Manmohan Desai. Three other successful releases in 1977 had already made the public familiar with his name. With *Amar Akbar Anthony* he moved from being a well-known director into the role of a producer-director who wielded a great deal of power in the Hindi film industry. Manmohan Desai explained the inception of the film and his own new role:

> I didn't want to produce *Amar Akbar Anthony*. I didn't want to become a producer because I'm too outspoken, too blunt. I call a spade a spade and don't take any shit from anybody. But a producer has to be patient and diplomatic. Unfortunately, I'm not a diplomat. That's one of the major reasons why I'm not popular. I was afraid I'd have trouble with my artistes. But my wife and Prayag Raj said, 'No, become a producer.' When I did, nobody gave me any trouble.
>
> We were sitting here (in his office). Prayag Raj came by. He wanted to take the keys to my farm 50 miles from here to spend the weekend there with his wife. I said, 'Have a drink.' And between 7.00 and 10.00 p.m., I swear, we made the plot for *Amar Akbar Anthony*—the title, the

characters, the story. Prayag was drunk. He said, 'Come on Manmohan, the films you've made for others, you can make for yourself.'

I said, 'No, no, I'm scared.'

My wife said, 'Come on, make it.'

My little boy put in his word. He also joined the chorus, 'Yeah, make it, make it, Daddy; produce it.'

I don't drink, but they gave me a little half-peg of whiskey and I think I was intoxicated with that. So I was carried away, and I said, 'Okay, I'm making it.' At 10.30 in the night I decided to produce this film. In three hours the rough plot of *Amar Akbar Anthony* was formed here.

Desai went on to explain that *Amar Akbar Anthony* was partially rooted in fact:

I got the idea for *Amar Akbar Anthony* from a news item in an evening paper. An alcoholic named Jackson was fed up with life and one day packed his three children in a car and dropped them off in a park. I twisted this around, forgot the alcoholic bit and separated the three children. I also built in a miracle, the blind mother gets her eyesight back. This isn't bunk. Miracles have taken place, haven't they? There are faith healers, pundits, astrologers. Why do people believe in them?

The inspiration for Anthony came from someone closer to home:

There was a narrow strip of gutter between those two buildings across the street. Antav, the Anthony character, came from there. He used to wear a funny hat and was very rowdy. That's where the bootlegging went on for twenty years. All the Anthony characters used to operate there out in the night, out in the roads.

Because of the technical finish of *Amar Akbar Anthony* and the cleverness of the script, because it was the first time that Amitabh had so shone as a comedian, and because it went on to a Golden Jubilee, the critics took note of the film. Many did not like it, but some did, and the film became a reference point in Indian cinema history, mentioned whether in admiration or in horror, along with *Sholay*, as one of the most prominent films of the seventies. Since then, it has gone on to become a classic, recalled in admiration by many and discovered by newer generations.

The combination of hard work, luck, and a spark of genius that made *Amar Akbar Anthony* such a success was perhaps not independent of the general boom of the Hindi film industry in the second half of the seventies. Those were the Amitabh years, the big money, big cast and big audience years. Cinema was still flourishing before video started eating away at the market and before the initial force and inspiration behind the top films of the period were buried under the debris of some lifeless imitations.

the plot

The plot of *Amar Akbar Anthony* is almost mathematical in its logic, almost geometrical in its complexity. The first twenty minutes before the credits constitute a prelude during which we follow Kishanlal (Pran) through a series of misadventures that bring about the separation of all five members of his family. This first part of the film has a somewhat rougher look than the rest and is flawed by an excess of speed and melodrama, especially in the sound track. Those twenty minutes, nevertheless, set the stage for all that is to follow. The nature of each character is established and many detailed bits of information are introduced which will later prove significant in linking the dispersed family members. This introduction to *Amar Akbar Anthony* also represents the essence of Desai's work inasmuch as the number of happenings and turnarounds in that one event-filled day is mind-boggling. Each individual scene is necessarily very short as the story line moves from the fate of one family member to another in quick succession. Let us examine the beginning, then, scene by scene.

Kishanlal is released from the Central Jail.

Upon returning to his humble street, he learns from a neighbour that his wife has contracted tuberculosis. In their two-room house his three young sons are fighting over a bit of bread. He distributes presents to them; the oldest son buries the toy pistol he is given to prevent the second son from stealing it away. His coughing wife Bharti (Nirupa Roy), with deep circles under her eyes, explains that Robert (Jeevan) went back on his word, refusing to give even one coin to the care of Kishanlal's family, this despite the fact that Kishanlal, as Robert's chauffeur, had taken the blame for an accident Robert had caused.

Enraged, Kishanlal goes to Robert's luxurious house to find him elegantly dressed, surrounded by strong men and calmly sipping imported whiskey. 'Don't you remember your promise?' Kishanlal asks.

Robert callously answers that he remembers nothing except that he has forgotten the ice for his whiskey. Then pouring a bit onto his shoe, he orders Kishanlal down on his knees to dry it off. Afterwards, adding insult to injury, he smugly tosses Kishanlal a one-*anna* coin and tells his men to throw him out. In a fury Kishanlal grabs a gun from a guard and shoots Robert in the chest. Robert slumps over, then rises with a triumphant laugh and dramatically opens his shirt to expose his bulletproof vest. With a couple of karate chops, Kishanlal frees himself and crashes through a window. In the garage he steals one of Robert's cars. Robert, horrified that Kishanlal has chosen a car with gold hidden in the boot, orders his men out in quick pursuit.

Fearing for his family's lives, Kishanlal stops at his home. Bharti has disappeared, leaving behind a suicide note and a Jai Santoshi Mata medallion on a chain. Kishanlal gathers the three children and hurries off in the car. A policeman neighbour, seeing them, gives a look of surprise and then a shrug. A hot chase follows until Kishanlal comes to Borivali Park where he leaves the three boys at the foot of the Mahatma Gandhi statue.

Amar, the oldest, at first agrees to stay in the park, but when he sees his father drive away, he runs behind until he is knocked down by the car carrying Robert's men.

Bharti, running madly along a tree-lined street, is caught in a sudden storm. Lightning strikes and a branch falls, knocking her unconscious.

Back in the park the baby is crying inconsolably. The second son offers to find his little brother some food.

Kishanlal runs off the road; his car slides down a hill. The boot of the car springs open. The gold flies out, and the car bursts into flames. Robert's men prepare to go down to recuperate the gold when the police arrive and forbid access to the burning car. One of the policemen at the site is Kishanlal's neighbour who now supposes Kishanlal and the three boys to be dead.

At the park again, a Muslim kneeling on a pray mat, hands uplifted, is finishing his prayer when the baby's cries catch his attention. He gently lifts the child, then, lamenting what a sorry world it is in which parents abandon their offspring, takes the baby home with him.

The middle brother now returns to the park with a bit of bread, but he finds himself all alone.

The Muslim, driving down the street, finds the road blocked by a fallen branch. When he tries to move it out of his way, he discovers Bharti. She regains consciousness, but realizes that she has become blind. God has punished her thus, she believes, because she wanted to kill herself. The Muslim kindly drives her home. In the car she hears, but cannot see the baby he has just adopted.

Kishanlal seems to have been miraculously thrown clear of the wrecked and burning car because when the flames die down, he is seen stealthily gathering up the box of gold before making his way back to town.

Back at the park, a sudden downpour forces the lonely middle brother to seek refuge on the nearby church steps where he sits shivering, cold and afraid.

Bharti arrives at her empty home and is informed by her neighbour of the death of her husband and children.

The next morning a priest opens the door and finds a feverish little boy.

A passing patrol jeep comes upon the oldest son still lying wounded on the street. A police inspector, with a look of pity and concern, carries the boy to his jeep and drives away.

Kishanlal returns to the park, and beneath the Gandhi statue he calls out for his sons; the park remains silent and empty.

In the church the middle child, looking a bit older, is kneeling beside the confession booth. He tells the priest who has adopted him that he has sold his schoolbooks. 'What! Sold your school books!? Why??' the priest scolds the child.

'I sold them to give money for a funeral,' he answers, and the priest smiles tenderly, warmed by the boy's good heart.

The next cut serves to make the 22-year jump through time that takes us into the main story of the film. We see an aged priest and a grown Anthony (Amitabh Bachchan), still kneeling in confession. Thus ends the prelude proper, but the film credits are several scenes away.

The priest begs Anthony to give up the alcohol trade before he finds himself in serious trouble with the police. Anthony answers, pointing to Christ on the cross, that the matter is between himself and his 'partner' to whom he gives fifty percent of his earnings. The priest accuses him of trying to bribe heaven, but before their discussion can continue, Anthony is called outside. A woman—Bharti—is lying on the ground, the victim of a hit-and-run accident. Anthony whistles for a taxi to take her to the hospital.

At the police station the grown older son Inspector Amar (Vinod Khanna) receives a call informing him of the accident and of the name of the hospital where the woman has been taken.

Akbar (Rishi Kapoor) is at the hospital for his daily visit to the pretty doctor Salma (Neetu Singh). She listens to his heart with a stethoscope, announces he is perfectly fit, and tells him to leave. Akbar admits he has only come to hand deliver her invitation to his *qawwali* programme. She would like to attend, she says, but her father will refuse unless the entire household accompanies her. A nurse interrupts to say that the wounded woman needs a blood transfusion. Salma asks Akbar, as a personal favour, to help. For Salma, Akbar declares, he would willingly give not only his blood, but his life!

In another ward, a man in a white coat with a patient chart asks Salma the names of the three men stretched out on hospital beds, red tubes leaving their arms as they donate blood. Salma answers, 'Their names are...' The camera travels from bed to bed as the young men announce in turn, 'Amar,' 'Akbar,' 'Anthony,' while below each appears the corresponding actor's name. An echo after the names heralds our entry into an epic world, clearly not meant to be mistaken for reality. Irony is central in the song that accompanies the credits, '*Khoon khoon hotaa hai paani nahin*' (Blood is blood, not water) comes the line, '*Yeh sach hai, koi kahaani nahin*' (This is true; it's no story). The camera guides our eyes about the room. Bharti, a bandage on her head, is lying on a table to the front and centre. Medical reality yields before symbolism. Three separate tubes carry the men's blood to a suspended bottle from which only one tube relays blood into Bharti's vein.

The song and the credits end. The main story begins in earnest.

The plot line proceeds with the implacable logic that only fiction can provide. The three young men continue to come in contact. Anthony attends Akbar's *qawwali* show. Amar, the policeman, jails Anthony, the barkeeper, for withholding information about the smuggler Robert. The mother, thankful to all three for saving her life, appears with flowers for each. The three brothers, of course, must find true love. Amar saves Lakshmi (Shabana Azmi) and her grandmother from her wicked stepmother (Nadira) and conniving stepbrother (Ranjeet) and has the two move in with him. Akbar sings and dances to woo Salma; her father (Mukri) firmly refuses the match until Akbar comes Tarzan-like to the rescue of father and daughter caught in a burning building. Anthony and Jenny (Parveen Babi) fall in love, but Jenny's bodyguard Zebisco (Hercules) and her real father, the gangster Robert, interfere; the final fight removes the barriers to their romance, sends the bad guys to jail and provides for the originally separated family's happy reunion, the only letdown being that Kishanlal, having turned smuggler himself, must go to jail along with Robert.

the religious component

In contrast to certain other Desai films in which religion receives barely a passing nod, in *Amar Akbar Anthony* it is constantly present, whether for its own sake or for the sake of promoting tolerance and mutual respect among those of different religions. That the separation of Kishanlal and his three sons should take place at the foot of Gandhi's statue is appropriate given Gandhi's role both as preacher of communal harmony and as father of the movement to end colonial rule. Kishanlal's family is broken up precisely on Independence Day, August 15, a day that in Indian history evokes both the joy of freedom and the pain of Partition with a subsequent legacy of rioting, massacres and the massive relocations of population. An individual family melodrama includes a national morality tale. Though circumstances have given the three boys different religions, they have remained brothers. An extrapolation could easily be made, the lesson quickly understood, that all Indians, regardless of religion, are *brothers*. The three-religion theme in *Amar Akbar Anthony*— four when there is a mention of the Sikhs—is insistent and carefully repeated throughout the plot, in the dialogue, through character traits, and also in the visuals. During the credits, for example, in the blood transfusion scene in the hospital, behind Amar's bed is a window looking onto a Hindu temple; behind Akbar we see a mosque; behind Anthony, a church.

All three religions are represented. Nevertheless, with scenes shot on location at a church in Bandra and with Amitabh playing the role of the Christian, the film appears weighed towards Christianity. Statues in the church are used dramatically to underline two moments of crisis. First, when the future Anthony is found on the church steps, the priest gathers him in his arms, takes him inside, and says, 'The Lord will protect you.' The camera focuses and rests on a statue of Mary holding the infant Jesus. Later, when Robert lifts his knife menacingly against the priest, we do not witness the fatal stabbing as such. Instead, a cut is made to a statue of the crucified Christ from whose wounds blood has begun to flow.

Islam is present, above all, in Akbar's speech, which is peppered with allusions to his faith. Interestingly, Akbar is a pacifist. During the final fight he supports his battling brothers from the sidelines, using the rhythm of his accordion to punctuate their blows. When he is about to deliver the final, decisive punch that lands Robert in jail, he first apologizes to Allah; up to that point, he says, he has only lifted his hands in prayer. If a certain warrior tradition exists historically in Islam, delving into Islam in South Asia reveals a situation of great complexity. Akbar is perhaps a reminder of the wide impact of the Chisti Sufis with their emphasis on love and devotion and their openness to accommodation. Also, consciously or unconsciously, Akbar's portrayal may be intended to soothe and comfort those in the audience who could feel threatened by a more aggressive stance from a member of a large minority.

Hinduism in the film is more personal and more diffuse. Beyond clear evocative markers like Amar's hands formed for prayer or Bharti's Jai Santoshi Ma medallion a certain Hindu worldview, exemplified by tolerance and respect for other religions, sets the tone of the film. The theme of communal harmony has often been present in post-colonial Indian cinema but has never been so memorably illustrated as in *Amar Akbar Anthony*. Responding to a question concerning the communal harmony message urged in the film, Manmohan Desai said:

> Had I stood on a platform preaching 'Hindu-Muslim *bhai-bhai*, Hindu-Christian *bhai-bhai* (brother-brother),' they would have said, 'We don't want to hear that bullshit from you.' So I said, best give it in a very palatable, say, homeopathic pill. We gave a sugar-coated pill; they took it. They liked it. So we had communal harmony in it.

But is the Hindu worldview that emphasizes tolerance at times prone to religious immobility in Manmohan Desai's films? The Hindu Kishanlal kidnaps Robert's baby daughter Jenny, yet he has her raised as a Catholic like her father. Unlike for both Muslims and Christians, conversion, for Hindus, is a term without meaning. Akbar and Anthony, though raised in other religions, are still considered Hindus by Hindu viewers. Therefore, as Desai explained, even though Akbar and Anthony marry a Muslim and a Christian respectively, it was preferable not to offend sensibilities by actually showing the wedding ceremonies taking place.

If religious tolerance has often existed side by side in India with an insistence on maintaining distinctions, these two features have often paradoxically and interestingly combined with a third, that, in appearance, is in direct opposition to the other two, *i.e.*, a tendency towards syncretism. A confusion over the boundaries between different religions is used to comic effect when Anthony, disguised as a priest, leaves the villains perplexed by claiming to have performed Akbar's four weddings. A more serious form of religious overlapping is found in the figure of Sai Baba. In a small country temple decorated with symbols of both Hinduism and Islam, Akbar leads a group of the faithful in a song of worship, '*Shirdiwale Sai Baba.*'

Desai spoke about Sai Baba and explained how the saint found his way into *Amar Akbar Anthony*:

It was never clear about Sai Baba whether he was a Hindu or a Muslim. Until now it is not clear who he was because he believed in both Islam and in Hinduism. Hence he did not get himself cremated. He attained *samaadhi* (liberation) and he was entombed in a place. So Muslims also believe in Sai Baba, as do Hindus and Parsees. Sai Baba is considered a very big saint in Maharashtra. The pilgrimage place is in Shirdi which I visit every year on the 13th of April, the day my wife died. I go to pay homage and to pray for my wife's soul. She was a great, great believer in Sai Baba. I remember having many photos of Sai Baba in my house. She used to read Sai Baba *granth* (book), and whenever my son would fall sick, she would always say, 'Sai Baba, Sai Baba.' She would get *vibhuti* (ashes) from a temple and put it on my son's forehead.

She was a great believer in Sai Baba; hence that rubbed off on me. She said, 'Why don't we bring Sai Baba into our film?' And so when we had to show a deity who performed a miracle in *Amar Akbar Anthony*, I thought why don't we show Sai Baba. Quite a few Muslims, Parsees and Hindus go to Shirdi.

Sai Baba, then, represents harmony and syncretism, a site and a symbol of the meeting, blending and intertwining of religions. What carries one interpretation in India, however, can provoke different reactions abroad. The sight of Akbar singing and praying along with other believers before a statue in a human form comes as a shock to some Muslims. One Pakistani, for instance, found the encompassing nature of the Hindu religion as shown in *Amar Akbar Anthony* to be a threat to his religion and expressed his concern over the tendency of people from his country to incorporate Hindu practices into Islam as a result of regularly viewing Hindu-based films from India. A Kuwaiti, having seen the same film, took a more casual view. Questioned specifically about the scene in which Akbar prays to Sai Baba, he said, 'According to my religion, I'm not even supposed to go to the movies. What difference does it make what I see when I get there?!' In another Muslim country, Dubai, the censors failed even to notice or to object to the more essential Hindu nature of the film, drawn as they were by the more obvious, concrete presence of the church.

The Sai Baba scene is one of the richest in the film. At one level, it is simply good cinema—well acted by both stars and junior artistes, well filmed, with good music, good special effects, and with a good balance between action and emotion. The scene is also pivotal to the story line. Bharti, still blind, is being chased by Robert and a member of his gang. The singing from Shirdi attracts her; she makes her way inside in search of safety. The gangsters who try to pursue her are stopped when a cobra on a sacred mission suddenly blocks the entrance to the shrine, menacingly puffing out its hood. As the music swells with emotion, two small, flickering flames appear, first in the eyes of the Sai Baba statue, and then in Bharti's eyes. Slowly, Sai Baba comes into focus for her, and superimposed, are her three young children beckoning her forward. She crawls to the statue, kisses it in deep gratitude, and announces the miracle to the amazed gathering. Cinema audiences over the years have either marvelled at or been annoyed by this miracle. Actor Om Puri, for example, complained:

> If Manmohan Desai were to deal only with fantasy, I would have more regard for him. But he claims to base his films on newspaper clippings and real happenings. In *Amar Akbar Anthony* he has a scene where the blind Nirupa Roy goes to a temple. Two shafts of light emerge from the eyes of the deity and Nirupa gets her sight back. These sorts of miracles are very dangerous things to show. Filmmakers have no right to play around with people's blind faith.[1]

Manmohan Desai revealed his own feelings about blindness and the miracle of sight regained thus:

> You see, blindness, I feel, is the real curse of God. There is no greater handicap than blindness. My heart always goes out to somebody who

is blind. A person without hands, legs can exist, can see. Just imagine a person who cannot see, who can hear—who can hear the laughter of children, hear a river or brook—they can hear so many nice things but they cannot see… . It's a curse of God. And I have always felt that if you show a blind person (on screen), there are millions of people like me whose heart goes out for the blind. And if you show a blind person regaining his sight…! I wish there was some way that all the blind people in the world could see, as there is no greater handicap or torture. I have used blindness time and again because, as I said, my sympathy goes out for them and whatever I may be doing in my life (in the way of charity), I try to do it for the blind.

losing and finding

While *Amar Akbar Anthony* is rich in thematic goals, the ambitions of the plot are simpler: to reunite the separated family members, to bring love to the three brothers of the story and to give the spectators a bundle of surprises in the context of an otherwise predictable cops-and-robbers, lost-found story. This last goal is reached brilliantly in a number of scenes. One astute sequence is worth noting.

A group of coolies are transporting smuggled goods up from a boat on the waterfront. Among the men struggling under a heavy load is Robert, now greatly reduced from his former position of money and power. Robert trips over the foot of a well-dressed man. The camera travels up to the man's face and we discover that the smuggling chief is none other than Kishanlal, present to supervise the handling of the latest shipment of contraband. Robert is wearing a simple white uniform, just as Kishanlal was at the beginning of the film, and Kishanlal is wearing exactly the same elegant black pin-striped suit, red vest, white shirt, red silk tie, and dressy black shoes that Robert wore when he was first introduced. Robert throws himself at Kishanlal's feet, begging to know the whereabouts of his daughter Jenny. 'Don't you remember?' Robert asks before recounting how Kishanlal stole his child away while she was just a baby. Kishanlal answers in a perfect imitation of Robert's voice and accent, precisely as he was told 22 years earlier, 'Oh yes, I remember; I forgot to put ice in my whiskey.' Some has spilled on his shoe; he has Robert stoop down on his knees to clean it off. He then tosses a one-*anna* coin to Robert, exactly the same coin that Robert cruelly threw to Kishanlal at the beginning of the story. In a split second Robert's pleas turn to anger and, like Kishanlal before him, he grabs a gun and shoots Kishanlal in the back. Kishanlal slumps over, but soon stands up straight, takes off his jacket, and, as we might have expected, reveals his bulletproof vest. But now comes the punch line, 'Robert, I knew that against you I had to cover my *back*, not my chest.' Kishanlal, then, has become like Robert, but only up to a point. Like many other Desai fathers, Kishanlal is moderately good. He has indeed become a smuggler, having metamorphosed into an apparent carbon copy of Robert; yet he retains a sense of integrity. He must go to prison, but he will go honorably.

Making a good lost-found story requires talent. Desai described the difficulty:

> It is the art of losing in the first two reels and how you reunite them; that is the secret; that is the catch. If you do it beautifully, it holds the audience's interest. Many other people have done it, but they haven't been able to make it click It is very difficult to bring about the union in a different way every time.

Rarely has any rejoining involved the complexity it has in *Amar Akbar Anthony*. The lost individual with an identifying mark is a timeworn gimmick in Indian cinema. *Amar Akbar Anthony* explodes this device into a huge array of crucial props and signs and key bits of information, as varied as the cast is large. The toy gun provides the link between Amar and his father; the Jai Santoshi Ma medallion and the suicide note join Kishanlal and

Anthony; Akbar's photo taken soon after his adoption serves as proof to Bharti that he is her son. Salma overhears Robert name Bharti as Kishanlal's wife; Akbar then helps Bharti find her lost husband.

All the pieces fit into the puzzle just in the time for the three brothers to band together to save Jenny from her father who, to save himself, wants to marry her to the calculating Zebisco. The title song mocks the villains congregated for a wedding—that will not take place—and consecrates the reunion of the three young men, accompanied by the women they love: 'Ek, ek se bhale do; do, do se bhale teen...Amar Akbar Anthony.' (Two is better than one; three is better than two...Amar Akbar Anthony.) The song ends. A fast and funny fight begins. Amar and Anthony send Robert's strong men banging against one another as though they were billiard balls. Akbar's blow lands Robert in jail, in the same cell as Kishanlal. Bharti cries outside his cell, sad to have found her husband only to lose him again. Kishanlal consolingly reminds her that she has her three sons once more and three daughters-in-law too. Kishanlal receives permission to hug his sons. And the three young couples go riding off into the sunset in Akbar's car, to the refrain of the title song *Amar Akbar Anthony.*

Amar Akbar Anthony's importance is multifaceted. Certainly, though, one lasting effect of the film's success was to confirm Amitabh Bachchan's box office supremacy and to solidify the Manmohan Desai-Amitabh Bachchan working relationship. Let us, then, give the final word to Amitabh Bachchan who, while listing his favourite Manmohan Desai film roles in January 1984, evaluated his part in *Amar Akbar Anthony* thus:

> Well, I would certainly put the one in *Amar Akbar Anthony* as something that's right on top of the list because it was something totally fresh from the point of view of filmmaking, of commercial filmmaking in India. It was also very fresh as a role for me because I hadn't done something that light-hearted, something as frivolous as

that. I'd been doing some rather intense work before that and it opened up a totally new field for me and a new kind of audience. And ever since then I think that particular characterization has always been very popular. At least as far as Manmohan Desai's concerned, we've always tried to bring some shades of that (character) back into all his films because he (Manmohan Desai) is one who believes in trying to go back to something that's already proved successful once. And his logic and his thinking haven't proved wrong so far.

Manmohan Desai, the irrepressible raconteur.

1960: Chhalia *marked Desai's directorial debut. He was a great fan of Raj Kapoor and Nutan. Photo: Hyphen Films Ltd.*

Bollywood filmstar of the '60s, Shammi Kapoor played the lead role in Desai's Bluffmaster *and* Budtameez. *Photo: Hyphen Films Ltd.*

1973: Desai on the sets of Aa Gale Lag Jaa *with Shobha Khote and Shashi Kapoor.*

1973: The publicity folder of Bhai Ho To Aisa. *Through self-sacrifice, the younger brother (Jeetendra) sparks repentance in the older brother (Shatrughan Sinha).*

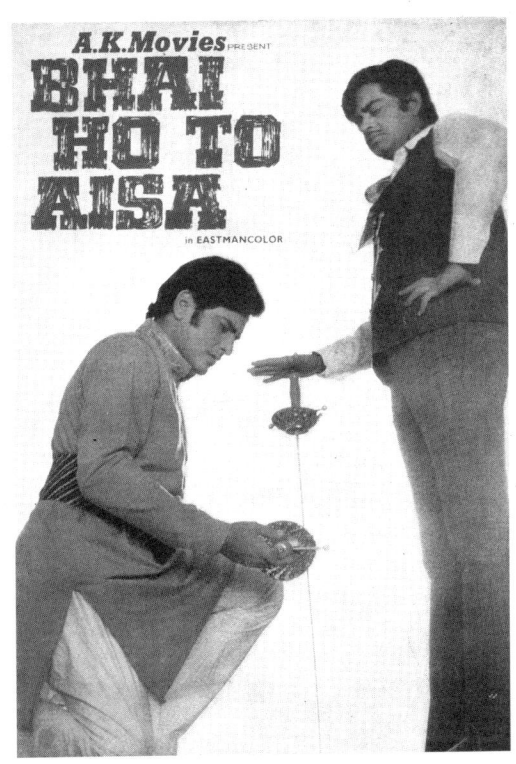

1973: Master Tito, playing a polio-stricken boy, saves his father (Shashi Kapoor) in Aa Gale Lag Jaa.

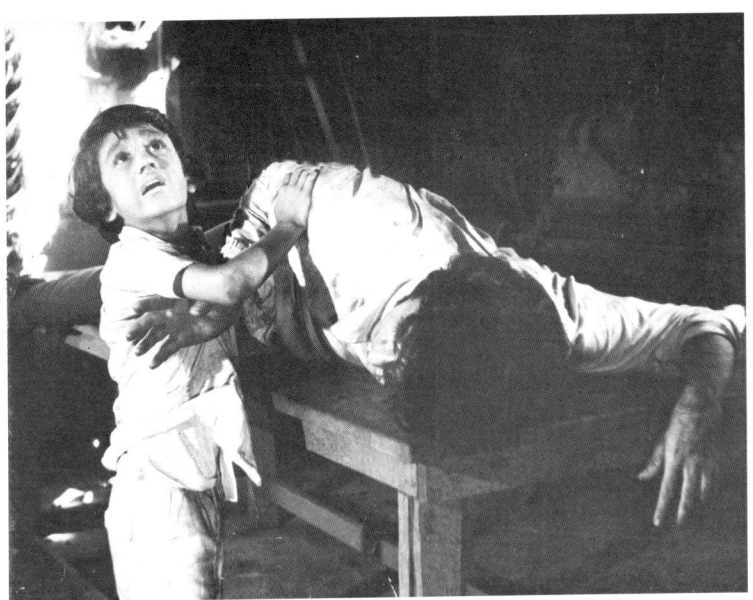

Desai during his days of struggle with Shashi Kapoor in the early '70s.

1974: Mumtaz disguised as a holy man with Rajesh Khanna and Desai on the sets of Roti. *Desai had cast Rajesh Khanna in a double role in* Sachaa Jhutha *(1970).*

1977: Speaking of his son's role in Dharam-Veer, *Dharmendra's* father said, 'I fed and raised my son just for this film.'

1977: Desai finalizing cues on the sets of Dharam-Veer.

1977: Joala (Pran), the hunter, with Wonder Bird Sheroo on the sets of Dharam-Veer.

1977: Indrani Mukherjee and Pran in discussion with Desai on the sets of Dharam-Veer.

1977: Desai explains a scene to Zeenat Aman on the sets of Dharam-Veer.

1977: Brothers separated by malice, reunited by fate: Dharmendra and Jeetendra in Dharam-Veer.

'Laugh at me today,' Desai would tell his detractors good-naturedly, 'but mark my words, you'll appreciate my work some day, even if it's too late.'

1977: The publicity folder for Amar Akbar Anthony.

1977: Vinod Khanna, the one-man band, ready with music and muscle in Amar Akbar Anthony.

1977: Desai with Rishi Kapoor, getting ready to shoot the song 'Pardah hai' *for* Amar Akbar Anthony.

1977: Desai on the sets of Amar Akbar Anthony *sharing a light moment with Rishi Kapoor.*

1977: Desai with Parveen Babi during the shooting of the song 'Humko tumse ho gaya hai pyar' for Amar Akbar Anthony.

1979: (Left) The brochure for Suhaag; *(Right) Amitabh Bachchan as the chappal-waving drunk in the courtesan's palace in* Suhaag.

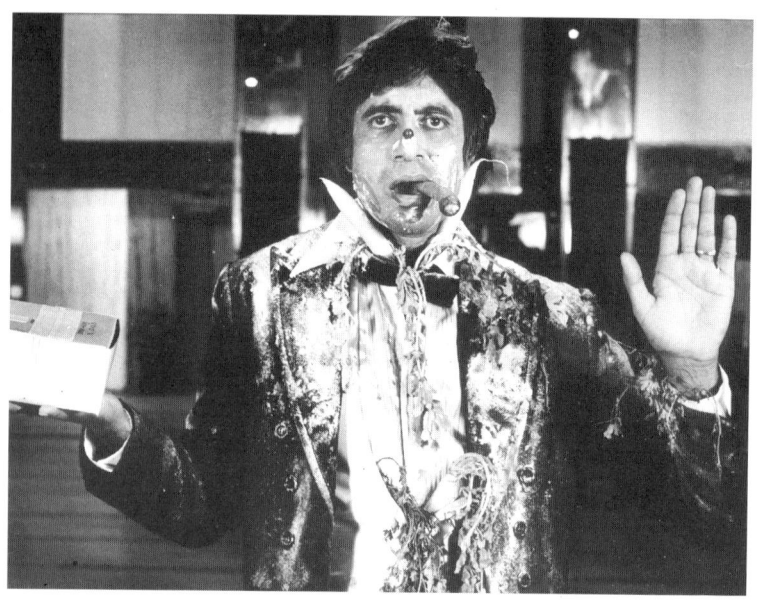

1981: Amitabh Bachchan as the pie-in-the-face clown in Naseeb.

1981: (Left) Hema Malini as Miss Asha, the singer in Naseeb; *(Right) Spunky women band together: Reena Roy, Hema Malini and Kim in* Naseeb.

1981: Amitabh Bachchan as John Jani Janardhan in Naseeb. *'Such an actor comes only once in 76 years,' said Desai of Amitabh Bachchan.*

1981: The deceptive 'friend,' played by Amjad Khan in Naseeb.

1982: Poster of Desh Premee.

(Bottom clockwise) Coolie, *1983: Divine protection renders Iqbal (Amitabh Bachchan) invincible; Rati Agnihotri and Amitabh Bachchan dancing to the song* 'Allarakha'; *Amitabh Bachchan, Rishi Kapoor and Shoma Anand in the song* 'Lambuji Tinguji'.

1985: Desai relaxes during the shooting of Mard *with Bob Christo (extreme left) and Amitabh Bachchan.*

1985: Desai on the sets of Mard *with Amitabh Bachchan and his stunt double.*

1985: Amitabh Bachchan and Desai on the sets of Mard.

1985: Amitabh Bachchan on horseback in Mard. *Desai averred, 'I'd even say Amit is my alter ego.'*

coolie

Manmohan Desai claimed a life-long fascination with Islam and Islamic culture. Living just blocks away from the Bhendi Bazaar, the largest Muslim neighbourhood in Bombay, he was always in contact with Muslims. He wanted to make a film for his 100 million Muslim compatriots. Manmohan Desai described the inception of *Coolie*:

> My office is in a crowded area near Bombay Central, so we'd see these coolies in their red shirts and dhotis and pyjamas in and out, in and out. Very often we'd see them when we'd go by train. They are very fascinating characters. They would never go out of turn. They would sit in a queue, then run when the train comes. Each one would take his compartment. They all have their badges. There's no infighting amongst them. And I'm told, as a matter of fact, towards the end of the day they all sit together, they pool their money, and then they divide the money equally. I said, look, Amitabh has been identified as Anthony (the bootlegger); Amitabh has been identified in *Naseeb* as a waiter, why not bring the characters down to earth so people can identify with them easily… I said, I have not touched upon a Muslim social, so why not bring in a Muslim character? I told it to the writer Prayag Raj, and the whole fabrication of *Coolie* was started. Then we

felt, why not bring in a falcon? That is the national emblem of the United Arab Emirates. So we brought all these things that appeal to the Muslims, and we put one Hindu character there, Chintu, that is, Rishi Kapoor.

Interestingly, in his piece 'Muslim Ethos in Indian Cinema' critic Iqbal Masud enriches the interpretation of the falcon and proves yet again that no matter what film a director may intend to make, the interaction between the story onscreen and the accumulated knowledge and experience of each individual member of the audience is such that a personal and partially unique film will be constructed in the mind of each viewer. Iqbal Masud says:

> The old Mehboob syndrome of Muslim radicalism is reproduced in *Coolie*. Amitabh carries a hawk named Allah Rakha on his wrist. This is a direct reference to poet Iqbal's hawk (Shaheen)—a central symbol in his poetry. Shaheen for Iqbal represented the aspiring, soaring spirit of man as in the line. *Tu Shaheen hai parwaz hai kaam tera*, (you are a hawk, your destiny is flight).[1]

Along with his noble motives, Desai, as usual, combined good business sense. Muslims are movie-goers, regular clients who could fill the coffers of the box offices, and Muslims live throughout India. Desai thus hoped to have in *Coolie* an even bigger grosser than his extremely successful *Amar Akbar Anthony*. Desai's detractors ignored his higher motives altogether and accused him of simply pandering to the moneybags of Middle Eastern countries. And though 1983 to early 1984 was a relatively calm time communally, the centrality of a Muslim figure did not seem to please everyone. Certain airport workers, for example, stated stiffly that, because of its emphasis on Islam, they would not see *Coolie*. Still, it was impossible to imagine at that time that less than a decade later, Bombay would be in flames as politicians played the communal card and public discourse turned towards rejection of 'the other.'

A wide public did, however, accept Desai's film with its portrayal of a poor Muslim hero, women realistically wearing burkhas and praying five times a day, and in which Muslim festivals play a central part. This is not to say that the Muslim hierarchy immediately felt honoured by the attention paid to Islam in the film. The pre-release publicity alone almost gave rise to riots. On posters plastered around Bombay, Amitabh Bachchan was shown with the Koran at his side rather than, as the religious leaders felt seemly, above him in its rightful place. Under pressure, Desai ordered all of the posters in Bombay torn down and replaced with less offensive publicity. Even on the new posters, though, Amitabh Bachchan was draped, as in the film, in a sacred shawl normally reserved only for holy men. Desai again tried to placate the leaders by telling them to see the film before passing judgment. After a great deal of official Muslim reticence, the tables turned drastically. The Muslim public began to see the film, and like the Christians at the release of *Amar Akbar Anthony*, they were overjoyed, 'See our *Coolie*; see our Iqbal Bhai!' Manmohan Desai added:

> Trade journals are saying now that this is a Muslim mythological. The correct impression of the impact of *Coolie* on Muslim audiences comes from watching the film at the Alankar Theatre (at the edge of the Bhendi Bazaar neighbourhood). I knew that once the ladies in pardah started filling that theatre, making the house full daily, that the film was a hit. The Muslims have taken that film to their hearts. Otherwise, the Muslim ladies wouldn't be out there. They're very orthodox. They're not allowed to see any Tom Dick and Harry film by the family, unless the male members see it and approve.

Manmohan Desai, thrilled at its success, said, 'I wish I could make a pilgrimage to Mecca to offer thanks.' As always, a magnanimous caring for the masses for whom his films were destined and a concern for quality filmmaking concurred with very real, bottom-line self-interest: a film must bring in crowds; it must make money. This *Coolie* did, being one of the biggest grossers of 1983-84 (or the biggest, depending upon the figures to which one refers).

video threat

After the threatened Muslim boycott, another menace loomed over *Coolie*, just as over all films post-1980. The long-feared video threat finally materialized into a real loss of revenue at the box office and dried up a once booming Indian film circuit. Foreign markets, especially in England and the Middle East, gave way almost entirely before a cheap, easily available, abundant stock of films on cassette. Films were soon being released on video, either in official or in pirated form, well before theatre premieres.

For several years, industry planners blithely continued to bank on the domestic market, the logic being that in a country as poor as India, the masses would never have access to video technology. Human ingenuity proved the forecasters wrong. Tea-stall owners, even in the heart of slums, went into debt to buy video players; the money from increased business quickly made repayment possible. Servants, who had before negotiated access to television, began giving first preference to employers with VCRs. The irony, of course, is that people the world over began watching many more Hindi films at a time when making them was becoming an increasingly precarious business.

Like other film directors of the eighties, Desai was petrified of the video menace. In his fighting moments he wanted to see video pirates flogged. When feeling more resigned, he said simply, 'You can't fight technology.' To a certain extent, though, he did fight, and, at least for *Coolie*, he won a minor victory. Draconian measures, including police raids of video shops, were taken to insure that no pirated copies reached the shelves until several weeks after the *Coolie*'s theatre release. Even in Europe *Coolie* was seen on big screens before entering people's living rooms.

the making of the film

Coolie was the first film that Manmohan Desai co-directed. His long-time associate Prayag Raj sat in the director's seat for many of the scenes shot. *Coolie* is an MKD film, produced by Manmohan's son Ketan Desai. Like *Amar Akbar Anthony* and *Naseeb*, *Coolie* had the benefit of Desai's own financing. Desai believed in spending money on a film if the expense could be made to show. With many on-site locations, a huge cast including 2000-3000 extras, and a record 245 prints of the film distributed simultaneously, no expense was spared in the effort to make *Coolie* stand apart from the rest of popular film production. Because of the huge investment *Coolie* represented, Manmohan Desai was biting his fingernails, so to speak, before its release and telling journalists that his new film had better be a hit because otherwise he and his son Ketan might find themselves working as coolies at Victoria Station.

Manmohan Desai described the budding of the idea for *Coolie*, the efforts needed to give the film authenticity, and the organizational skills necessary to turn an idea into an onscreen reality:

> I decided to construct a story on a railway porter, but after constructing it, we realized it was going to be very difficult to shoot with Amitabh Bachchan at any railway station. It would be absolutely impossible. How to control the crowds! Then we decided to go to Bangalore. We had a friend called Manjunath Hegde in Bangalore who came to our rescue. He said, 'I'll make all the arrangements with the police and the necessary permissions; you can shoot in Bangalore.' Believe me, we had our hearts in our mouths. We shot there for 20 days, and the government gave us a lot of facilities. We had about 350 armed policemen at the railway station... . People down south are

more cultured, refined. They have seen a lot of shooting of their regional films, so it was nothing new to them. They were so well behaved that when we used to request them to move out when we were coming in for a shot, they would listen. We hardly had any problems for 20 days. The railways were also kind enough to let us shoot there... . We thought we would never be able to get the long shots, but with the good crowd arrangement, the good response of the people and the railways, we could shoot everything, and I don't think anybody before this film had ever shot like this on a railway station, and I don't think anybody can do it again... . Let's just say, we were very, very lucky, and we thanked Manjunath Hegde and the government of Karnataka at that time to allow us to shoot this film.

We had to take a lot of extras, junior artistes, from Bombay. We gave them the clothes of the coolies and we asked them to study the habits of the coolies. We used to linger around the railway stations for days together, much before the shooting, and see how they would smoke the *bidi*... . They would sit in a line when the train would be approaching the railway station, and then they would run towards it.... We have made the junior artists study them, and it looks so very natural that nobody has been able to make out that they were not the real coolies.

Cities mean crowds, and we make generous use of extras because if you do not use extras, if you try to crib and cringe and try to save money on them, you cannot create the atmosphere... . A station is always crammed, so we had to bring extras. The extras that we used at the station were from Bangalore itself. We didn't get them from Bombay. The only junior artists we took from Bombay were to play the coolies. We took about 20 of them, and that was quite sufficient for the Bangalore city station. I used a lot of extras, and that was how we could create the impact... . That's why I have five to six assistant directors, and they would look after the extras, and instruct them. These assistant directors have to instruct the junior artists about what they should do, and it was quite easy to organize the extras in the song 'saari duniya' because they were briefed much in advance as to what each one had to do.

a media event

Coolie was not simply a film. It was an important media event and as such was well-publicized entirely by chance long before its release. It was on 25 July 1982 on the sets of *Coolie* that Amitabh Bachchan had his near-fatal accident; an overly realistic punch in the stomach and a fall against a sharp-edged table led to life-endangering complications. *Coolie* might very well never have been finished. On the one hand, Desai deplored the morbid publicity—'publicity not paid for by me,' as he said. On the other hand, following a well-established pattern, he brought reality into the fiction of his film to let the public participate through the film in the miracle of Amitabh Bachchan's recovery. 'Cashing in on the accident,' his detractors called it. 'Satisfying the public,' Desai considered it. Amitabh Bachchan not only recovered, but he returned to the sets of *Coolie* to take up the fight at the place where shooting had left off. As this fight appears on the screen, two freeze shots have been included to let viewers know exactly the jab in the belly and the landing on a table corner that were responsible for Amitabh's ruptured intestine. Printed on the screen in English, in Hindi, and in Urdu is, 'This is the shot in which Amitabh Bachchan was seriously injured.' If we place ourselves well into the future or far in space from India and Indian audiences, the intervention of reality in the midst of a screen story might seem an unnecessary distraction, but for the masses of India who had prayed for Amitabh Bachchan's recovery, Manmohan Desai knew that speculation about the moment of the accident would be inevitable. By freezing the action and informing the public of the exact moment the blows took place, he was clarifying what could have continued to be clouded in rumours and guesses.

Iqbal Coolie, the character played by Amitabh Bachchan, was originally scripted to die at the end of the story. However, after Amitabh's brush with death, Desai did not feel he could maintain the fatal ending of the story and still face his ever-faithful child audience. He could imagine them cornering him with, 'Uncle, we prayed and Amitabh Bachchan lived and now *you* have killed him.' Iqbal's experience, then, was infused with details from Amitabh's real-life experience. In the film we see Hindus, Muslims, Christians and Sikhs praying for Iqbal's recovery, just as in real life members of the four major religions prayed for Amitabh Bachchan. Iqbal's recovery, like Amitabh's, borders on the miraculous. At one point, Iqbal waves at the crowd from the balcony under which we see the sign 'St. Philomena's Hospital,' a reference to the hospital in Bangalore in which Amitabh Bachchan was first operated on before his transfer to Breach Candy in Bombay for another two-months' stay. Around Iqbal's neck are symbols of the four religions. In real life Amitabh Bachchan returned, once he was well, to St. Philomena's on a pilgrimage and prayed at each of the centres of worship, giving thanks to all of those whose prayers had, it seemed, reached their destinations.

Part of the original idea for *Coolie* was inspired by the true story of a family separated by religion. A woman had been married twice. One husband was Jewish, the other Muslim, and with each she had a son. One husband forbade his son to enter the house of the other husband, and yet the two stepbrothers, despite their different religions, were secretly the best of friends. Simple and altogether real, that seed—two youths whose friendship was blind to religion—flowered into a story as complex as the cast of *Coolie* is large.

the story

Arch-demon Zafar (Kadar Khan), a villain who knows no bounds, bursts a dam and floods a village in order to kill Aslam (Satyen Kappu) and steal his wife Salma (Waheeda Rehman). Her son Iqbal (Master Ravi) is left motherless. A family friend Maruti (Nilu Phule), a Hindu coolie separated from his own wife and baby during the flood, raises Iqbal to follow in his footsteps, carrying heavy loads at Victoria Terminus in Bombay. Allahrakha, the almost magic falcon who has always served Iqbal's family, remains Iqbal's special pet, ready to swoop down whenever Iqbal is in need of rescue or counsel. Salma, mute and amnesiac, spends her life with the tyrannical Zafar.

Salma and Zafar's adopted son Sunny (played as an adult by Rishi Kapoor) is, in accordance with Desai's logic, none other than the lost son of the coolie Maruti. The boy grows up to be an alcohol-imbibing newspaper reporter, forever blue after being separated from his childhood sweetheart Deepa (Shoma Anand), who likewise turns alcoholic during her years of pining for Sunny.

The rich heiress Julie (Rati Agnihotri) has a conspiring legal guardian (Om Shivpuri), a building promoter involved in housing frauds. He would like his son Vicki (Suresh Oberoi) to marry Julie in order to gain lasting control over her fortune. Fate, of course, has her fall in love with Iqbal (Amitabh Bachchan), the penniless but fearless and dashing coolie. Julie refuses to marry anyone, however, until she has avenged her father's (Amrish Puri) murder, committed—she believes—by Aslam, Iqbal's real father, who was taken on in the service of Julie's father after surviving Zafar's attempt on his life. Aslam is, of course, innocent, having been framed by the wicked Zafar. The first half of the film introduces the characters, defines their relationships and sees them separated. In the second half, little by little, they are reunited, and, finally, justice is made to reign through the death of Zafar and his colleagues in crime.

Desai describes his films as old wine in new bottles. Indeed, we are on familiar ground in *Coolie* with one more convoluted lost-found story and a careful blend of the nine *rasas* (sentiments or aesthetic pleasures), the criteria that have been the basis for well-rounded drama since the beginnings of Sanskrit theatre. While *Coolie* contains ingredients to please many and varied tastes, three elements are salient: religion, revolution and comedy.

religion, revolution and comedy

Numerous details lend a Muslim religiosity to *Coolie*. The opening scene has Iqbal's father presenting his mother a green scarf for Id (a Muslim religious festival). Later, when Iqbal, still a child, returns alone to his flooded, abandoned house, the Koran falls from a shelf into his arms, a sign for him not to give up hope or belief. Having grown to adulthood and become a coolie, Iqbal's porter badge bears the holy number 786. And the magic falcon Allahrakha wears a gold necklace with sacred lettering.

The exaltation of religious feeling is also central to the ongoing plot. Salma overhears Zafar scheming to take Iqbal's life; she runs to warn Iqbal of the impending danger and in the process is hit by the bullet meant for him. As she wavers near death in the hospital, the reflection of Allahrakha's necklace shines on Iqbal's face and the sound track changes to a chant *'Allah Huma,'* (the community of Islam), a formula that incites Iqbal to attempt a pilgrimage to Mecca to pray for his mother's life. The emotion-filled scene that follows, though strictly Muslim, appeals across the barriers of formal religions. Iqbal is prepared for his journey, but before he can enter the ship with thousands of other faithful, the official travel doctor declares him too feverish to make the voyage. A *maulvi* (religious leader) recommends that he use his ticket wisely, that he give it to someone too poor to make the Haj (pilgrimage); his good deed will insure that his prayers are heard. As fate would have it, the man the maulvi indicates is none other than Iqbal's own long-lost father. When the ship departs carrying his father and the other blessed pilgrims, Iqbal sings, 'Mubarak ho tum subko haj ka mahina, na thi meri kismat ki dekhoon Madina; Madinewale se mera salaam kehna.' (May the month of Haj be auspicious for you all. It was not my destiny to see Medina; give my greetings to the Prophet.)

Near the end of *Coolie* it is a religious miracle that restores Salma's speech. As she visits Iqbal's empty home, a heavy draft and rattling walls caused by a passing train chance to send down the holy plaque above the door hard onto her head. After 20 years of silence Salma cries her first words: '*Ya Allah!*'

The final fight scene in *Coolie* takes place in the Haji Ali Shrine in Bombay. The villain Zafar Khan mounts the steps to escape from Iqbal. A wind carries the green holy shawl off the *durgah* (shrine) and drapes it around Iqbal like a shield. Zafar's bullets penetrate the shawl and wound Iqbal, but like one obsessed, Iqbal fights on, invincible. With each shot Iqbal cries out sacred verses in Arabic from the Koran. An echo and a crescendo produced by a heavenly choir chanting in minor key increase the impression that we are witnessing a divine intervention. With superhuman force Iqbal topples Zafar from the highest floor of the minaret and then falls into his mother's lap and haltingly uses his bloodied finger to write the name of Allah on a nearby wall.

Religious feeling in the film is not limited to Islamic fervour. Maruti fights off a villain (Puneet Issar) with a mace (the symbol of Hanuman or Maruti). Also, when the wicked Zafar carries off the virtuous Salma, Hindus are reminded of Ravana capturing Seeta. As in the *Ramayana*, a bird (here Allahrakha) reacts to this infamy by attacking Ravana's chariot in the sky (here Zafar's helicopter). The evil that Zafar represents is total and irredeemable. And like Ravana, he must be eliminated entirely.

The most powerful message, however, is not *for* one religion or another, but rather *to* all religions. Once more, Desai makes a plea for communal harmony. A Hindu boy is raised by a Muslim mother and a Muslim boy by a Hindu father. Iqbal and Sunny share Salma as their mother, just as Hindus and Muslims share one motherland and should for this reason—the message is clear—look upon one another as brothers. The presence of Julie, the Christian girl, provides a nod in the direction of the second largest minority in India.

If religion is close to the hearts of most viewers, the triumph of the poor and downtrodden is equally cheered. The bustling train station is shown as the place where coolies wait for trains, carry heavy loads, wash up, eat, celebrate religious festivals, find themselves mistreated, go on strike, and even lie down in front of a moving train to obtain recognition for their just cause. Talking freely about revolt and the fight for justice, Manmohan Desai expressed his interest in the Polish situation as it obtained in 1983:

> What's happening in Poland is very nice. They're being oppressed, and they want to come out for solidarity; it's good drama material: revolution and religion mixed together. I'm saying revolution and God exist together. If you can do that, like in *Coolie*, you can have box office success.

Desai makes another historical comparison:

> The coolies storm that house; they bash things up. It's nothing but October Revolution, storming the Winter Palace. It's been done in history by the masses. In their small way these people are doing the same thing.

Of course, the 'revolution' in *Coolie* does not change the status quo. Iqbal shouts, *'Kal tumhara, aaj hamaara!'* (Yesterday was yours; today is ours.) Tomorrow is not mentioned, and really it need not be since Hindi carries the unusual ambiguity of having the same word *(kal)* to express both yesterday and tomorrow. Iqbal's slogan in Hindi has no verb, hence no tense. 'Today is ours' is clear, but *'kal tumhaara'* could mean either 'yesterday was yours' or 'tomorrow will be yours' or both. In fact, the coolies have only a temporary victory; in keeping with the carnival spirit, they reign only one day. Manmohan Desai admitted:

> I'm not encouraging revolution. I say let them let their steam off. Don't oppress them all the time so that they can never rebel, so they can't speak their mind or express themselves. Let them speak out. Let

them also feel for a change, 'All right, we are somebody.' Why do you want to make them suffer, to grind them to dust all the time. They (art directors) are trying to grind their characters deeper and deeper into the ground. Let the steam be vented. It's not the October Revolution; it's not storming the Winter Palace, but in their own small way, the coolies have a great time there. They're asking for their deeds; they were cheated out of their houses. They say, 'We will not leave till we get our money back or we get our homes; if not, we'll have a spot of fun.' It's done everywhere in the world, and I've shown it in a lighter way. If I showed the same thing in a serious way, nobody would like it. In a lighter way, people laugh; they enjoy it. The chap on the ground, down on the street, says, 'Ha! We've shown that imperialist chap; we've shown that rich man a thing or two.'

Interestingly, Mani Ratnam's Tamil film *Nayakan* (made four years later) has a scene which, though similar, is played, like the entire film, in total seriousness. The slum dwellers who invade the rich man's house also begin by breaking a chandelier and a mirror before they go on to destroy all his furniture in a chilling act of intimidation that ensures the slum dwellers will not be displaced to make way for a factory. Mani Ratnam gives us a slice of reality. Desai gives us a lighter version in keeping with the mood of his film, the result both of his desire to entertain and of his iconoclastic streak. Yet one can never tell how the poor in the audiences might react even to such sugarcoated messages, whether they will simply laugh and forget or whether they will feel emboldened to fight in turn. Certainly, some governments found even this circus-like revolution to be threatening: scenes with the hammer and sickle were preventively cut before *Coolie* was sent to certain sensitive Middle Eastern countries.

The second half of the film deals more seriously with issues faced by the poor and the oppressed. Desai had decided to update his formula; everyone, he felt, was tired of cops and smugglers. In *Coolie* the bad guys are the corrupt politicians, chit fund embezzlers, and dishonest housing promoters. These villains seem to have learned a cynical lesson, that robbing the poor is more profitable than robbing the rich; the wealthy may possess more money per capita, but the poor, simply because of their numbers offer a boon that can be milked to greater advantage. In response, Iqbal gives up his railway platform to stand on the election platform. As Iqbal urges the voters to elect him, his speech includes the line 'The world belongs to the poor!' To this, the cinema audiences at the time in India responded with enthusiastic applause. Having Amitabh Bachchan play the electioneering Iqbal showed prescience. 'All the workers will vote for you,' Iqbal is told. In real life, after having denied for years that he would ever leave acting for politics, Amitabh Bachchan stood for a seat in parliament in the late 1984 election that followed Mrs. Gandhi's assassination and Rajiv Gandhi's step into power. In his hometown of Allahabad all the workers must have voted for him because his victory was indeed sweeping.

Some might accuse Desai of compliantly following a trend in *Coolie* in bringing politics to the fore. 1983-84 were fertile years for politically oriented films. Yet as early as 1974 in *Roti* political shenanigans were denounced. '*Public jo public hai sub jaante hain; andar kyaa hai; baahar kyaa hai; ye sub kuch pehchaante hain.*' (The public knows all; they recognize the difference between what is on the inside and on the outside, *i.e.*, what appears to be and what is.) So sings the character played by Rajesh Khanna as he shines light on those who talk of public service but who act in their own self-interest.

Coolie is not actually a revolutionary film, but a certain attitude is nevertheless recommended: a simple person can refuse to submit humbly to injustice. Our principal focus throughout the film is on super-coolie Amitabh Bachchan, who, faithful to his persona, can right all wrongs single-handedly. However, the film's strike sequence, though it lasts only a few minutes during the credits, shows coolies achieving their goal of justice without the help of a superhero. Amitabh Bachchan is missing, and yet by using their numbers and their cohesive strength, the coolies carry through a serious revolt, not simply a carnivalesque one-day seizure of power. Those in the comfortable confines of society are forced to realize to what extent they are dependent on those 'who carry the loads of the world'. Well-dressed arriving passengers puff, pant and wipe sweat from their brows as they manage their own bags. The coolie strike effectively reminds those at the top of society's hierarchy that they must not take for granted the services of those at the bottom. Such a scene was most uncharacteristic of popular cinema of the period. The very notion of 'hero' is largely incompatible with democratic group action. The next major cinematic reminder of the effectiveness of a pooling of efforts would come in 2001 with Ashutosh Gowariker's *Lagaan*.

Desai did not consider images of revolt to be his principal contribution to the underprivileged among his audiences. Rather, he hoped to lighten their loads by entertaining them. And the comedy in *Coolie* is droll. From broad slapstick, which keeps even the youngest enthralled, to more subtle visual and verbal humour that engages alert minds, *Coolie* overflows with clever comic ideas. After the coolies invade the building promoter's house, Iqbal captures the rich heiress Julie, slings her over his shoulder like a sack of potatoes and carries her to his home. Handcuffed in place, she is to serve as collateral, not to be released until her uncle has fulfilled his promise to sell homes to the coolies at the originally agreed upon prices. After playing the tough, smart, unbeatable hero, however, nonsense becomes dominant and Iqbal morphs into a bumbling idiot in this young woman's presence. While Iqbal is trying to prepare a French omelette by following the instructions of a radio cooking lesson (to the letter), Julie discovers that a slight nudge to the knob will tune in a yoga lesson; by switching quickly back and forth from station to station she can regain the upper hand. In a series of short gags with enhancing sound effects we see him, for example, breathing pepper deeply until steam comes out of his ears, trying to throw an onion into the frying pan while standing on his head, or sitting on an egg he has placed on the floor...till out hatches a baby chick. The handcuff key then falls from his pocket; Julie fishes it over and frees herself while Iqbal remains immobilized, his legs inextricably entwined about his neck.

Desai's humour was not without a cutting edge. High and low alike could find themselves victims of his wit. Many journalists felt that Desai made the Rishi Kapoor character Sunny into the caricature of a newspaperman in order to mock the people of the press with whom Desai had every reason to want to settle scores. Sunny arrives along with the coolies at the rich promoter's home. When the promoter asks, 'Who are you?' Sunny retorts with smug self-assurance, 'What! You don't know me? I'm Sunny, the *great* reporter!' He then flaunts the power of the press, *i.e.*, the prerogative to give bad publicity. During the circus of an interview his questions are singularly lacking in substance. The tone is light-hearted and funny, but some journalists bristled at what they suspected to be a real undercurrent of aggression.

Coolie, in many ways, is one of Desai's most accomplished films. Camera angles enhance the viewers' emotions. Transitions are often clever and elaborate. The music is memorable, and the song picturizations show thought, care, and a mastery of the medium. This being said, scripting continued to be Desai's weakness. Certain basic plot assumptions, though fundamental to the development of the story, are incomprehensible. Sunny is born a Hindu and adopted as a baby by a pious Muslim woman who, we are led to believe, considers the baby entirely her own. Sunny himself obviously does not know of his Hindu origin since we see him flabbergasted to learn over half-way through the film that he is not Salma and Zafar's child. Yet he never shows any sign of having been taught a single feature of Muslim worship. Through such plot illogic Desai no doubt achieves his primary goal, that of not offending Hindu spectators who consider Sunny to have remained a Hindu. The drawback, however, is that Sunny's character is greatly weakened by the basic confusion over precisely who and what he is.

Coolie's pacing, too, is faulty. At moments, the film simply offers too much of a good thing—one too many fights, one too many hospital scenes, one too many songs at close intervals, and a final chase scene that attempts to force a sense of suspense. Judicious cutting could have given a shorter, stronger film.

Reactions to *Coolie* varied. One Bombay dweller saw coolies in a new light, 'Before, I felt coolies were just a normal part of the environment of a train station, but after seeing the film, I look at each one as an individual.' Among the press, reactions were rather predictable. All the critics who disliked Desai's work generally, and this included the majority of Indian reviewers, were no more favorable to *Coolie* than to Desai's earlier films. In Europe *Coolie* attracted more positive attention. It was shown as part of the official selection of the twenty-first Mostra Internationale del Cinema Nuovo (the Pesaro Film Festival) in Italy in June 1985. This is not to say that its presence was appreciated by all. Several invited Indian filmmakers representing New Wave cinema (Mani Kaul among others) expressed their shock that the festival would serve as a forum for such 'crass commercial cinema'. *Coolie* nevertheless ran to a full house in Pesaro where the local townspeople made up an important part of the apparently contented audience. Afterwards, Desai showed his usual verve when speaking of Pesaro, 'I couldn't go to the festival because I was down with flu; if I had been there, I would have definitely pulled off Mr. Mani Kaul's dhoti!'

In other areas abroad the reception of *Coolie* depended on the particular situation of the communities of Indian origin who were often the principal viewers of exported Hindi popular films. In certain parts of Africa where Muslim-Hindu tensions are close to the surface, the film could not be publicized at all for fear of exacerbating communal discord. In sections of East Africa the title itself was objectionable, *'coolie'* being a derogatory term applied locally to all Indians.

Back in India, Desai assessed *Coolie*'s strong points and analyzed its success in view of his following film *Mard*:

> The first half is all nice comedy. The first three reels of the film, I feel, are brilliant. The flood scenes are something new for the audience. Also, there's the sentiment for the mother, and the scene of the yoga where the radio line changes. Then the sequence of the Haj; I think it's a classical sequence for Hindi films. It's considered very pious if you send your parents on a pilgrimage; this boy unintentionally sends his father on a pilgrimage. This along with the election scene where Amitabh Bachchan hits out at the rich—it's a sure formula here. There are 80% poor and 10% rich, right? And then the Haji Ali Shrine sequence with the name of God upon his shoulder, when he recites the lines of the Koran. These things have clicked in a big way. That's why I'm trying to fashion *Mard* on that line, but I'm not getting it that way.
>
> The Haj reel is an immortal reel in my opinion. I've incorporated a Hindu item in *Mard*, a very beautiful reel, but it will not be in the class of this Haj sequence. This just happens, you know. It's like a masterpiece. You don't plan a masterpiece. It just happens. You can't reproduce that thing again. So I've become very conscious of my film *Coolie* now. Will my film *Mard* have the same items? Will it have the same appeal as *Coolie*? *Coolie* is first half comedy; first three reels are emotional, comedy, comedy, comedy, then trrrrraaa...: emotion, drama, action, everything going in like this in correct portions.

a wide angle on
manmohan desai's work

kaleidoscope

chhalia

Very early, Desai established his own preferences as a filmmaker and, to varying degrees from film to film, left his cinematic signature on his work through recognizable recurring marks of his style. At a glance, the differences between Desai's first film, the 1960-released *Chhalia* and his big hits of the seventies and eighties are striking.[1] *Chhalia*, in black and white, is a simple triangular love story with three main characters and two minor ones, quite unlike the multi-layered, complex maze of subplot within subplot that would distinguish most of Desai's later stories. *Chhalia* has the look of the fifties. Drama is central. There is no farce, and comedy is reduced to passing moments. Yet a closer look at *Chhalia* will reveal that it bears the Manmohan Desai imprint as surely as does *Coolie*.

At the heart of the film is the problem of communal conflict set against Partition and its aftermath. Shaanti (Nutan), a young Hindu woman finds herself in Pakistan where she bears her husband's (Rehman) child. The Hindu child has been given the name Anwar and raised as a Muslim. In his dual religious allegiance, he is a forerunner of Akbar in *Amar Akbar Anthony*, and to a certain degree, of John Jani Janardhan in *Naseeb*. Anwar's father refuses to believe that Anwar is his son. Imagining that his wife has been unfaithful during her stay in Pakistan, he casts her out as unjustly as Ram sent Sita on her lonely way. Desai's reference to the epics situates him within a long tradition in popular cinema. The homeless Shaanti is befriended by Chhalia, a character played by Raj Kapoor as a continuation of Raju from Raj Kapoor's own *Shree 420* (1955).

The error of communal bickering is driven boldly home in a powerful scene. Little Anwar, following the lead of his Hindu schoolmates, throws rocks at a passing Pathan. Then, catching a glimpse of the Pathan's face, he realizes that his victim is none other than his 'father,' the Muslim who raised him during his time in Pakistan and one of the people he most cherishes in the world. He runs to Akbar Khan (Pran), throws his arms around him and cries that he will never throw rocks at anyone again.

Another recurring, highly emotive element in Desai's cinema is the absent mother, the lost, longed-after one. Little Anwar is separated from his mother early on and spends much of the film pining for her. He finds himself studying in a boarding school where, by chance, his real father is the teacher. During reading class one day, Anwar is called upon to read a text about a mother. The boy breaks down sobbing midway through the lesson. His father-teacher, who has so far remained cold towards the child, is touched to the point that, in spite of himself, he consoles his rejected son. Anwar's response is similar to young Rahul's later in *Aa Gale Lag Jaa*; he refuses to accept his father's love if he cannot also have his mother's.

Certain Desai heroes are hopelessly romantic. Like Prem (Shashi Kapoor) in *Aa Gale Lag Jaa* or Dharam (Dharmendra) in *Dharam-Veer*, Chhalia is unabashedly in love. Yet such is his nobility and his respect for fidelity, that he unhesitatingly steps aside, yielding before his beloved's desire to remain true to her husband, cruel though the husband may earlier have been. Religion is a constant; family is another, and the reunification of this separated family—of Anwar, his father and his mother—is essential.

Already in *Chhalia*, Desai strikes a balance between his portrayal of the rich and the poor. Both husband and wife come from well-to-do families; when her future husband first calls upon Shaanti, he arrives in an expensive automobile. But later, when Chhalia gives her shelter in his humble hut, Shaanti joins the ranks of women whose lives are full of toil and devoid of luxury.

Desai's strengths are clear from his first film. The songs are lovely and are beautifully filmed. Ellipses create speed and a sense of magic. In the song '*Dum dum diga diga*,' for instance, the ladder Chhalia is climbing starts to fall, but in the following shot he is comfortably seated, as if by miracle, on the shoulders of a passing man. At another point, Shaanti has prepared Chhalia's supper and is waiting for him to eat. She timidly lowers her eyes. In the next shot, she is lifting her head, but time has passed; she is now outside praying that her husband will return. Briefly and cinematically, the conflict between her current situation and her desire to be reunited with her husband is made clear.

If many of Desai's qualities as a director are apparent from the beginning, what will prove to be a lasting weakness is also present in his first film. Like much or perhaps most of Hindi popular cinema, Desai's films testify to more care having gone into individual scenes than into plot lines as a whole. The result is that one can take pleasure watching a film out of order; likewise, certain scenes can be outstanding enough to draw spectators again and again. The disadvantage is that holes often appear in the story line; some questions remain unanswered; other answers defy common sense. Shaanti, for example, inexplicably seems to forget, when she attempts suicide, that she has a son to care for. Also, as Pran, the actor who played the Pathan, pointed out, it is the Pathan who should finally bring Shaanti and her husband back together; only he can explain what happened to her in Pakistan. Instead, in the last scene, he remains in the background as Raj Kapoor, the star playing Chhalia, runs to rescue Shaanti from the toppling figure of a fiery Ravana before dramatically forcing her into her husband's arms.

One could compare Desai's work to a kaleidoscope with its seemingly infinite possibilities for change within precise limits. In the toy, amazing variety in geometric form and colour is produced with bits of glass that, themselves, never change but are simply rearranged. In the same way, Indian fabrics exhibit elements of predictability in patterns and colours; yet intricate variations assure each textile design surprising individuality. So it is that from film to film Desai wove similar themes, characters and, at times, even identical lines of dialogue. As he emphasized certain motifs, refined others and elaborated upon still others, each film became distinct.

self-plagiarism

Desai is not the only filmmaker to have repeated himself. Alfred Hitchcock recognized and ennobled the artist's tendency to feed off of himself. 'Self-plagiarism,' he said, 'is style.' Several of Howard Hawks' films, too, (*e.g., Only Angels Have Wings, To Have And To Have Not,* and *Rio Bravo*), though of different genres, have similar plots, themes, interrelationships between the sexes, and often repeated bits of dialogue. Repeating oneself can be a sign of laziness, of consistency, of prudence, of the need to make a point or to exorcise a problem, or indeed, simply a matter of style. Shabana Azmi, when asked how she would classify Manmohan Desai's films, answered, 'The genre is a Manmohan Desai film.' His critics, of course, used words such as 'rehash' to describe this repetitive tendency, which in a more positive light, could be seen as an opportunity for a second chance, an opportunity to improve. Examples of Desai's returning to similar ideas abound in his work. In *Roti* Jagdeep is forced to swallow a housing deed; in *Coolie* Rishi Kapoor gets even more laughs when he is force-fed a newspaper. In one scene in *Amar Akbar Anthony* Amitabh Bachchan comes out of an Easter egg to dance at a party; in another scene, he is dressed as a priest and is playing a violin. In *Mard* the two ideas are joined when Amitabh Bachchan comes out of a birthday cake—violin first—dressed as Father Anthony and repeating several lines he spoke in the earlier film.

Animals are frequently used as part of the narrative. Both the secular falcon in *Dharam-Veer* and the more religious falcon in *Coolie* have semi-magic powers that allow them to swoop down to their masters' rescue. Dogs, cobras, horses and tigers recur. Music is also re-used, sometimes as an economy measure for the producer, sometimes to create an in-joke with the audience. First heard in *Suhaag*, the *'chappal'* music is the background against which Amit (Amitabh Bachchan) repeatedly pulls off his leather sandal and poses the riddle of his shoe size as an excuse to lay into the unwary and witless characters he encounters. In *Desh Premee* the same music clues the audience to an oncoming confrontation between Raju (Amitabh Bachchan) and a couple of petty criminals who, listening to Raju's polite formal speech, do not realize that blows are about to rain. In *Coolie* the musical warning takes a third distancing step; it would appear that this time the screen villain, too, has seen *Suhaag* and *Desh Premee*. It suffices that Iqbal (still Amitabh Bachchan) take off his sandal to the well-known tune to restore a man faking a heart attack (Om Shivpuri) to good health.

Whenever past material is reused, the formula is generally followed only to a certain point. The repeated lines, the evocative costumes, the background music or other inside references become a succinct form of communication, little telegraphic messages sent to audiences, the equivalent of the mean-looking stranger entering the local saloon in a cowboy film or the beautiful but dangerous-looking brunette trying to entice the detective in a *film noir*. An interesting *film noir* or a good cowboy film will show the cliché but will not stop with it. The time saved through the use of the familiar is, at best, spent developing the novel or unexpected. If Desai's detractors railed against him for repeating himself, Amitabh Bachchan's assessment was different:

> It's interesting seeing him going back to some of the stuff he's already made. There's no harm in following a given technique or a given formula. You know that what you're seeing is totally illogical, but he has always managed to put it forward in such a convincing manner that you tend to forget logic. And so beautifully done. You can see the pains that he's taken in putting something so illogical into something which you eventually tend to believe within the course of three hours. That must surely be the work of a genius.

kinetics

He doesn't like wasting time.... He wants a lot of pace in whatever he does.

—*Amitabh Bachchan, April 1987*

energy

If the focus in certain periods and among certain directors has been on the tragedy of the human condition, *e.g.*, as illustrated in Bimal Roy's *Devdas* or in Guru Dutt's *Pyaasa*, another important trend in Hindi cinema has been toward lighthearted, lively exuberance. Desai, no doubt because of his own speedy temperament, carried this tradition a step further. A fast talker, a quick mover, Manmohan Desai constructed his cinema in keeping with his own inherent impatience. As Shabana Azmi noted, when a cameraman tried to do some slow trolley work during one of his shootings, Desai immediately yelled, 'Hey, what are you doing? This is not a Bengali film; this is a Manmohan Desai film!' His films are not meant to be watched languidly, one's eyes caressing the screen. Rather, many scenes are so rich in detail and so quickly paced that multiple viewings are necessary to grasp their full content.

Desai was a person who used energy, who gave it off, who passed it on, who stirred it up in his team. At the end of the chain it is the public who receives this accumulated vitality in the final work that appears on screen. The limitation of working as he did came at the moment of discerning the delicate distinction between energizing stimulation and a sense-numbing excess of bright colors, loud music, and quick movement. Perfect pacing is necessary to maintain a balance on the tightrope towards an exhilarating high. A few too many seconds in a dynamic scene can plunge audiences into a jittery low, similar to that produced by an excess of caffeine. At times Desai probably did not get off stage, as it were, soon enough. At other times he judiciously offered welcome breathers. In *Desh Premee*, for instance, Navin Nischol, playing a policeman, has come to search Parveen Babi's house for stolen diamonds planted in her bag. Mistakenly believing him to be a criminal, she grabs her father's gun and pursues him in a fast, funny, action-filled scene. Abruptly, the mood changes. In the midst of the scuffle come a close-up and a slowing down, marked by romantic music, as the two suddenly touch, gaze into one another's eyes, and realize their physical attraction. Viewers need such pauses, and Manmohan Desai often, but not always, gave them.

It is possible that some of the hostility on the part of the intelligentsia to Manmohan Desai, even if it was never stated as such, could be traced to Desai's very use of time, which was, in many respects, at odds with a traditional sense of Indianness. Satyajit Ray's *Shatranj ke Khilari* (The Chess Players, 1977) illustrates this gap in sensibilities when, as British troops march in after crushing the 1857 Revolt, the two chess players agree on the need for a faster, more modern game of chess. Writer Mark Kingwell considers speed to be part of an existential malaise, a doomed human effort to escape death:

> ...desperate attempt to get away from ourselves. And I think that's really what boredom is. It's a sort of deep unhappiness or restlessness

with the fact of one's own existence. Speed isn't the answer because it simply doesn't solve the problem, but of course it's very difficult to see that when you're in the grips of boredom.[1]

Leaving possible motivations aside, what is observable is the way in which Desai dismantled the time-space connection through quick cutting. His characters appear freed of the laws of physics and transported about as if in dreams. In *Suhaag* soon after their first encounter, Shashi Kapoor and Amitabh Bachchan must fight a bully who has attacked them both. To light, fast background music, they kick the man down a flight of stairs; miraculously, before he lands, one of the two heroes is waiting below. Desai's time is double time, magic time, Superman time. It is cinematic time writ large.

Everyday life is full of boring repetition and tedious humdrum activities, the very stuff that adds to our 'existential malaise', our sense of the limited nature of life itself. Fiction, generally, tends to eliminate the daily grind. Indian popular cinema, unlike much of art cinema, is particularly unmindful of realistic time considerations. In the seventies and eighties, the fashion of the multi-starrer required ever-greater speed to maintain the progression of all of the characters' stories. Thematically, Desai's series of items are often lumpy at the linking points. Cinematographically, however, many of the lumps are smoothed and the action further speeded through the use of clever transitions. In *Naseeb* alcohol is poured for Vicki (Shatrughan Sinha) in London; the next shot takes us to India where a drink is placed on the table by Bombay waiter John Jani Janardhan (Amitabh Bachchan). Alcohol serves as a more meaningful link when Vicki breaks a bottle on the street, a sign that he has decided to give up his debilitating habit. Two shots later, we see John, the teetotaller, now drunk, circling an intact bottle of whisky on a table. Alcoholism, like a virus, has passed from friend to friend.

Desai offers an array of locomotion, from stilts to elephants, from submarines to balloons. In *Aa Gale Lag Jaa*, the final fight takes place on roller skates. And in *Naseeb* the restaurant revolves! Manmohan Desai pointed with pride to the motion in his motion pictures, 'We commercial filmmakers make *movies*. Something moves on screen and within you.'

accumulation and invention

Accumulation, the art of packing every scene with as many details as possible is the fruit of hard work and a quick mind. This most essential, most characteristic element of Desai's style can result in a geometric complexity of relationships, as in the picturization of the song *'Pardah hai'* from *Amar Akbar Anthony*, one of the director's favourites. It would have been funny enough to see tiny Taiyabali (Mukri) waddle into the auditorium for the *qawwali* programme or funny enough again to see him accompanied by a tall daughter. But he is followed by six tall daughters, all clad in black burkhas; together, they fill an entire row. A series of links is established throughout the song; first, between Akbar (Rishi Kapoor) and his musicians, then, between Akbar and Salma (Neetu Singh), the daughter he is attempting to woo, between Salma's infatuated sisters and Akbar, between Anthony (Amitabh Bachchan) and the woman he calls 'Ma' (Nirupa Roy), between Anthony and Taiyabali, who must be physically restrained from walking out, between Anthony and Akbar as Anthony unexpectedly belts out *'Akbar tera naam nahin hai'* (Then your name isn't Akbar), and finally between the on-screen audience and Akbar and Salma when, at the end of the song, they cheer the triumph of love over paternal authority. The props offer further embellishments: the daughters' black veils lift in unison under Akbar's spell until Taiyabali's cane brings them down with one quick thrust; Taiyabali's eyebrows bob as Anthony rhythmically pulls a garland of money from his shirt, and like a magician, Akbar produces a series of poetic items—coloured veils, a rose, a mirror, wine and fire—to bring the words of the song alive.

Desai explained the development process:

> It was only after the song was recorded that I and Mr. Kamal sat down for days together to think about these ideas. Hence the props came into the picturization after the song was recorded and not before. So the credit for the recording goes to Laxmikant and Anand Bakshi. And we did full justice to it by putting props according to the lines of the song.... Taiyabali's bobbing eyebrows was Mr. Kamal's idea.... It took about five days to picturize the song. We had only one camera.

We might react to one of Desai's complex, idea-packed scenes somewhat as we would to a group of acrobats constructing a human pyramid. With the ascent of each additional member of the troop, we become progressively more awe-struck. A five-member pyramid impresses us. The troupe that succeeds in building a ten-member pyramid amazes us. So it is that Manmohan Desai added one element after another to make not a good scene, but an outstanding one. And in his best work, like a good circus group, he stopped when he was thrilling us, a moment before the entire construction would have collapsed under its own weight.

technical choices

the audio component

> Cinematic sound is that which does not simply add to, but multiplies, two or three times, the effect of the image.
>
> —*Akira Kurosawa*[1]

A particularity of Indian cinema is the importance given to the 'audio' aspect of this audiovisual medium. Audience interest in Hindi cinema dialogues, music, and songs probably has no counterpart in the world. Background music and sound, which audiences are less consciously aware of, are also an essential part of the package. Desai explained:

> Now, you cannot visualize the film today without good, appropriate background music. I'll give you an instance. In the Bond films, there is just a simple shot of James Bond walking through those pipe-like things. (Desai imitates the music.) The public starts tapping. There is nothing in that shot. The man is just walking, and he takes a gun and fires at the viewer. But that background music, when it comes on, people start tapping; they start clapping... . Now without the background music that shot would not carry any weight. Any American film, any

action sequence without sound effects or without background music falls flat. Absolutely flat. You can judge from the silent films.

It is only in the last decade, that is, after *Sholay*, that people in India have started realizing the meaning and effect that the sound track can have. When they did the 70 mm stereo mixing of *Sholay*, they made you hear even the toss of the coin. Since then, we have been trying to put as many sound effects as possible in films. In my films it takes 30 days to do the re-recording—I think that is the maximum anyone takes in India—because we want to put even the minutest footsteps or the click of a button and everything possible to heighten the effect.

Laxmikant and Pyarelal were responsible for the music, *i.e.*, the songs and background score, of nine of Desai's twenty films—*Roti*, *Chacha Bhatija*, *Parvarish*, *Dharam-Veer*, *Amar Akbar Anthony*, *Suhaag*, *Naseeb*, *Desh Premee*, and *Coolie*. Manmohan Desai discussed their collaborative effort:

First, we have to have the script ready.... Then we work on the song situations. Then we go and narrate it to the music director. They give an idea. I've been working with Lamikant for about 10 to 12 years, so I give him the story first; then he hears the song situations. Then he works on the tune; he calls me after a couple of days. In the meantime, I also try to hum out some tunes. Though I don't know classical music, nor can I play piano or harmonium, I have an instinct, a flair you can call it, to compose tunes. And I also try to hum out some tunes. When I meet my music director, he plays a few numbers, and I select one of them. Sometimes, it's not okay, and he may have to make more tunes. But I always share an excellent rapport with Laxmikant. And sometimes, when he hums out one line, I feel the next line comes out from me. I remember in *Amar Akbar Anthony* there were so many numbers that we sat down together, and at every sitting we could take out a song.

First of all, you must inspire the music director. After that, there are two ways. First, you have a tune, and you get the lyrics written out. For the other, you get the lyrics and then make the tune. In my case,

I would like the tune to be composed first, and then we fit in the lyrics.

So with Laxmikant I had a very beautiful rapport, and we could come up with something nice... . During the process of recording, I start to think what I'm going to do in the song, where I'm going to start the song, where I'm going to end the song, and I start thinking of the gags and business in the song because if the song is not picturized well, the Indian public—they like to hear songs; they care for music—but if they don't like it, they'll walk out of the theatre. You'll find half the auditorium out. So in order for them to be seated, not only the tune has to be catchy, but the situation has to be good. They should feel, 'Yes, a song should come at this situation,' and if it's well picturized, they'll laugh and they'll clap.

When you share an excellent rapport with the music director, then it becomes sort of teamwork. So we got along famously and had many hit songs. The credit is entirely Laxmikant's... . Now Mr. Pyarelal comes into the film during the interludes of the song... . Laxmikant is the one who composes the tunes, the *mukhra* (introduction, leading phrase) and the *antra* (any verse other than the first). The interludes of the song and the background music are done by Mr. Pyarelal... . He sees the film, assesses the film and then gives me an idea of what he wants to do. Like, say, for instance in *Coolie* Pyarelal worked at great lengths, took four or five shifts only to compose the last background music where Coolie, that is Amitabh Bachchan, has been hit by four bullets and he's still going on and on and hits the villain. Pyarelal gave fabulous voices, choir music. It gave an eerie feeling to the whole sequence. His background music and Amitabh's voice reciting those passages from the Koran lifted the sequence sky high.

The precision of language required for the Arabic in this scene required Amitabh Bachchan to spend two full days for dubbing a few lines. Attention to the sound track is expensive, as Desai explained:

Pyarelal watches the film, notes the footage, says that from here to here is eighty feet or about two and a half minutes, then composes and times it. An eight-hour music shift costs Rs. 20,000 to 25,000. A film needs a minimum of twelve shifts. *Coolie* took 23 to 25 shifts. The background music for it cost rupees eight lakh.

The high cost of the music component no doubt explains the repetition of some background music from one Desai film to another. Much time, energy and money went into developing the music for *Amar Akbar Anthony*. In *Suhaag* and *Desh Premee*, bits of the *Amar Akbar Anthony* score were brought out and refurbished.

An excellent analysis of the importance of music in Indian cinema comes from composer Vanraj Bhatia who explained the operatic nature of Indian cinema:

> The most dramatic moments in our films are often those where all the action stops and the song takes over, expressing every shade of emotional reverberation, and doing it far more effectively than the spoken word or the studied gesture. The situational songs in the films of Guru Dutt, in *Bobby*[2], and in *Amar Akbar Anthony* work extremely well as condensations of dramatic action... .[3]

Songs being a must, good lyrics are essential. Many of Anand Bakshi's rhymes are an alliterative joy, as in the *'jise meri yaad aaye jab chahe chale aaye'* line (the one who thinks of me may come to meet me whenever she wants) in *'My name is Anthony Gonsalves'* from *Amar Akbar Anthony*. The success of a song depends not only on its writer but also on its interpreter. Manmohan Desai had his favourite singers:

> Singers like Lata Mangeshkar and Mohammed Rafi can make even an ordinary tune nice whereas a bad singer... it would not be fair of me to name the singer, but in *Coolie* I had an experience. I recorded the song 'Sari duniya ka bojh' by another playback singer, and I was not satisfied, so I had to change the playback singer and give it to Shabbir who sang it fairly well. So a good tune can be enhanced by a

good singer, and in the same way a good tune can be spoilt by a bad singer.

Rafi sang many songs in my films because I was a great admirer, you can say a devotee, of this man. I remember even when I was a kid, I used to go to somebody's recording; I would inquire if it was Mohammed Rafi's recording. I would go to hear him and then go and touch his feet... I think that was the voice of God... . The man was so versatile! Give him a sad song; give him a light song; give him a song with a low bass, a high pitch; he would excel in all of them. At the same time, he was a great human being... . The amazing thing about Rafi sahib was that he could change his voice. He would always ask at the recording, 'This song is being picturized on which actor?' Now, on Shammi Kapoor, he would sing it the Shammi Kapoor way. On Dharmendra, he would sing it the Dharmendra way. On Amitabh, he would sing it his way. His versatility was truly amazing. And he was excellent in high notes as well as in bass... . So my childhood idols were Lata Mangeshkar and Mohammed Rafi, and I have said that even God got jealous of his voice and wanted to hear him in person; that's why He called him up at such a young age.[4] I don't compare anybody with Rafi and with the going away of Rafi, I am at a great loss. I don't have any good singers who have a voice like Rafi, who could do justice to my songs. It's a great loss to me as well as a great loss to his family.

There was a time when many of the big music directors boycotted Mohammed Rafi for three or four years, and they projected Mr. Kishore Kumar in a big way after *Aradhana*. But when I made *Amar Akbar Anthony*, and even during the time of *Dharam-Veer* I told Laxmikant Pyarelal that I wanted only Mohammed Rafi to sing my songs and nobody else. They were a little hesitant, but then they agreed, and they asked me whether he would be ready to sing for them because he was almost boycotted for a couple of years. I went to Rafi Saab and I said, 'Saab, this is my first film; these are the films I'm making. I'm coming up in a big way. Would you please sing for me?'

And I remember Rafi Saab telling me, 'Manmohan, for your sake I am willing to sing for these people; otherwise, I would never sing for them.'

I said, 'If you want, I will ask them to come to your place for rehearsals.'

He said, 'No, I will go to the music director's place and rehearse.' In a way you can say Rafi's comeback in 1975 was due to Manmohan Desai because I insisted on bringing him back with a song in *Dharam-Veer*—'O meri mehbooba.' After that, Rafi Saab never looked back again. Due to certain power politics he was shunned by the music directors, and when I brought him back in *Amar Akbar Anthony*, everybody flocked to Mohammed Rafi again, and rightly so.

On the subject of film music Manmohan Desai expressed himself well. He could analyze, tell anecdotes, sing beautifully himself, or turn sentimental. Very opinionated, he could also become livid on the subject bad habits within the industry:

The one who set this trend of too many musicians was Naushad. He used 100 musicians in *Mughal-e-Azam*, for background music and even in songs. Now everybody has started to do that. But do you *need* 100 musicians? There's a hall in Tardeo. The capacity is only 60, but they take 100 because Naushad took 100. Twenty of those musicians are sitting on the road and playing, I think. Or else, they sit outside and eat *paan!* And the poor producer has to pay the bill for them. So this shouldn't be done. When you need 100 musicians, you take 100 musicians! Then you need a hall that big.

Biddu proved that you can make a song with eight or 10 musicians. He made the song *'Aap jaisa koi'.*[5] How many were there, eight to 10 musicians? My brother made a film called *Janam Janam Ke Phere.* There was a song called *'Zara saamne to aao chhaliye'* It became a big rage in 1958. It was recorded in Basant studio—no recording hall, mind you. It was a studio stage where you close the iron doors and outside you can hear the birds. Musicians would sit there at Chembur. There was a small recording room where there would be two knobs only. That song was recorded on only two tracks and it became a legend. It's not the recording that is important. That's only a fad. Music directors sometimes complain that the recording did not come out right. What has it got to do with the recording?? What is your *mukhra*? If your *mukhra* is no good, you can keep recording it: four tracks or eight tracks won't make any difference. So basically, it's your tune, your *mukhra*. The *antra* can be anything. Nobody sings the *antra;* they sing the *mukhra*. Today with all the electronic equipment you have, a clever musician can make it with 15-20 musicians. When you need choirs and violins, okay. Otherwise, (if you have a big orchestra), you end up with eight people playing the tabla. Never heard of such a thing!

Sound, of course, includes dialogues. Kadar Khan, whose work for a large sector of the industry in great part defined dialogue writing during the seventies and eighties, is credited for the dialogue of seven Desai films—from *Roti* to *Coolie*. Desai recognized his debt to Kadar Khan and gave a name to the language that developed from their association:

If I use roadside dialogue, it is because it is easy to follow. Of all the dialogue writers I've worked with, Kadar Khan is easily the best. He knows the colloquial idiom. I've learned a lot from him.[6]

Extra sounds that it would be difficult to categorize complete the audio tableau. Many are unforgettable. During the chase in the leper colony in *Desh Premee*, for example, a manual cotton separator sets the jarring pace of the scene. In *Coolie* a sound like percolating water complements the actors' body work as Sunny the reporter (Rishi Kapoor) and the newspaper owner (Mukri) bob up and shoot down on opposite sides of the desk in a chance game of see-saw-like hide and seek.

Once sounds, music and dialogue tracks are created, they must be 'mixed' or put into their final form shortly before a film is released. A rather extraordinary man was for a very long time the key figure at this stage in the filmmaking process. Until 15 October 1985, when Mangesh Desai died at the age of 62, he was the chief recordist, the person responsible for almost all of the re-recording in Hindi cinema. This man, whom Manmohan Desai referred to as 'an ace sound technician', began his career working with V. Shantaram at Rajkamal Studio. With 35 years in the industry he had a determining role in the development of sound technology in Indian cinema. For six days a week, nine hours a day he sat at his button-panelled desk in Bombay watching the best and the worst of the films produced and taking the decisions that would increase the four tracks of sound furnished by the sound editor to the twelve tracks that would go on the finished film. With ears so finely tuned that he could immediately pick out a tiny flaw in the mixing, Mangesh Desai, at the same time, made a conscious effort to identify with ordinary people in order to imagine exactly how the inexpert listener-viewer would react during a showing. Mangesh Desai testified to Manmohan Desai's desire to perfect the sound tracks of his films. 'The average film is mixed in eight to ten days,' he said. 'Mixing *Coolie* took a full thirty days. Manmohan Desai sometimes gets new ideas as he goes along and follows them up. He spares no effort to get the sound just right.'

visuals

Desai proudly remembered the scenes that involved difficult but successful visual work, *e.g.*, the scene in *Dharam-Veer* in which Indrani Mukherjee and Pran ride a horse around the ramparts of a castle wall before their escape from the palace grounds. Likewise, he was the first to notice and regret scenes that lacked a perfect finish. Both *Dharam-Veer* and *Parvarish*, made during the Emergency, suffered from the limitations set on filmmaking at that time. Desai lamented:

> There was a rule then. There must not be more than 150 feet of action at a time. The end of *Dharam-Veer* is disjointed because of this. The linking shots have been cut. Also, when Zeenat hits Dharmendra, I had to cut the shot before the whip hit the skin. It looked ridiculous.

Visuals were important for Manmohan Desai, but not exaggeratedly so. If he was totally implicated in the audio component of his filmmaking, he was less involved with the camera:

> I like to handle everything in a film except the cinematography. I still don't know how to light up a shot. Editing is my forte, music, scripting, and the performances of my artistes.
>
> I don't like to monkey with the camera. Like Chaplin said, the camera is mainly there to record what you want to film. It shouldn't be used like a monkey... Your scene must convey what you want. If it's an emotional scene, it must convey emotions. The camera is there only to record. Don't use it as a gimmick or a gadget. Look at Billy Wilder's taking; it's simple.
>
> In a comedy scene, let the artistes perform. I don't give that many points to the camera, like 90% of our directors are doing here. The reason they do this is because they don't know what to do with a scene. Needless trolley shots, needless zooming—zooming has become a fad. Raj Kapoor: here is a man who does good neat camera work.

Desai insisted on the importance of content over form when he fumed against the almost pure form that has sometimes defined art cinema:

> People like Mani Kaul should understand the difference between a movie and a still. Giving 100 marks to good photography is like giving 100 marks to good handwriting. But what is the director saying? It's no easy job to entertain, to cater to 400 million people. You need a careful study of their psychology, their likes and dislikes.

Like Desai, cameraman Peter Pereira, who shot *Sachaa Jhutha, Aa Gale Lag Jaa, Amar Akbar Anthony, Desh Premee, Coolie,* and *Mard,* and N. Satyen who did *Chhalia* and *Bluff Master,* all learned camerawork and special effects under Babubhai Mistry, director of many mythologicals[7] and revered as a special effects artist. Pereira's work was consistently pleasing to the eye. Likewise, in *Bhai Ho To Aisa* and in *Dharam-Veer* N.V. Srinivas' work maintains a recognizable quality and continuity of style.

The choice of background and the composition of frame can make a film visually memorable. Among Desai's earlier films, *Bhai Ho To Aisa* stands out in this domain. Shooting on location in such a beautiful setting as Laxmi Vilas palace in Baroda was unusual in the seventies. The choice of these premises for a drama of a traditional (read: reactionary) Thakur family lent a rare magnificence and credibility to what could otherwise have been a cliché-filled story. The final confrontation in which the good brother Bharat (Jeetendra) must defend himself in a sword fight against his corrupt older brother Ram Singh (Shatrughan Sinha) could easily be rated the best serious climax Desai made. Neither too violent nor overlong, the sequence is shot from a multitude of angles so as to bring the palace alive. Not only does the camera carry us along with the two men as they duel from parapet to turret to terrace to ledge, but longer shots catch the shadows that the two towers cast on the lawn below, bigger than life images that reinforce the drama of human conflict taking place above. Significantly, Desai's teacher Babubhai Mistry is credited with the special effects for this film.

In contrast to this excellent filming, two of Manmohan Desai's films are particularly lacking in plastic beauty. In *Raampur Ka Lakshman* (director of photography: Sudhin Mazumdar) and in *Chacha Bhatija* (director of photography: V. Durga Prasad) colours are poorly blended; some scenes look cluttered, and the decors of the expensive villas that often serve as settings are less than tasteful.

colour

Some directors and some genres are more effective in black and white than in colour. Suspense films, *films noirs*, and any film that relies on the use of *chiaroscuro* for a haunting, shadowy atmosphere can benefit from shades of grey, *e.g.*, Guru Dutt's beautifully lit *Kaagaz ke Phool* (1959). Certain scenes in *Chhalia*, such as the one of the couple alone in the ruins, have a romantic quality that would have been jarred by the addition of colour. However, apart from this and a few other exceptions, the absence of colour in Desai's three black and white films is precisely that, an absence. From the time of *Kismat* in 1968, all of Desai's films were in colour. Quality varied in the late sixties and seventies, probably partly in keeping with the talent of different cameramen, partly depending on the film stock used. The colours in *Dharam-Veer* provide the rainbow array that one would expect in a long-ago-and-far-away never-never land tale. During the gypsy dance, the dresses and turbans splash the arena with the pink and yellow, assuring an atmosphere of gay abandon. Of all Desai's films, *Coolie* probably presents the most thorough control of colour, calculated to add beauty and to show character progression as well. When we meet her, Julie's (Rati Agnihotri) spoilt-rich-girl image is reinforced by her white dress and simple red accessories to match her red car. Later, as the avenger on the motorcycle, she is appropriately attired in red and black. When she declares her love to Iqbal, though, she is wearing a yellow dress, as sunny as her newfound disposition. During the song *'Allah-rakha'*, the consecration of their love, she appears in one colourful costume after another, as bright as a garden of flowers.

the players

Acting is supreme when it is done by a madman or a child.
—*Shashi Kapoor*

In Joseph Mankiewicz's *The Barefoot Contessa* (1954) the fictitious film director Harry Dawes (Humphrey Bogart) is asked by the promising discovery Maria Vargas (Ava Gardner), 'Could you teach me to act, Mr. Dawes?'

'If you can act,' he answers, 'I can help you. If you can't, nobody can teach you.'

Manmohan Desai considered his ability to get the best performances from his artistes to be one of his fortes. Italian filmmaker Federico Fellini searched the streets for the face to match the scene, then turned the person behind the face into an actor for the time needed for the shooting. Desai did not go so far, but it is clear that he generally chose actors and junior artistes carefully and guided them well. Like Harry Dawes, he could not teach just anyone to act. Dan Dhanoa, the young villain in *Mard*, was not a professional actor before *Mard*, and his presence is a distraction. Likewise, though it is commonplace to see actors working well outside their age range in Hindi cinema, the practice is often confusing and always annoying. In *Naseeb* Prem Chopra plays the son of Kadar Khan even though both actors are approximately the same age.

Generally, though, his performers gave their best. Shabana Azmi described how Desai often whipped his actors into a sort of altered state by radiating energy and fervour. Looking back at her work in *Parvarish* and *Amar Akbar Anthony*, she said:

> He was extremely demanding with his stars. He would shout, 'Don't go into remote control. Come on! What am I paying you for?!' He would encourage us to take risks to get the best performances. When we did a good job, he would be full of praise. He would say, 'You're my doll!' He is completely convinced of what he is doing. He shows great involvement and his enthusiasm is contagious. He jumps up and down, yells, claps his hands. He infuses the actors with a sense of fun. I had a ball working with him.

Later, speaking with Nasreen Munni Kabir, Shabana Azmi described the draw of working in popular cinema:

> ...Your imagination is tested in the extreme. For instance, there was Manmohan Desai's film *Parvarish*, for which we had to shoot the climax for thirty days. And Neetu Singh and I had to hang in the villain's den over a river where any moment a crocodile could eat off our legs. So can you imagine trying to pretend this whole thing is real, and to do it with any degree of conviction? That's quite, quite wonderful. I think that what commercial cinema does is to require you to create an alternative reality. And to bring any semblance of truth to that alternative reality is a real challenge for an actor. You have to suspend your belief system entirely, and go along with it.[1]

Desai tended to call on certain actors and actresses repeatedly. Desai was full of praise for Hema Malini, who starred in four of his films:

> Hema Malini is the most beautiful actress we have in India, a very

good dancer, and besides, I think she is a very good actress too. In *Desh Premee* we had one sequence with Amitabh in which the old Amitabh brings this girl home and tells his son to find the boy who has ditched this girl—though he doesn't know the boy is his own son. The scene where they talk to each other without seeing each other and she describes the boy who has ditched her—and it's the same boy—was taken in one shot only. The way she performed that scene, I think, is absolutely incredible and I remember sending her flowers afterwards.

Desai could be unrepentantly exacting:

I remember an incident, where he (Shammi Kapoor) had to walk across a roof. He said, 'I can't walk on the roof. How can I do that?' I said, 'All right, I'll go up. If I can do it, you can do it.' So I went up on the roof and did the shot. I said, 'If I've done it, now you do it.' And he went up and did the shot.

During the seventies, when Desai made the maximum number of films, Kadar Khan, Nirupa Roy, Amjad Khan, Indrani Mukherjee, Pran and Ranjeet appeared frequently, always giving very good supporting performances. Another regular during this same period was Jeevan, who worked in eight Desai films: *Bhai Ho To Aisa, Roti, Dharam-Veer, Chacha Bhatija, Amar Akbar Anthony, Suhaag, Naseeb,* and *Desh Premee.* At the risk of oversimplification, one could separate actors into two basic categories: the instinctive and the analytic. Nirupa Roy was an actress who gave excellent performances, apparently intuitively. She enjoyed working on films with good story lines and interestingly developed relationships between characters. Jeevan, on the other hand, was cerebral in his approach. He analyzed his roles and asked directors for background information on his characters; his performances were studied. In real life, Jeevan would hardly have caught one's attention. On screen he was another person entirely. His nasal twang and spectacular gestures were calculated to call attention to himself, as well as to add to our pleasure. In *Amar Akbar Anthony*, during a police raid on a group of smugglers, as Robert, he shoots a policeman and hides behind a rock to avoid arrest. Now, many thousands of actors have ducked behind rocks in film history, but rarely have any thrusting and dipping been so eye-catching. This bodywork, rather fashioned on mime, lasts only a second; yet the discrepancy between the effort needed and the energy mobilized enlivens the entire scene. His use of voice, like his bodywork, was often unforgettable, as in *Dharam-Veer* when he liltingly calls out *behn* to his sister just before treacherously hurling a knife at her.

Generally in Desai's films, the stars tend to harmonize with one another, with the supporting actors and with the extras. Shabana Azmi offered an explanation for the liveliness Desai achieved in group scenes:

> Manmohan Desai really encourages everyone on his sets. I remember after one shot he went to a junior artiste way back on the sixth row and told him what a good job he had done. The man was elated. He couldn't believe that the director, who must have his eyes on the whole set and especially on the stars, would notice the efforts of one person in the background.

While he cared about all the actors on screen, Desai knew that big name stars sold his films. The semi-deification that stars undergo, in India more than elsewhere, is a fascinating phenomenon. Stars are not simply actors. They are the repositories for the public's hopes and fantasies, and probably more importantly, to a certain extent, blow-ups of our individual dream selves. It has been said that cinema puts our dreams on screen, the implication generally being that cinema relates to our waking dreams. A much deeper connection, and one that explains part of the power of cinema, is to be found in our sleeping dreams. Several times a night each person's subconscious takes on the role of film director, creating images and playing out scenes, often with much better special effects than have yet been invented for the seventh art itself. The dreaming individual is more often than not the central player in these disorganized 'movies.' We are, in fact, the stars of our own 'unconscious' scripts. A real film can 'flesh out' not only certain of our daydreams but also some small percentage of our sleeping dreams. We are programmed, then, for living within stories, whether they be mysteriously self-generated or fabricated by the hundreds of people who have worked to bring a film into being. The same confusion that exists when we are half awake and cannot tell dream from reality can also take place in the theatre. A great part of a film's success depends on the extent to which each member of the audience steps into the hero's or the heroine's shoes. The oft-mentioned 'star quality' is above all this ability to engage people's psyches, to elicit identification, to give people a bigger-than-life view of how they envision themselves. A good actor can make a woman identify with a man, a man with a woman, a young person with an elder; a grandparent can suddenly feel like a 20-year old with the youth-like raging emotions of attraction, anger, or desire for justice. The switches from identification to identification can take place in fractions of seconds within our brains. Or our left brains can put us into analytic mode. With a thud we land in reality. We are in a movie theatre, suddenly aware of ourselves, aware that the life we have been living with the screen characters is but fiction. We notice an itch or a leg that has gone to sleep. We wonder how long it took the heroine to change costumes and hairstyles. The magic spell of the screen is momentarily broken until, as often happens, the characters and the story whisk us back once more to live through them.

amitabh bachchan

When Manmohan Desai spoke of the importance of keeping the audience in their seats, it was no doubt this complete immersion in the film that he was aiming for. He had many tricks to maintain audience attention, but probably none outweighed the draw of the star and the star's role. Individual taste on the part of members of the public must be factored in; nevertheless, the saleability of top stars supposes that certain actors, at certain times in their careers, have a much greater percentage of the public under their spell.

Amitabh Bachchan's screen magic is legendary. His collaboration with Manmohan Desai brought success both to him and to the director. From the time of *Parvarish* to that of *Gangaa Jamunaa Saraswathi*, Amitabh Bachchan appeared in and gradually became the cement for every successive film that Manmohan Desai directed. Desai did not simply employ him as an actor; he organized entire films in keeping with Amitabh's talents. In the search for 'items', the salient moments that the scenario linked together to form each film, Desai and his team would prime their creative pumps by asking themselves what the audience had never before seen Amitabh Bachchan do on screen.

Amitabh Bachchan's screen image for his Desai films was as fluctuating as the moods from scene to scene—now a daring fighter and able acrobat, now a rowdy good-for-nothing, now a noble friend and devoted son, now a front-bench-appealing drunk, now a sentimental romantic, now an effervescent singer and dancer. *Amar Akbar Anthony* marked a turning point, not only in Desai's filmmaking and in Amitabh's own career, but also in Hindi cinema in general. As Amitabh Bachchan noted, Desai incorporated bits of Anthony into every new role he gave Amitabh, as did many other Bombay film directors from that time forward.

Amitabh as Anthony or Anthony's reincarnations most often played a street-wise tough guy. Life has dealt him a hard blow; he has lost his family and has had to make his way against stiff odds. He is a success in that he is often the *dada* (the don) of his neighborhood. He can establish justice with his fists; hence, others give him at least grudging respect. In *Suhaag* he is a street-dweller who has earned a degree. In *Naseeb* he is a poor waiter, but he wins boxing matches after work and pays for his brother's studies. Gangsters and policemen can turn him from an intrepid hero into a grinning, salaaming sycophant. He is both powerful and powerless. He is a hard-skinned fellow who goes soft in the face of womenfolk. In *Desh Premee* he is a sophisticated gambler and counterfeit money dealer, but he also plays a clumsy policeman in a Peter-Sellers-Inspector-Clouseau imitation. He can be romantic to the point that violins play in his heart when the woman of his life steps into view for the first time. He can succumb to alcohol, but he also has the force of character to overcome the power of the bottle. He can turn villains into fools, but small, inanimate objects take on a life of their own to make him a bumbling buffoon.

Manmohan Desai's relationship with Amitabh Bachchan was one of mutual respect, mutual need, and mutual inspiration to outdo past achievements. Desai addressed Amitabh as '*Raja*,' the king, and his confidence in him as a drawing card was thorough.

> Before *Amar Akbar Anthony* my concept of a hero was almost entirely modelled on Raj Kapoor whom I had cast in my very first film *Chhalia* made in 1959 when I was just 22. It's only in *Amar Akbar Anthony* that Amitabh got Raj Kapoor out of my system. Now I have got Amitabh in my system and cannot think of anyone other than him. Amitabh is the only complete actor we have. He has star charisma. His presence is magnetic and the man has tremendous histrionic ability. He is like Haley's Comet. Such an actor comes only once in 76 years. We have seen one this century. We don't know when we will see another again.

Desai's connection to the Amit character is also worth noting:

> My heroes are like me. All the impossible feats I've dreamed of, they perform for me on the screen. I'd even say Amit is my alter ego.

When told that Manmohan Desai banked on him, Amitabh modestly replied, 'It's more the contrary that is true.'

If Desai used Amitabh Bachchan well, it could also be argued that he sometimes overused him. According to Desai, Vinod Khanna had the best role in *Parvarish*. In *Amar Akbar Anthony* the situation is reversed. Yet as the older brother, Vinod Khanna maintains a certain authority, and with three male stars and three female stars, Amitabh's role, though highlighted, does not overshadow all others. When Vinod Khanna arrives at the end of *Amar Akbar Anthony* disguised for the wedding sequence as a one-man band, hands, arms and legs full of musical instruments, he looks like an appropriate metaphor for the tendency to load individual stars with an inordinate share of work and of responsibility for a film's success. '*Hum three in one hain; Hindu, Muslim, Sikh, Issai, subhi to hain bhai-bhai,*' (I'm three in one; Hindu, Muslim, Sikh and Christian, all are brothers), he announces, and his words seem to predict the future. As John Jani Janardhan Amitabh envelops all three characters represented by Amar, Akbar and Anthony.

The tendency gained momentum with each succeeding film. In *Desh Premee* Amitabh doubled his impact by playing a dual role. In *Coolie*, in spite of a large and excellent cast, his dominance was undisputed. In *Mard* he was a superman without a competent foil, male or female. Significantly, the credits of these last two films do not list him among the stars. Rather, his name is above and separate from theirs—'M.K.D. Films and Aasia Films present Amitabh Bachchan as' *Coolie* and *Mard* respectively. The Hindi film industry encourages monopolies. The competition among actors to 'reach the top' is a well-publicized aspect of the pyramid thinking that flourishes in every area of production, the pinnacle of each pyramid being clearly delineated in rupees.

Manmohan Desai's increasing reliance on Amitabh Bachchan was not without drawbacks. Amitabh's excellence need not have precluded his sharing the screen. In *Suhaag*, made between the time of *Amar Akbar Anthony* and *Naseeb*, his presence was ably balanced by Shashi Kapoor. One of Amitabh Bachchan's favourite scenes from a Manmohan Desai film, in fact, sees the two in perfect tandem. The tempestuous Amit has just fought Kishan (Shashi) to a draw. Yet upon learning that Kishan is a police officer, his tone changes abruptly; he begs and pleads and pleads some more with the policeman not to make an official report of the fight until, at last, Kishan, theatrically losing his temper, almost blows Amit over in a thunderous '*Tum jao!!*' (Go away!) Audiences not only enjoyed watching Amitabh act; they also took pleasure in waiting for him to appear, and they appreciated the cumulative punch that came from his facing other strong personalities.

Just such a marvellous moment comes near the end of *Amar Akbar Anthony* shortly before the title song. All the main characters are reunited at the gangster's home. Amitabh Bachchan interacts with each in turn in a series of lively, witty dialogues. He then whisks up a winding flight of stairs, violin in hand, his priest's habit swaying. In a memorable two-second scene he holds our gaze; with assured concentration, like a conductor leading an orchestra, he solemnly motions for a pair of curtains to close. As if by magic, the curtains oblige. With perfect timing, he whirls; his moment alone has ended; another group scene follows. Our joy is great as we feel our eyes move nimbly across the screen from this marvellous actor to two beautiful and enchanting actresses, Parveen Babi and Shabana Azmi, and back again. The dialogues, the decors, the costumes, the colours, the background music create an ensemble for our pleasure, but, finally, it is the players who are responsible for transporting us in and for making us live the story with and through them.

the child

When I was a child, the movies brought the vistas of a desirable adulthood tantalizingly close; as an adult, I find that they help to keep the road to childhood open.

—*Sudhir Kakar*[1]

One could rightly conclude after a few visits to Bombay movie theatres that the average audience is overwhelmingly composed of adult males. A theatre playing a Manmohan Desai film, however, generally exuded quite a different atmosphere. Babies' cries, toddlers' pattering feet, older children's giggles, and women's chuckles blended with hearty male laughter. Women and children may not actually have outnumbered the adult males, but their presence assured a more balanced public. Desai liked children and he respected them as spectators. As he said:

> Children form a majority of my audience. I aim my films at them especially, and then for all ages. It is my attempt to provide clean stuff. I try my best to avoid rapes and other scenes where women are badly treated. I avoid blood-curdling scenes because I want those who have come to the theatre to have their eyes up there on the screen, not down. The day children stop coming to my films I will give up and go away.

Manmohan Desai's motivations were double. His noble concerns were coupled with solid business sense. Desai looked to women as a barometer to gauge the success of his films, 'Once the women in purdah (heavily veiled) start coming, I know my film will be a hit.' His logic was the result of simple arithmetic; by adding a sizable number of women and children to one's audience, the potential box office returns more than double.

Children not only appreciate Desai's films for their magic, their animals, their colourful stories, and their humor; they also identify with the child characters he put on screen. With stories often stretched over two or three generations, child actors have long been a staple of Hindi cinema. Desai was quite faithful to this cinematic tradition. Children appeared in the majority of his films, most often as future adults to be played by stars (*Raampur Ka Lakshman, Roti, Amar Akbar Anthony, Chacha Bhatija, Parvarish, Dharam-Veer, Suhaag, Naseeb, Desh Premee,* and *Coolie*). In other films the children appear as their own characters, either in small roles (*Bluff Master, Bhai Ho To Aisa, Desh Premee,* and *Shararat*), or in more important roles (*Aa Gale Lag Jaa, Chhalia,* and *Roti*).

the child artistes

Desai was a director who systematically got the best from his child actors, avoiding the tendency to have children play stiff, unnatural goody-goodies. The quality he attained was on two levels: convincingly drawn characters and lively performances. In *Parvarish*, for instance, the boys (Master Tito and Master Ratan) must confess to their father (Shammi Kapoor) that they have played hooky from school to go to the movies. With their attempts to lie and their show of guilt when they are forced to tell the truth, the boys help to turn a preparatory, background scene into a memorable moment in the film.

Master Tito was only six years old when he first worked with Manmohan Desai. Yet, he had already been acting for over four years. Under his father's guidance, the child had learned early to tune in to the proper emotions he would play. Desai liked the boy at once. With his twinkling eyes, his ready smile and his natural tears, Master Tito gave one of the great child performances of cinema history in *Aa Gale Lag Jaa*. He would go on to to do smaller but noteworthy parts in *Roti*, *Parvarish*, *Suhaag*, and *Naseeb*. Looking back, Master Tito (Tito Khatri) described the enjoyable working atmosphere on the sets where Desai tickled, teased and played with him. His first scene with Manmohan Desai was especially memorable. In *Aa Gale Lag Jaa* his character is a child who has never known his mother. A bit depressed one night, the child asks to see his mother's picture. His father (Shashi Kapoor), very preoccupied with his own problems, lashes out at his son in anger. Taken aback and hurt, the boy cries, 'But I don't want my mummy. I only want to see a picture of her.' Suddenly, the father realizes how harsh and unfair he has been and sensitively consoles his suffering son. The weight of this tight and emotional scene rests almost entirely on the actors. Desai was so thrilled with Master Tito's performance that the next day he called the child in and offered him whatever he wanted as a reward for a job well done. 'But I have everything I need,' Master Tito answered.

Desai insisted, 'Let me give you something. Tell me anything you'd like to have.'

After a long hesitation, little Tito said, 'Well, I don't have a watch.' Of course, Manmohan Desai gave him one.

Grandchildren held a special place in Desai's heart. Discussing the beautifully filmed scene in *Aa Gale Lag Jaa* in which a cold, rejecting grandfather warms over a game of marbles with his grandson, Desai said:

> Every grandfather loves his grandchild. Like today, I crave to see my grandchild. Whether I'm shooting or not, I must see my grandchildren every day. In Hindi we say the interest is more valuable than the actual amount given (the capital). So the grandchild is like the interest on the

child you have. You love your own child, but you'll love your grandchild more.

the inner child

Desai worked well with children, partly because like many creative people, he never entirely outgrew the child he was. Shashi Kapoor recognized this trait. Manmohan Desai related it thus, 'Once Shashi Kapoor said something very nice about me, "We have outgrown our childhood; you have not outgrown your childhood." I am still a child, and I don't mind being a child.' And indeed, behind the work that appeared on the screen was a childlike, imaginative spirit. Lurking inside the apparent adult was a naughty boy, ready to poke out his head and, with a devilish gleam in his eye, grin with glee at his own mischief. Imagination supposes a touch of anarchy, a willingness to turn rules inside out, to stand the world on its head in order to see it from a different angle. Like his films, Desai, in one breath, was straight-faced and whole-heartedly earnest in his defense of his valued beliefs, especially the sanctity of religion and family. In the next breath he was mocking society's rules, institutions and power symbols.

A certain social irresponsibility appears and reappears in Desai's films. Chhalia, the pickpocket, is unabashedly unrepentant. It was only at the censors' insistence that his song was transformed from *'Chhalia mera naam, chhalna mera kaam;'* (Deception is my name; deceiving is my game;) to *'Chhalia mera naam; Chhalia mera naam.'* The censors were less fussy at the release of *Parvarish*. The heroines not only pick pockets but also brazenly sing a song in defence of their livelihood. Crime pays, too. Neither Chhalia nor the girls are ever punished for their deeds (in sharp contrast with some of the characters in Hrishikesh Mukherjee's films who go against one parental order and spend half of the film asking to be forgiven). Desai's characters are not bad. They are simply a bit naughty, like spirited children who are too rambunctious to be kept firmly under adult control.

In *Coolie* this touch of social anarchy is carried into a rich man's (Om Shivpuri) home. Iqbal (Amitabh Bachchan) leads a group of coolies who use their numbers and their lack of respect for the unspoken rule—that the rich and poor must not mingle—in order to turn the rich man's luxurious dwelling topsy-turvy. The coolies play lively music, make merry, drink alcohol prepared for the rich man's guests, use his swimming pool to bathe—with soap—and to wash their clothes. They carry civil disobedience into the homes of the rich oppressors not in anger, but simply having left aside their inborn fear of and respect for the established order.

Most spectators seem to enjoy this scene, but it is surely the children who laugh the hardest. The coolies, in fact, are acting like misbehaving youngsters who take pleasure in wreaking havoc on the ordered adult world. When questioned about the uneasiness the rich might feel while viewing the scene, Manmohan Desai himself got a devilish look in his eye and rubbed his hands together with relish. Desai not only put his mischief on screen; he also had his larks in daily life. He was, of course, a well-known personality in his Khetwadi neighbourhood. If a fight broke out, the people of the area urged him to use his influence to put an end to the dispute. However, more than once he postponed acting as a mediator in order to enjoy the spectacle for a while. Eventually, he called a halt, separated the fighters and insisted that they shake hands and go away as brothers, but not until after he had had his own ringside thrills.

Desai gave us a little boy in *Chhalia* whose reaction is similar. Little Anwar, Shaanti's (Nutan) son, is at a boarding school. Being one of the youngest boys there, Anwar is too frightened to sleep one night. To bolster his courage, he sits on his knees in bed and begins to pray loudly and fervently. Angry to be awakened, the other boys try to teach Anwar a lesson; the result is a general brawl. The threat is no longer imaginary demons but rather real boys. He scampers under the bed and, from his safe position, forgets all of his worries as he gives bent to his pleasure in encouraging the warring camps.

Desai's feisty, misbehaving screen children are not without precedent in Hindi cinema. There is another naughty, but enchanting little boy in a film that Desai greatly appreciated, Mehboob Khan's *Mother India* (1957). Birju (Master Sajjid), Radha's (Nargis) second child, is active, fearless, at times insolent, quick to react to injustice, and ready to work like a man when circumstances demand. Manmohan Desai's film children follow his lively lead.

Desai did some striking work with children in a group, thereby multiplying the naughtiness. *Roti*, an uneven film, weighed down by melodrama and overwrought suspense, is saved by the light-hearted, fast-paced schoolroom sequence in which an entire classroom of boys light up the screen with their verve. Mangal Singh (Rajesh Khanna) inadvertently becomes a schoolmaster in a Kashmiri village. The boys he must face, like mischief-loving children around the world, take a special joy in initiating their new teacher with their devilry. The first two days of class give rise to a battle of wits over who will reign. Mangal is greeted with firecrackers popping about the room, a traditional welcome, he is told, in that area. The boys, in seeming obsequiousness, invite him to sit while they stand, hardly containing their impatience to see him fall to the floor from the chair from which they have partially sawed off the legs. When Mangal asks their names, they reply the days of the week. When he asks them to tell the truth, they answer that these days milk is false, ghee (clarified butter) is false, everything is false, so why should they tell the truth! The second morning of class they take bets on whether their teacher will dare to show up again. What the boys cannot guess is that, in spite of his adult appearance, Mangal, acting as Desai's alter ego, is himself simply a big, naughty child. He takes a delight as great as theirs in replaying their practical jokes on them. The pupils are dumbfounded. 'We're even,' he says, 'no winners, no losers.'

Manmohan Desai's feelings about school were aptly portrayed in *Roti* when Mangal Singh, trapped into taking a teaching job, has to be led protesting to the schoolhouse. A mocking background score emphasizes the irony of his predicament. Bijli (Mumtaz), the village belle, tries to calm him, 'There's no reason to be afraid. You're not going to jail.'

'I can get out of jail,' he answers, more truthfully than she realizes, 'but from here, how do I escape?'

Desai looked back at his own years of 'imprisonment' thus:

> I was very bad. In school I was turned out three or four times. My elder brother used to go and apologize to the principal. He would slap me in front of the principal, hit me and say, 'He won't do it again.' I didn't like to study. Even now, you know, some people say they regret they didn't study more. I don't regret a bit. I wish I hadn't ever gone to school ... I used to go to school only for the sake of playing cricket.... Every Thursday and Sunday at St. Xavier's I played cricket. Cricket, cricket, cricket. Table tennis and badminton...I never used to study.... But somehow I stayed in—because I was very good in cricket. That's why they didn't fail me.... I was taken at college because I was the school captain. From St. Xavier's School I was sent to St. Xavier's College with a note, though I had 35% total. That's a borderline case. But then I was chasing girls, so they realized I wasn't even playing cricket.... After two years I was thrown out. I failed. I was bound to fail. It was a university exam, and I failed in Hindi, can you believe! So I said, 'Good riddance!' And I took up work as an assistant director.
>
> School I hated! I detest it even now. My logic is very simple. If a father and mother are paying their school fees on time, why should the school fail a student? ...I don't agree to the exam system either. You teach, you do your job, and get lost. All that studying is going to give children big heads and underdeveloped bodies.

A scene in *Naseeb* gives a witty illustration of Desai's disdain for the grading system. Sunny (Rishi Kapoor) is twice a rogue when he threatens the headmaster (Jeevan) by saying that he will jump from the roof if the headmaster does not raise his grade to passing. First, he blackmails the teacher, 'If I jump, I'll die. If I die, it will be in the papers. If it's in the papers, the school will get a bad name. If the school gets a bad name, parents won't send their children here, and the school will have to close.' Secondly, the threat is but pretence. Sunny has a rope carefully tied around his waist to prevent even an accidental fall. It is significant, too, that when the girls arrive from the neighbouring school, the boys scurry away, leaving Sunny to argue his case alone. Chasing girls is not only more important than schoolwork; it is also more important than Sunny's 'life-and-death' spectacle.

Manmohan Desai put his own pranks on screen so that we who have joined the serious world of adults might go back to childhood for a short time during his films. His playfulness was rooted in his lively imagination, the positive side of the illogic with which his name was almost synonymous. Children are thrilled by the outlandish: 'Wouldn't it be funny if the sky were green and trees were blue, if snow were hot, and if we had two mouths, one for eating and one for talking so that we could do both at the same time?' It is as though Desai played the 'Wouldn't it be funny if?' game on screen. As he gave implausible or impossible situations, he awakened our imaginative, un-staid selves, the part in each of us that knows how to enjoy, the same part, in fact, that is open enough to consider the world with fresh eyes, to learn, and to be creative. Desai gave us provocative possibilities: suppose someone could learn to read lips and could then use a telescope to decipher the plans of a group of evil doers talking in a building across the street (*Naseeb*); suppose a villain could immobilize an entire gathering of police by serving a hypnotic drink that would turn each person into a statue momentarily (*Sachaa Jhutha*); suppose a pet falcon could break an arrow in mid-flight in order to protect its master (*Dharam-Veer*).

The structural basis of each of Desai's films is the result of a game of wild hypotheses. Games, though, are also present in a more prosaic forms in many of the films. Desai never put his own favorite game, cricket, on screen. (One wishes he could have lived to see Ashutosh Gowariker's 2001 cricket-centered film *Lagaan*.) Desai, nevertheless, regularly filmed other forms of play. From the beginning, this inclination was clear. In *Chhalia* during the main song sequence, 'Chhalia Mera Naam,' Raj Kapoor takes a little spin around the bazaar on a child's push scooter. In *Naseeb* young men and women play 'hu-tu-tu-tu' as a choreographed song and dance. And an imaginative game of musical chairs was one of Desai's favourite scenes from *Aa Gale Lag Jaa*.

'Let's pretend' is repeatedly played with dress-up added to enliven the game. Dharam in *Dharam-Veer* dresses as a *jyotishi*, an astrologer, to convince the hesitant princess that her kiss is needed to bring the supposedly dead Dharam back to life. The dress-up found throughout Desai's cinema is especially delectable to the children in the audience. First, the surprise element of an apparently new character on screen awakes us. Then comes the job of recognition, a process which for adults may take only a split second, but which may last several seconds, even minutes, for children. Finally, there is the expansion of identification. Children play dress-up in order to try on different identities. Through disguise, the screen characters split and multiply, providing spectators with an abundance of personae to respond to. There is an expansion, too, of wishful thinking. Wouldn't it be nice if in real life one could trick the bad guys through costume and play-acting? Life is indeed a stage, but not always the bard's tragic sort. Rather, it can be full of fun and delight and a child's sense of discovery. To give us this sort of experience, Desai had to appreciate pleasure; he then had to toil to bring it to the screen.

comedy

There's a lot to be said for making people laugh.

—*Gerald Mast*[1]

A clue to Manmohan Desai's ability to make his audiences laugh might be found in his vivacious, yet rather anxious nature. Asked whether he saw his films with audiences, he revealingly replied:

> No, no, I'm petrified. I'm petrified because if anyone gets up to go to the loo, I feel he's doing it intentionally. And then I might pick a brawl. I almost did. Can you believe that when *Amar Akbar Anthony* was running the 70th week in the Opera House, I used to go to see songs? But anybody who'd get up, well…I called one man and said, 'Why are you getting up?' He said, 'I'm going to the bathroom.' I said, 'Don't go to the bathroom in my song!!! You want to make loo, you do it here. Don't go to the bathroom!' He said, 'But I want to go to the bathroom!' So then the manager said, 'Look, Mr. Desai, you can't do that. You see, they've paid money.' And I cooled down, and I realized I better not go to theatres. I'll sit at home and hear the reviews. Since then, I've never seen any of my films in the auditorium. I won't see them. I get damned scared if anyone gets up.

Like many people with a comic gift, Desai was not a light-hearted, easy-going person. And if he recognized his flair for music, he could be somewhat dismissive in describing the humour in his films. 'Gags,' he called them, 'nonsense.' He certainly did not see himself as a maker of comedies. Amitabh Bachchan agreed, 'You wouldn't put *Amar Akbar Anthony* into the comic cadre. It was a complete film. It had shades of almost everything.' Yet if one defines comedy as 'the comic element,' and if one remembers that the cream of the comic genre are films structured to keep the audience passing in and out of various emotions, then Desai would deserve to be remembered as the 'King of comedy,' for no other Hindi film director has regularly matched his wit.

Comedy gives us immediate pleasure. We are caught in the moment. Our laughter is spontaneous and instantaneous. We find ourselves in the situation of a two-year old crossing a colourful field. An adult would, above all, be interested in arriving at the road beyond. A small child, on the other hand, is concerned with the step-by-step process of walking and the pleasure of seeing along the way. A truly frivolous, superficial comedy is nothing more than a passing moment, a genial jaunt across a field, but one that leaves no memory. A comedy with substance, offers the instant delight of watching and the pleasure of having watched, as bits of food for thought—often tucked almost out of sight—continue to nourish us long after the theatre lights go out.

Manmohan Desai's films could never be considered profound; yet neither could they be dismissed as merely transitory, agreeable moments. At the beginning of *Dharam-Veer*, wickedness is on the loose. The plotting brother (Jeevan) of the queen (Indrani Mukherjee) would win power and save himself at the expense of his sister's happiness, even her life. Though neither the *Mahabharata* nor Manmohan Desai would use the term 'dysfunctional family', we find ourselves plunged into such resulting dark feelings—the makings of a tragedy—with Fate playing a major role. Yet the mood that reigns in *Dharam-Veer*, as in the majority of Desai's films, is light and funny. The heavier moments lend a fullness and depth to the canvas on which comedy is painted brightly in the foreground. The effectiveness of comedy in the film comes precisely from the interweaving of the serious and the nonsensical. Early in *Dharam-Veer* the evil character played by Jeevan hurls his sister's newborn baby from a high castle window into the void below, to certain death... . Yet out of nowhere a magic falcon appears and snatches the falling bundle from its doom. And the audience laughs! We laugh in surprise at the unexpected twist; we laugh, too, to realize we have entered into a realm beyond logic where fear is only a passing emotion. Desai explained his philosophy thus:

> There are a lot of problems on this earth, like where the next meal is coming from, but the man who spends even four rupees to see a movie has every right to my esteem... . The person who comes to the movies should be happy to see whatever he's seeing.

the nobility of laughter

Desai was not alone as he manned the barricades in defence of the pleasure principle. The 1982 award-winning comedy *Tootsie* is based on similar reasoning. Actor Michael Dorsey (Dustin Hoffman) wants to raise the money necessary to put on his roommate's deep and meaningful play, *The Return of the Love Canal*. His agent (played by the director Sidney Pollack) tries to make Michael see financial reality, 'Nobody is going to do that play.'

'Why?' Michael asks.

'Because it's a downer; that's why. Because nobody wants to produce a play about a couple that move back to Love Canal.'

'But that actually happened!' Michael insists indignantly.

'Who gives a shit! Nobody wants to pay $20 to watch people living next to chemical wastes. They can see that in New Jersey!'

We also feel the jab at naturalistic, profound, arty theatre as we watch the writer and future director (Bill Murray) of *Return of the Love Canal* pontificating self-righteously, 'I don't want a full house... I want 90 people who just came in out of the worst rainstorm in the city's history. These are people who are alive on the planet until they dry off.' His pretentiousness is nauseating. We the audience of *Tootsie*, of course, never see the heavy and sobering *Return of the Love Canal*. We simply see a brilliant comedy.

Looking back in time, a comparison could be made between Desai's comic entertainment and that of Hollywood during the 1930s. With the Depression at its deepest and 25% of the U.S. working population unemployed, America was enthralled by musicals and screwball comedies. Fred Astaire danced in coat and tails; Ernst Lubitsch gave us unlikely romances between rich, continental sophisticates (*Ninotchka*, released in 1939, to name but one). Howard Hawks had Katherine Hepburn and Cary Grant chasing about after a millionaire widow's pet leopard in the ultimate screwball comedy, *Bringing Up Baby* (1937). America had a sobering reality to escape from and Hollywood offered joy-inducing fantasy to escape to. Such cinema is obviously not on the cutting edge of social reform; yet it is in its own way lasting. In the 1970s, the decade when cinema appreciation was at its height, it was in art theatres that a new generation found an opportunity to jubilate over the quality-made nonsense of Hollywood in its heyday.

Tagore's proverb, 'God respects me when I work, but he loves me when I sing,' could be applied to our perception of movies. 'Serious' films, *i.e.*, drama and tragedy, by their very nature, tend to be held in regard. Comedies, though often loved, are rarely respected. Comedy is often distinguished from drama not so much in the material and themes treated as in the distancing effect offered to the audience. A solemn film might treat the same lost-and-found family traumas that Desai's films are noted for. Yet with calculated regularity, Desai seriously involved us with a character's dilemmas only to have us stand back a moment later and laugh. In *Parvarish* Inspector Amit (Amitabh Bachchan) has finally cornered the smuggler who has been eluding him for months. In a darkened hotel the end of the chase is near; Amit shoots the offender in the leg. During the man's resulting temporary paralysis, a light falls upon his face, and Amit realizes that the long-pursued criminal is none other than his own brother Kishan (Vinod Khanna). The cliché would have been a lightning bolt to indicate the emotional blow Amit receives upon learning the truth. Instead, we join Amit for a moment in his horror and agonize with the tracked and desperate Kishan. Then, in the midst of this intense scene we are visually whisked away, outside the hotel, outside the story and inside the director's visual language joke: above the roof a neon sign is flashing 'Bhai-Bhai (brothers) Hotel.' Audience identification cannot continue. The heavy mood is broken. The director pulls the viewers to his side to laugh along with him at his story that, he reminds us, is after all only a story. Desai's 'in' jokes are like a director's winks at the spectators.

Double meanings, sight gags, pratfalls, mockery, twists, and satire are but a few of the tools in Desai's comic bag. Parody is another. One of Desai's favourite scenes in *Amar Akbar Anthony* was the confrontation between Amar (Vinod Khanna) and Anthony (Amitabh Bachchan) in Anthonywadi. Pyarelal's musical score offers a brilliant pastiche. As the two he-men stand threateningly face-to-face in the open air at mid-day, drums roll, like the call to war on an 18th-century European battlefield. Next comes the Mexican-style trumpet followed by the guitar in a perfect evocation of Morricone's famous spaghetti western music. Amar begins the fight with a judo flip that sends Anthony sprawling behind him and the Italian western notes immediately give way to shades of the Far East, bringing to mind Bruce Lee and his fellow martial arts experts. Amitabh Bachchan clowns his way through the scene, playing off straight man Vinod Khanna who remains true to the tough, macho image of the fight films—

as well as maintaining his elder brother status. The music adds an extra, nonsensical dimension to Amitabh's clowning; as we hook in to the two literally deadly genres evoked, the contrast between their seriousness and Amitabh's lack of it gels in our minds into something absurdly incongruous, the essence of parody.

the comic actors

— Those who create laughter on the stage or on the screen do not stoop. Quite the contrary. Bringing laughter into the hearts of those who return from the fields, their hands too calloused to close, those who leave their offices bent-shouldered, having forgotten the pleasure of breathing, those who come back from the factories hanging their heads, their nails broken, the cracked skin of their fingers black with oil; to make those laugh who have lost their mother or who will lose her…
— And who are they?
— Everyone. Those who have not lost their mother will lose her one day. He who for one minute causes them to forget little hardships, fatigue, worry, and death—he who brings laughter to people with so many reasons to cry, gives them the strength to live, and they love him as a benefactor.
— Even if to make them laugh he degrades himself before them??
— But if he must degrade himself and if he consents, his merit is even greater because he sacrifices his pride to lighten our suffering. We should say that to Molière. We could say that to Charlie Chaplin.[2]

Thus in his 1937 film *The Schpountz*, writer-director Marcel Pagnol has Françoise (Orane Demazis) convince the hesitant Iréné (Fernandel) of the worthiness of playing the clown. If the comic is a noble character according to Pagnol, the laughter the comic elicits is equally estimable: 'Laughter is God-given and belongs only to human beings, perhaps to console them for being intelligent.'

Shammi Kapoor acted in four Manmohan Desai-directed films, *Bluff Master*, *Budtameez*, *Parvarish*, and *Desh Premee*. In the sixties, before becoming the 'older man,' Shammi Kapoor was a much-in-demand hero. The high point in his career, however, corresponded with Manmohan Desai's low. It was between the time of *Bluff Master* in 1962 and *Budtameez* in 1966, both starring Shammi Kapoor, that Desai waited in vain for a producer to knock at his door. It is interesting to speculate what the cinematic results might have been if both Shammi Kapoor and Manmohan Desai had hit their peaks simultaneously, and Shammi Kapoor had starred not in two, but in four or five Desai films. Given their evident compatibility, such a series would no doubt have been memorable. Shammi Kapoor himself looks upon *Bluff Master* as the best Desai-directed film in which he has acted. But in *Budtameez*, too, he is extraordinary, his style of clowning fitting perfectly into Desai's circus-like entertainment.

An actor brings his whole being to his work. How expressive a face and voice, how finely tuned a body, how bright a mind and how much of an inner spark he has are measures of an actor's capacity. As a star, Shammi Kapoor possessed all of these. With a contagious vitality, he literally threw himself into his roles, displaying openness, generosity, and gay abandon. At the summit of his popularity he was capable of a surprising variety of entertaining, if not subtle, facial and body movements, including a Groucho Marx-style duck walk! His size and shape, even at that time, led one to expect awkwardness. And, occasionally, he did stumble about. But soon afterwards this same man was showing grace, ease and a wonderful sense of rhythm.

Shammi Kapoor, the star, had a gift for comedy that Shammi Kapoor, the character actor, has not lost. Asked to remember his best acting moment from *Parvarish*, Shammi Kapoor and his wife in real life gave their best marks to a comic scene: playing a police inspector, he lectures his wife (Indrani Mukherjee) and two grown sons on the importance of taking precautions against pickpockets. He scolds them from the lofty perch of his own smug self-assurance. How could *they* have been so foolish as to lose their belongings to two young women?! But pride, we know, goeth before the fall. When he checks his pocket and finds that he has no watch at the end of his chain, he realizes that he too has been duped. His eyes grow wide, and we can almost imagine him as a Tex Avery cartoon character on whose forehead the word 'chump' blinks in green and red neon.

Amitabh Bachchan was Manmohan Desai's other special comic star. The director recognized the actor's potential early on:

> During the making of *Parvarish* I realized this man has a fantastic sense of humour, an uncanny sense of humour… . So then we made this script of *Amar Akbar Anthony*… . And I asked Amit, 'Could you please do this film?' He said, 'By all means.' And I said, 'I'm giving you a comic image, and the only thing is the language.' He said, 'What language?' I said, 'Look, this is the language which I've been used to hearing in my school… . This is the language people speak in Bombay… .' I said, 'You speak this line.' And he did it so beautifully. I said, 'Just speak the way I'm speaking it.' And he did. And the fantastic timing he has for comedy! The whole role became hilarious.

Indeed, Amitabh Bachchan's gift for comedy was never so consistently and rousingly summoned forth as in Desai's films. Salim-Javed's scripts introduced us to Amitabh as Vijay—police officer, gangster or poor-boy-turned-rich—usually in trouble with family or society or both. Circumstances are cruel both to Vijay and to Amit or Anthony or John Jani Janardhan. But we ache with Vijay. We laugh with (and at) Amit-Anthony-John. It is not by chance that in real life a little girl in a near-coma state after a fall from a second story window mysteriously called out for a certain 'Anthony.' When the name was decoded, Amitabh Bachchan was contacted…and the star came in person bearing flowers.

A certain vein of Hindi cinema would have us laugh at pitiful characters. Desai gave us Amitabh Bachchan who is noble enough and fearless enough that we can wish to emulate him, and who is, at the same time, simple enough and silly enough in his weaker moments that we both identify *with* him and laugh *at* him. Amitabh Bachchan's frequent lack of dignity on screen forms a lively contrast with his real-life power and prestige. In Amitabh we have a man whose public and private images have been indelibly traced on the minds of many of his compatriots. Privately, he is known to be rich, handsome, intelligent, well educated, sensitive, from a good family. Publicly, he was the seventies' 'angry young man', the avenger, a man at odds with society, a hero who rights wrong with physical might—and who must often die in turn. The incongruity of seeing such a figure making a complete fool of himself doubles our laughter. To go back to Marcel Pagnol, 'If he must degrade himself and if he consents, his merit is even greater because he sacrifices his pride to lighten our suffering.'

As Amitabh Bachchan himself lists his favourite moments from the various Manmohan Desai films in which he worked, he as often as not mentions a highly sentimental scene like the one in *Desh Premee* in which, as old Master Dinanath, he is reunited in a prison cell with his long-lost leprous wife (Sharmila Tagore) only moments before she dies in his arms. Still, it was a comic scene in *Amar Akbar Anthony* that for both Manmohan Desai and Amitabh Bachchan, headed the list of unforgettable moments: for trying to drink and fight at the same time, Anthony has been punched up, brought down, and (temporarily) beaten out of his girl. Steadying himself in front of his mirror back home, he surveys the results of his own inanity, soundly berates himself, and then doctors his cuts and bruises by carefully applying iodine and a bandage...to the mirror! When all is said and done, the Manmohan Desai-Amitabh Bachchan association is likely to be best remembered precisely for this distinctive, highly perfected style of comedy that Desai so cleverly imagined and organized and that Amitabh Bachchan embodied and brought to life on the screen.

serious undertones

Good entertainment values account for much but not all of the success of Manmohan Desai films. Substantive issues pepper his films—individual morality, the role of family, poverty, politics, law, and patriotism. Many of these elements appear to be intended to increase emotional effect. However, if questions such as those of good and evil can rouse viewers to heightened emotional response, they can also encourage thought. Empathy, an emotion filmmakers generally seek to encourage, can flow from scenes that also involve social commentary. The suffering of innocents offers rich possibilities for audience concern. The ill not brought on by diabolical fiends is frequently wreaked by nature; flood and famine drive peasants off the land and into the city (*Sachaa Jhutha, Suhaag*) where they are prey to cunning confidence artists (*Sachaa Jhutha, Shararat, Raampur Ka Lakshman*). Behind the widespread hunger are the grain hoarders, the profiteers of misery who fabricate scarcity in order to push up prices (*Roti, Chacha Bhatija*). Politicians offer hollow promises of improvement in exchange for votes (*Roti*). Housing is precarious; a *basti* (slum) can be razed, its dwellers left heartless, in order to make way for a high-rise apartment building for wealthy residents (*Chacha Bhatija*).

Desai's innocent characters are victims of individual selfishness and greed, of an unjust system, of cruel elements and, often, of sadistic, even demonic violence. The attention Desai gave to the lambs among the wolves maintains a certain tradition in Indian cinema. Mehboob Khan's *Mother India* (1957) and Bimal Roy's *Do Bigha Zamin* (1953) are two classics centred on good, honest people who are put to harsh tests by evil men and pitiless nature, but who stand firm, resisting the temptation to sacrifice their principles. However hard their lives may be, their dignity and self-esteem remain intact and serve as rewards for these courageous souls. Desai did not rely solely on cinematic tradition for his inspiration. His understanding of the problems of simple folks also came from his own Khetwadi neighbourhood:

> I stayed here. I was raised here, and up to four years back, on Sundays I used to play cricket on the lanes and bylanes here. You're not allowed to play on the streets. But on Sunday there's no traffic One day we were arrested. We were all put in a police van, the whole team, and taken to the police station. The inspector told me, 'Mr. Desai what are you doing here?'
>
> I said, 'I was arrested with the other boys.'
>
> The constable said, 'Let Mr. Desai go.'
>
> I said, 'No, you let all the boys go, not me alone. We have committed no crime. There is no playground. That's why we have played here. If you arrest them, you put me in, or else, free all of us.'
>
> ...I know their frustrations. I know their likes. I know their dislikes. I know what makes them beat. Small things make them happy. You see, all my characters are from the lower middle class, characters who are down-to-earth, who have seen life in the raw. If I had been born an aristocrat, I could never have made it.

For perspective, let us look at the way some of Desai's contemporaries treated the poor on screen. One angle, generally limited to a small percentage of films from alternate cinema, has been to wallow in wretchedness, to concentrate only on society's poorest, their pains, their hopelessness, their no-out existence. Another tendency has been to ignore the poor totally; extrapolating from such films to all of society, one could imagine India to be inhabited exclusively by the westernized well-to-do. (It must be remembered that Hollywood has often given a correspondingly false image of America.) Still another group of filmmakers have presented the poor as conniving, low-class villains out to dispossess the rich—with whom we are made to side—of their legitimate wealth. Desai is an excellent representative of other filmmakers who have woven their tales around poor, but not ignoble characters and who have included many of these people's everyday concerns in their films. Some films in this category are dramatic, seeing the hero to his tragic death. Others—and most of Desai's films could be catalogued here—give improbable, if not impossible, solutions to the characters' problems. In Jack-and-the-Beanstalk-style happy endings villains are disposed of, material worries are vanquished, and blessed couples are formed. K.B. Pathak, one of Desai's regular screenplay writers *(Shararat, Raampur Ka Lakshman, Bhai Ho To Aisa, Aa Gale Lag Jaa, Roti, Dharam-Veer, Naseeb, Desh Premee)*, defended this approach to the dispossessed:

> The atmosphere in the slums is repulsive. The art film people show it just like that. We, on the other hand, look into every hut for the good feature in this dirt. Finally, we find it. It may be a little girl nursing her sick father. Maybe she works in a mill in the day and goes to a night school in the evening. We are the real idealists. No matter whether the film is a stunt film, a social, a historical or mythological, the one common feature that you will find in them is the victory of good over evil. Our hero wins single-handedly against twenty villains because he has the power of truth with him. This is the message which the *Ramayana*, the *Mahabharata*, the *Koran* and the *Bible* give.[1]

screen violence

A qualification now must be made concerning Desai's portrayal of the innocents and their problems. Police brutality raises a moral dilemma. In *Amar Akbar Anthony*, *Parvarish*, and *Desh Premee* the use of torture in order to extract information is seen as normal, even valorous, inasmuch as our strong heroic police officer is doing the beating, and then only for the worthy cause of assuring the downfall of dangerous criminals. In spite of the fact that such scenes remain macho without actually becoming gory, the message conveyed is one of tacit permission to ignore basic human rights, which include freedom from torture. Desai himself had no second thoughts and no regrets about his portrayal of the prisoner-beating police officer. To his mind, such practices were both commonplace and justifiable. He was apparently immune to any concern that police brutality, with its contempt for human beings, might corrupt society as a whole. Accessorily, it is a bit mysterious that over the years the Censor Board has, it seems, not taken exception to the police officer depicted as torturer, be he hero or anti-hero, whether in Desai's films or in those of other directors.

Media-caused or media-influenced violence, though widely studied in the U.S. and Europe, remains a subject fraught with controversy. Psychologists have never been able to prove to the satisfaction of U.S. courts, for instance, that a film can cause someone to act violently. A particularly notorious case was filed against Oliver Stone and the producers of the film *Natural Born Killers* (1994) for 'product liability' and incitation to murder after a couple of young people saw the film, dropped acid and went on a multi-state rampage. Interestingly, the case went through several levels of the court system before being struck down on the basis of First Amendment rights. A decade after the film's release, discussions continue, particularly on the large number of websites devoted to the film.

In 'The Trend of Violence on the Indian Screen & Its Influence on Children' Kanti Kumar (1999) reviews the literature on screen violence and expresses personal concern over its effect in India:

> If violence is glamorized, sanitized or made to seem routine, then the message is communicated that it is acceptable, perhaps even desirable... . The types of violence that affect children depends on their age, but children of all ages are at risk of learning to be aggressive when they see:
> - 'heroes' winning by being violent
> - violence being presented in a humorous way
> - violence not causing pain
> - violence inflicted on children, adults and animals
>
> Research conducted over the past 40 years leads to the inescapable conclusion that televised violence does affect viewers' attitudes, values, and behaviour. In general, there seem to be three main classes of effects: aggression, desensitization, and fearfulness.[2]

The word 'risk' is important in Kumar's discussion. Speculation is great, and much anecdotal evidence is indeed troubling. More clear-cut is the case against the film industry and the depiction of cigarette use. In 'Bollywood Told to Stub It Out' the BBC reported that the UN World Health Organization had studied Bombay films of the last 10 years and found that three fourths showed tobacco use and that teenagers who watched films in which stars smoked were three times more likely to try cigarettes.

> It also said teenagers whose favourite star smoked on screen were 16 times more likely to have positive attitudes towards cigarettes. It is estimated that 15 million people a day watch Bollywood films, either at the cinema or on television. Many see the stars as a leading cultural influence. India now accounts for almost a third of the world's smoking-related deaths.[3]

Given this data on films and tobacco, one could extrapolate and assume that other actions and attitudes on the part of film heroes and heroines, *e.g.*, a proclivity for violence, are likewise imitated. A thoughtful, society-wide discussion of the issue of film violence could be beneficial. Interestingly, the Health Ministry reacted to the 2003 WHO smoking report by controversially introducing in May 2005 what seems to be the world's first on-screen smoking ban. The result was an impassioned debate as the media, the public and the film industry expressed diverging opinions on the wisdom of such an initiative and tried to imagine what enforcement might imply.

self-sacrificing or self-seeking

The subject of courage is omnipresent in cinema. In a discussion about art with friends, Ike, the Woody Allen character in *Manhattan* (1979) mocks himself even as he promotes a position that is recurrent in the director's films:

> Talent is luck. Tsch. I think the important thing in life is courage.... . Listen to this example I'm gonna give. If the four of us are walking home over a bridge and then there was a person drowning in the water, would we have the nerve, would one of us have the nerve to dive into the icy water and save the person from drowning? ...Because that's a—that's a key question. You know, I—I, of course, can't swim, so I never have to face it.

For all of us who have found ourselves in a crowd, observed the surrounding faces and attempted to guess who, if anyone, might come to our aid were we in need, were we, say, attacked by a mugger or should we faint, the question of courage is, indeed, 'the important thing in life'. The next and particularly poignant question arises as to how much courage we could summon when confronted by someone else's distress. These two basic questions—the courage of others and our own—pose challenges to us all. The quality is both rare and difficult to delineate. *Shattered Glass*, the 2003 film by Billy Ray, based on a true story, appears to focus on the young journalist Stephen Glass (Hayden Christensen), who is found to have fabricated half of his articles before he is dismissed from his magazine. In fact, the dishonest Glass, though flamboyant, is only of minor interest. Our hearts go out rather to his editor Charles 'Chuck' Lane (Peter Sarsgaard) who must grapple, painfully, with how best to exercise his own power fairly and to maintain the ethics of his profession. Had he been less courageous, he would have followed the comfortable path and ignored the situation entirely. 'I, of course, can't swim, so I never have to face it.'

> Literature, according to our rhetoricians, must instruct people; it should tell them that 'one should live as Rama did, and one should not live as Ravana.' Because it is literature, the same instruction is expected from drama as well.[4]

Thus Adya Rangacharya describes the moral and pedagogical function of traditional Indian theatre. Indian cinema, in keeping with these injunctions, was, at its beginnings, religiously and morally based. D.G. Phalke, considered the father of Indian cinema, constructed *Raja Harishchandra*, his first feature film (1913), on an episode from the *Mahabharata*. Since that time, the *Ramayana* and the *Mahabharata* have not ceased, directly or indirectly to inspire filmmakers. Desai readily acknowledged the *Mahabharata* as his principle source and called it 'the greatest piece of literature in the world, one hundred stories in one!' Karna from the *Mahabharata* was Desai's model:

> Karna was a noble character. He was a gallant man who believed in charity. Krishna came to him dressed as a beggar to trick him into giving up the power that could help him win the war. Karna knew it

was Krishna, but he gave anyway and said, 'Never let it be said that Karna did not give.' And that Krishna also waited to attack Karna when the wheel of Karna's carriage was stuck. It was against the rules of valour of the day. When you talk about a god, you talk about good and perfect. Krishna is no god for me.

I wanted to make Dharam as Karna (in *Dharam-Veer*), but I realized that people wouldn't like it if he were killed. I rate Karna that high in my life. When I say Billy Wilder is my god for filming and scripting, so I say Karna is my hero who I acknowledge as a master, a man who is charitable.

Charitable and also courageous. Martin Esslin in his *An Anatomy of Drama* (1976) says that an essential purpose of all forms of dramatic art is to present spectators with a variety of role models and thus to prepare them for situations they have not yet confronted in real life. *Desh Premee* (The Patriot), despite its many moments of fun and silliness, is arguably Desai's most serious, most message-filled film. Courage is central. Early on, when Master Dinanath (Amitabh Bachchan) sees that his school is being used as a warehouse for smuggled arms, he confronts Thakur Pratap Singh (Amjad Khan), the all-important man in the village. In exchange for silence, Thakur offers Dinanath a stack of bills which, though most tempting, would, if kept, destroy Dinanath's vision of himself as a man of principle. Throughout the night Dinanath ponders. The medal that he won as a freedom fighter against the British is hanging in the window, swaying in the breeze. It catches the light of the moon and shines on Dinanath's confusion, making his decision clear. Patriotism, he realizes, means not only fighting heroically in times of war but also being honest and working for the common good in times of peace. He takes his stand the following day by returning the money and exposing Thakur's doings to the police. Far from earning congratulations, his courage brings him great suffering. In retaliation, Thakur has Dinanath's house burned down and his wife (Sharmila Tagore) and daughter kidnapped. He is told that both have died. Homeless and penniless, his family devastated, Dinanath and his son must attempt to rebuild their lives in a dusty slum. As a freedom fighter who almost lost his life in his resistance to the British, he received respect and support for his courage and his efforts. When he uses the same moral standards and the same backbone to confront post-colonial corruption, the fickle public, often a bad judge of character, abandons him to his lonely fate. Being courageous means being prepared to accept the consequences.

At this point in his life, the patriot's miseries are temporarily eased. Yet many years later he must face a new disappointment, the realization that his own son Raju (Amitabh) has grown into a scoundrel, involved in extortion and counterfeiting and lacking the decency even to acknowledge the woman to whom he is married (Hema Malini). The ever-present, self-sacrificing hero of Hindi films often follows his ideals— being faithful to a friend, keeping a promise, refusing tyranny—to their logical conclusion. Master Dinanath dies by stepping in front of his newly repentant son Raju and taking a bullet in his stead. The good and courageous among the older generation protect the younger generation even to death if need be. We have only a second to dwell on Dinanath's tragic end however. His *'Hai Ram'* is followed immediately on the sound track by a baby's cry—Dinanath's grandson is born, a reminder of the continuity of life. For in spite of all the tribulations that Dinanath suffers, the film does not end on a pessimistic note with the older generation's sorrows and the younger generation's corruption. Like Ramesh Sippy's *Shakti* (1982), *Desh Premee* suggests hope for the future. In each film the sons repent, and the grandsons follow the paths traced by their honest grandfathers. After the young grandson proves his honesty by returning a dropped wallet, his father Raju, now reformed, hugs his son, takes him before the statue of the deceased Dinanath and proclaims, 'Who says you are no longer in this world? Patriotism cannot die. It is immortal. Today it has been born again in this house. Look at this child.' The uprightness of past generations is not lost. It has simply skipped a generation. In *Shree 420* (1955) the Raj Kapoor character passes through the same three stages in a few short years of his own life; first an honest villager, he becomes a crooked, street-wise city man, only to regain his lost integrity as the story ends.

Today's chauvinistic warriors, so common in recent Hindi cinema, bear little resemblance to Master Dinanath. His last words to his son make leprosy into a metaphor for the true enemy of the country, *i.e.*, corruption:

> *Tumhaari maa to kor se mar gai, bete. Magar, magar, is bhaarat maa ko kor mat hone dena. Is ke sine par kor phailaanevale vatan faroshon ko khatam kar dena. Khatam kar dena un vatan faroshon ko.*

> (Your mother died of leprosy, son, but, but don't let our motherland become leprous. Those who would sell our country and spread this leprosy, take them from among us and be done with them.)

If corruption threatens the nation, so too do the centrifugal forces pulling the nation apart. In *Desh Premee* Master Dinanath arrives delivering oil in the *basti* Bharat Nagar (literally, India town), clearly a symbolic name. He is met by discord, embodied by four leaders—a Bengali (Uttam Kumar), a Muslim (Parikshat Sahni), a Punjabi Sikh (Shammi Kapoor), and a South Indian (Prem Nath)—each with a separate accent, war cry, and religious symbol. All resemble one another, however, in their dishonest dealings and in their determination to gain advantage for their group at the expense of others. A heated argument erupts over who will be served oil first. Master Dinanath responds with the title song, '*Desh premion, aapas men prem karo, desh premion*' (you who love your country, love one another), a strong message to any who threaten to rend the Indian union. Much later, having been won over by Master

Dinanath's courage, the leaders turn their aggression away from one another and toward the common good, protecting their *basti* from outer villainy. Yet their specificity is maintained and dignified. When they are attacked, each in turn summons strength from a different source, the Bengali from Kali Ma, the Muslim from Mecca, the South Indian from Lord Balaji, the Punjabi from Guru Nanak. Symbols of differentiation and friction are transformed into positive forces to serve in a collective effort to combat evil. Communal harmony in Desai's films is most often associated with the three-religion theme which has its foundation in the understanding that the 'Mother land' of India is mother to all. Ignoring the variations that exist within Hinduism, researchers generally encompass over 80% of the Indian population under the appellation 'Hindu', while Muslims are thought to make up some 11% of the population, and Christians, 3%. The Sikhs, sometimes mentioned and occasionally present on screen, form an even smaller minority with only 2% of the population of the country, though their geographic concentration and historic importance increase their visibility. Polls have apparently not been taken nor statistics compiled concerning the possible positive effects of communal harmony messages in films. There are, however, opinions. A *Filmfare* reader from Goa, for instance, J.V. Abul Barkeeth, wrote in November 1981, 'Communal riots take place in every part of the country. In my opinion filmmakers do a lot to prevent these riots through their films which exhibit love and affection between different communities.'

Amitabh Bachchan voiced a similar view when he defended Hindi films precisely for their role in national integration, arguing that just as in films the hero and heroine overcome difficulties and love triumphs, in real life people should overcome caste and other differences and love should triumph. 'Hindi films are important to national integration. All over India people see the same films and sing the same songs even though they speak different languages and have different customs,' he said. Sociological studies on the effects on the public of such positive film messages would be most interesting. In their absence we are left with conjuncture about audience reactions to none other than Amitabh Bachchan as John Jani Janardhan singing, 'Yeh tinon naam hain mere; Allah, Jesus, Ram hain mere.' (These three names are mine; Allah, Jesus and Ram are mine.) A question must also be asked, a quarter of a century later, about the relative rarity of such inclusive messages coming from Bollywood today. Times have changed. The trend towards chauvinistic films is incompatible with the Hindu-Muslim *bhai-bhai* messages of the past. More recent films have, instead, focused on stories of tragedy resulting from love across religious boundaries. Mani Ratnam's *Bombay* (1995) and Lateef Binny's *Dahek* (1999) though clearly denouncing the ills wrought by narrow minds, nevertheless allow the narrow minded an opportunity to voice their intransigence towards 'the other.'

When Desai moralized, he remained true to a long-standing tradition, he brought the public sought-after values, and he was faithful to himself and to his own beliefs. One wonders, when Desai called Billy Wilder his god, the director from whom he learned the most valuable filmmaking lessons, to what extent Desai's admiration was of Wilder's form, to what extent of his content. Billy Wilder had tightly-knit stories, good editing with an intelligent use of ellipses, and a marvellous sense of comedy, all of which Desai appreciated. Yet it was perhaps, above all, as a moralizer that Wilder distinguished himself, and it was perhaps by putting his techniques into the service of his moral world view that Wilder most attracted Desai's admiration. In *The Apartment* Dr. Dreyfus advises Baxter (Jack Lemmon), 'Be a mensch, a human being.' In *The Big Carnival* the newspaper editor, representing unbending values, has 'Tell the Truth' stitched in needlepoint above his office desk; not surprisingly, he refuses to condone Chuck's (Kirk Douglas) unethical methods of self-advancement. In *Sunset Boulevard* the character played by William Holden is almost swayed from his self-destructive self-seeking by his colleague, a young woman who refuses to compromise her principles. Wilder would seem to have had enough cynicism to understand (and to make us understand) his morally flabby characters. At the same time, all of his characters have enough moral fibre to be touched by examples of integrity. In his tragedies his characters face their consciences too late. In the comedies the lesson is taken just in time. Hovering in the background would seem to be the Jewish proverb, 'If I don't think of myself, who will? But if I only think of myself, what good am I?' The emotional power of Wilder's films most often comes as his characters suffer while searching for moral courage.

Wilder's characters face their consciences in a more individual way. Desai's characters are not alone; they draw the strength necessary to stand firm or to reform from the family, an immutable value. In *Desh Premee*, Raju's family is at the heart of his reform. Because of his father's noble example, because of the memory of his mother, because of his wife's patient, faithful love, and for the sake of the son she bore him, Raju becomes the person he was always expected to be. In *Bluff Master*, typically, the mother reigns as the ultimate bastion against moral weakness. Ashok (Shammi Kapoor), a happy-go-lucky character, shamelessly goes about telling lies until his mother confronts him with the tangled maze he has constructed through deceit. She first screams of the need to uphold family honour, and then moving from the verbal to the physical, she beats her son, falls down unconscious herself, and awakes only at the sound of her repentant son's sobs and his promises never to lie again.

Families are valued, but they are not shown to be ideal. As Desai shows brother fighting against brother *(Bhai Ho To Aisa, Parvarish, Dharam-Veer)* or wives mistreated *(Bhai Ho To Aisa, Suhaag, Coolie)*, we are far from the saccharine vision of family as a haven of peace. Surprisingly often, the father is shown to be a threatening figure, someone who would (unwittingly) kill his son were he not stopped in the knick of time (*Dharam-Veer, Naseeb*) or who would (intentionally) subvert his daughter's happiness; in *Aa Gale Lag Jaa*, Preeti's (Sharmila Tagore) father separates her, first, from the father of her child, and then from the child she must bear out of wedlock. Interestingly, Manmohan Desai saw himself in the other father in *Aa Gale Lag Jaa*, Prem (Shashi Kapoor), warm loving, the biological father who adopts his own son:

> Yes, it (*Aa Gale Lag Jaa*) should have been called Father And Son. Father and son, just like Ketan and me. You know, people cannot believe that we are father and son. We are so close. We laugh and joke together all the time.

Alcoholism has long been seen as both cause and symptom of a family in trouble. One of the all time classic illustrations of the doom and degradation accompanying alcohol use—which in Indian cinema almost always supposes abuse—is in the Guru Dutt production *Sahib Bibi Aur Ghulam*, directed by Abrar Alvi in 1962. When the heroine (Meena Kumari) takes to drink, she forsakes her religious principles and becomes a slave to a force that would require superhuman power to overcome. Though alcohol is frequently present in Hindi cinema, generally associated either with villainy or with moral collapse, rarely has it appeared so regularly, so insistently, and, above all, with such increasing intensity as in Manmohan Desai's work. Desai was a vegetarian and a non-drinker. His brother died of cirrhosis of the liver. One may assume that the song '*Chal Mere Bhai*' in *Naseeb*, in which Sunny (Rishi Kapoor) pleads with his older brother (Amitabh Bachchan) to give up the bottle and come along home, gathers part of its strength from Desai's personal situation and heartfelt concern. From the time of *Amar Akbar Anthony* to the filming of *Coolie*, alcohol is seen as ever more debilitating and addictive. Anthony's drinking is above all an excuse for humour. Like Anthony, Amit in *Suhaag* is a funny drunk, but his habit prevents him from immediately implementing his decision to join the police force. Reducing his daily intake is not an option. Only total withdrawal, as painful as for any heroin addict, can make him a free man. Amitabh's talent for doing variations on the comic drunk is probably one reason for the recurrence of the alcohol imbibing character. However, when he plays the drunk for the third time for Desai in *Naseeb*, John Jani Janardhan's drinking provides laughter in only a couple of scenes; his attempts to box while drunk, on the other hand, merely elicit pity. Likewise, the liver ailment his friend Vicki (Shatrughan Sinha) suffers from is deadly serious; continued drinking, his doctor warns, will kill him. The song 'Chal Mere Bhai' in *Naseeb* blends two moods into tragi-comedy. The soft lighting and the old fashioned musical style mix a nostalgic sadness with a host of gags as Sunny begs, bullies, and then offers his drunken brother the ultimate, clinching argument: a threat to follow the brother's example and take to the bottle himself. In *Coolie* alcohol offers no laughs. Sunny's (Rishi Kapoor) health problem is even more serious than was Vicki's in *Naseeb*. Only a kidney transplant will save his life. Like many sick alcoholics, Sunny ignores the warnings given by his own body, by the doctors, and by his friends. With what appears to be suicidal determination, he continues to drink beyond all pleasure, beyond all logic. Significantly, it is his father who saves Sunny's life by donating one of his own kidneys. The (good) family—with its extension to brother-like friendship—is shown as the only solid ship that can help in weathering life's terrible storms. The solution, however, is a bit too neat, and we are left with a troubling sense of a family racked, in fact, by issues as grave as any faced by the characters in the *Mahabharata*.

Lessons of nobility, generosity, courage and self-sacrifice require counter examples. In *Parvarish* villain Mangal Singh (Amjad Khan) is incapable of any concern for humanity in general, limited as he is to thinking only in terms of blood.

Though he has considered Kishan (Vinod Khanna) his son for years, Mangal loses all interest in him the minute he learns that it is Amit rather than Kishan, who is his true descendent. He then pleads melodramatically for Amit to join him, but when, rather than answer the call of the bond of blood, Amit follows the teachings of the *Mahabharata*, remains a duty-bound police officer and attempts to bring his criminal father to justice, Mangal Singh reacts with utter cynicism. As he escapes, he turns to the young man to whom he has rather hypocritically offered his love only moments before, *'Afsos bete'* (Sorry, son); Amjad Khan's intonation perfectly projects the mean spirit of Mangal in whom not even a sense of family can foster a spirit of self-sacrifice. Karna is generous. 'Me' and 'mine' are Mangal Singh's only lasting values.

exclusion

In earlier decades, romance collided with caste barriers in films like Bombay Talkies' *Achhut Kanya* (Untouchable Girl, 1936) and Bimal Roy's *Sujata* (1959). Certain New Wave directors, too, centred their films on problems that *dalits* have faced (as Ketan Mehta did in *Bhavni Bhavai*, 1980). Like the majority of other commercial filmmakers of his generation, Desai never mentioned caste explicitly. His films do, however, make indirect references to questions of exclusion. If one extracts the smuggler-policeman-comedy elements from *Parvarish*, it has at its heart a reworking of the story of *Sujata*. Like Sujata, Amit is not related by blood to his parents; he is from a low family, a family of outlaws. Unlike Sujata, though, he is warmly welcomed by generous parents who make no distinction between their true son and their adopted son. The scene in which the parents in *Parvarish* decide to keep Amit, the *daaku's* (dacoit) baby, is worth observing in detail, so strikingly does it differ from the way in which, after her parents die, Sujata is permitted to stay in the high caste family's home, hesitantly, conditionally, and at a safe distance from the mother of the family and her own blood daughter. In *Parvarish* Shammi Kapoor plays a police officer who has been entrusted with the dacoit's child by its dying mother. When he arrives home, he finds his wife Asha (Indrani Mukherjee) nursing their son Kishan. He explains who the child is and expresses regret at the idea of sending the baby to an orphanage. Asha responds by suggesting they take the boy in. The police officer sighs with relief, saying that that had been his wish all along, but that he hadn't dared to ask. The child is the son of a dacoit after all; he has criminal blood running in his veins. She answers, '*To kyaa huaa. Insaan to hai na? Khoon kuch nahin hotaa... . Aaj is ghar se sirf vahi pyaar, vahi haq, vahi parvarish milenge jo mere Kishan ko milta hain.*' (So what? He's a human being, isn't he? Blood has nothing to do with it... . From now on he will have the same love, the same rights, the same care my Kishan has.) Her husband smiles broadly and responds in English, 'Asha, I'm so proud of you, so proud of you.' And he takes the son Asha has been nursing, places him beside the dacoit's baby and says, '*Aa Kishan beta, yeh le, aaj tujhe ek nayaa bhai milaa hai.*' (Come, Kishan, son, today you have a new brother.) The following shot shows the title *Parvarish*, i.e., 'nurture.'

Sujata's parents never let her forget her lower status. She is introduced repeatedly with the painful phrase, '*Sujata meri beti jaisi hai.*' (Sujata is like my daughter.) In *Parvarish*, Asha accidentally reveals to the adult Amit that he was adopted and then adds, '*Tu meraa betaa zarur hai, lekin mainne tujhe janam nahin diyaa.*' (You are indeed my son, but I didn't give birth to you.) Despite the differences in the two films, both *Sujata* and *Parvarish* are built on the same message, that one's bloodline does not determine one's character. Manmohan Desai loved Nutan as a performer and chose her for his first film *Chhalia*, which he made only one year after *Sujata* was released. One can only surmise that he was influenced by her role in *Sujata*. That

Desai did not name untouchability per se as an issue in any of his films does not lessen the power of his message. When Stanley Kramer made *Guess Who's Coming to Dinner* in 1967, the story was exclusively about race: a white girl brings home the Negro man (Sidney Poitier) she wants to marry and is astounded that her parents find this problematic. In contrast, in 1992, when Kevin Costner makes love with Whitney Houston in *The Body Guard*, the script makes no mention of shades of skin colouring. He's a handsome man; she is a beautiful woman. The story is elsewhere. Similarly, *Parvarish* makes only a brief mention of the subject that guides the plot of *Sujata*. Manmohan Desai's touch may be light, but his message carries weight.

An even bolder and unprecedented statement against exclusion in *Desh Premee* has not received the praise it deserves. Leprosy, a disease that more than any other has historically been seen as punishment from God rather than as the work of a bacteria, has, it would seem, never before nor since been featured in Hindi popular cinema. Though the mother (Sharmila Tagore) is afflicted with leprosy as the result of villainy and clearly not by divine retribution, she suffers as an outcast, spending the rest of her life far from the gaze and the touch of others. When one dark, rainy night she stealthily ventures into Bharat Nagar, she is seen, and when discovered to be a leper, is stoned by the *basti* dwellers. Though she lives apart and considers herself unclean, her daughter, her husband and her son all come in contact with her by chance 20 years after she has disappeared from their lives, and though they do not recognize her, none shrinks from her touch. The message is subtle, but powerful. If his stance in favour of communal harmony was recognized, Manmohan Desai's other messages against exclusion went unnoticed or at least unmentioned, perhaps because his fame as an entertainer so captured the attention of the viewing public and critics alike.

politics

Direct allusions to politics are not common in Desai's films. However, in *Dharam-Veer*, made during the Emergency (1975-1977), a Mrs. Gandhi-like figure appears in the form of Raani Ma (Indrani Mukherjee) who, though kind and good herself, reigns over a palace in which intrigue and hunger for power flourish. Her own brother[5] Sattar Singh (Jeevan) is seen scheming ruthlessly to put his son (Ranjeet) on the throne in place of the prince Veer (Jeetendra). Rather than attack Veer openly and directly, Sattar Singh adopts a sinuous plan to replace the harmonious friendship between Veer and the poor-but-noble-hearted Dharam (Dharmendra) with an enmity Sattar Singh is sure will destroy both Dharam and Veer. To this end, Sattar Singh has Dharam's adoptive father, the blacksmith, framed to appear responsible for the accident in which the queen's coachman loses his hands. Following the law of the land, '*khoon ke badle khoon*' (an eye for an eye or, literally, blood in return for blood), means Dharam's father must lose his hands. Dharam passionately cries out against this injustice in terms that give a foretaste of the language that Iqbal (Amitabh Bachchan) will use in his election platform speech several years later in *Coolie*. Dharam's words could be seen as having a special significance against the backdrop of the Emergency, 'If you continue to play with the lives of the poor, this reign will not continue. The fires of revolution will flare up in the hearts of the poor and this palace will be consumed.' When Raani Ma protests that all are equal before the law, that her law applies even to herself, Dharam answers with prescience, 'I'm awaiting the day when the law's thunderbolt will strike this palace. Then I will see whether the walls of this palace will crumble or whether, to save those inside, the law itself will crumble.' In a matter of speaking, the walls do crumble, and yet, at the same time, they do not. The film, while providing a forum in which the poor can rail against oppression and injustice does not implicate the good queen herself in any form of tyranny. Sattar Singh continues his treacherous plotting and has one of Veer's arrows, identifiable by the royal mark, kill Dharam's adoptive mother. In fury, Dharam marches into the palace, his dead mother in his arms, and demands justice in the terms established by the queen herself: *'Ma ke badle Ma.'* (A mother for a mother.) Exact retribution, to his mind, though, does not require that the queen mother die, but rather that she live to keep him company in his humble home in the place of his lost mother. She nobly agrees and, preparing to leave, appoints her son to rule in her stead. If Raani Ma is honourable to the end, her son Veer is shown capable of succumbing to the temptation offered by power. Veer, once on the throne, immediately attempts to use his new position to forbid his mother's departure and to order Dharam's arrest. It is Raani Ma who halts his tyranny, who refuses to allow him to place himself above the law, and who willingly walks out of the palace at Dharam's side. If one sees Mrs. Gandhi in Raani Ma (whose hair was likewise grey only on one side), one could interpret Veer's power abuse as a reminder of Sanjay Gandhi's heavy-handedness at the time of the Emergency. This possible reference to contemporary politics is not harsh however. Veer is, after all, basically good. After a flirt with power misuse, he proves his valour by joining forces with Dharam once again to fight the real villains upon whom evil, power lust and injustice are exclusively placed.

the law

As Desai said, foreign critics tend to read into his work concerns which he did not consciously intend. One such subject for reflection is common to popular Indian cinema in general. It is the recurring argument which, though rarely intellectually formulated, nevertheless frequently illustrates the split between what might be designated as 'the old law' and 'the new law.'

Quite simply, the new law is the modern legal system that came into being in 1947 and which, except for economic law, is largely inspired by the British model. It is enforced by the police and administered by the judiciary. Significantly, it is represented as a blindfolded woman. If blind justice holding the scales was originally intended to designate impartial judgments for all without fear or favour, it has been reinterpreted by Indian cinema as a symbol of the unjust court system that functions coldly and mechanically, impervious to individual needs and extenuating circumstances. B.R. Chopra's *Insaaf Ka Tarazu* (1982) gives precisely this reading to the statue which appears during the credits. Blind justice, rather than being seen as unbiased, is instead portrayed as one who uses the logic of the woman in Idries Shah's *The Exploits Of The Incomparable Mulla Nasrudin*:

> In a dark alleyway an agile pickpocket tried to snatch Nasrudin's purse. The Mulla was too quick for him, and there was a violent struggle.
>
> Eventually Nasrudin got his man down on the ground. At this moment a charitable woman passing called out: 'You bully! Let that little man get up and give him a chance.' 'Madam,' panted Nasrudin, 'You ignore the trouble which I have had getting him down.'

If the new law is clear cut and easily defined, the old law is multifaceted and somewhat hazy. At one level it is almost instinctive, prescribing the protection of the family at any price, even at the risk of endangering society at large. So it is that, up to a point, Radha (Nargis) in *Mother India* defends her son Birju (Sunil Dutt). He may become a violent dacoit without losing her loving protection. It is only when he infringes on what is for her an inviolable law and attempts to dishonour a village girl that he loses her support. Another characteristic of the old law is its demand for revenge. One who has been personally injured or had a friend or family member wronged, should, according to the old law, use no intermediary to establish justice. Films with revenge as a major or minor plot line abound in Hindi cinema. Ramesh Sippy's *Sholay* (1975) is one of the most notable examples, though the theme is likewise present in *Mother India* and many, many others.

An extension of the need for revenge is the potential for repentance and forgiveness. Upon seeing that a transgressor is truly sorry and prepared to change, a likely avenger may turn clement and leave justice to fate. In Mohan Segal's *Kartavya* (1979), for instance, the character played by Dharmendra recognizes Jacob's (Ranjeet) change of heart and, therefore, does not punish him for his actions of the past. The old law reserves vengeance for the truly evil and unrepentant. In contrast, the new law insists that anyone judged guilty be made to pay, whether or not the offender has, in the meantime, reformed. The clemency offered by the old law may be based on an understanding of a criminal's motivations. In K. Balachander's *Thaneer Thaneer* (1981) a community listens carefully to a man's explanations of the events that led him to commit a murder; they come to the consensus that his act was justified. Furthermore, because the villagers need his services, they follow the old law to its logical conclusion. They reject the new law entirely and take a solemn oath to hide the fugitive from the police. Thus a criminal is rehabilitated into normal society through group action, in direct opposition to the official legal system.

Vengeance, repentance, justification and rehabilitation are key aspects of the old law from the points of view of both the accuser and the accused. As a final resort, however, the old law rests on divine justice. In Sultan Ahmed's *Ganga Ki Saugand* (1978) a dishonest priest is spared by an avenging dacoit (Amitabh Bachchan) but killed by a sacred cobra. And in Bimal Roy's *Yahudi* (1958) 'Roman *qanoon*' is opposed to '*khuda ka qanoon*'. Roman law only appears all powerful; God's law is ultimately supreme.

Old and new law are often confusedly fused (or, it might be argued, harmoniously blended). In Raani Ma's (Indrani Mukherjee) kingdom in *Dharam-Veer*, with *'khoon ke badle khoon'* the most basic law of the land, revenge has been ennobled; what was originally an often savage form of self justice has been transformed into a guiding legal principle, condoned, controlled and executed by the state. It has also been expanded—for the sake of humour—to include non-violent areas of human interaction and contention. So it is that Roopa the gypsy girl (Neetu Singh) pleads to Raani Ma for justice in romance. Since her heart has been stolen, she says, a fair reading of the law would require another heart in exchange: *'Dil ke badle dil.'* Legally, Roopa's love for the prince (Jeetendra) cannot go unrequited. The lines of separation between the old law and the new are dangerously blurred in *Amar Akbar Anthony*. Police officer Amar (Vinod Khanna), representing the new law in all its coolness, has a hot, gut reaction when his superior officer (and adopted father) is shot by an escaping criminal. Amar's duty to the new law is simply to deliver the felon to the justice system. His uniform, however, provides him with the authority to achieve the ends of the old law, that is, to wreak vengeance against one who has harmed a member of his family. The means he uses—beating prisoners to obtain information—is more understandable, if not more excusable, in the light of his dual allegiance to two sorts of law.

In *Suhaag* the fusion operates in the opposite direction. In the line of duty, police officer Kishan (Shashi Kapoor) is blinded by a dangerous gangster (Amjad Khan). Amit wants immediate revenge and vows personally to find and punish the man who has taken his friend's sight. Kishan, however, rechannels this desire for justice. To Amit's talk of taking the law into his own hands, Kishan replies by holding up a police uniform. 'This is the answer,' he says. And Amit responds by joining the police force.

The modern legal system is not the only law that revokes the elementary notion of family above all. In the *Bhagvad Gita* Krishna counsels Arjun to forego family loyalty for the sake of a broader duty. In *Parvarish* (as in Yash Chopra's *Deewaar*, 1975) a policeman faces a situation similar to Arjun's. In each case, the teachings of the *Bhagvad Gita* hold sway, and the policeman pursues, rather than shields, his brother gone bad. One of the many complexities of *Parvarish* lies in the layered, intermingled loyalties the characters exhibit to three overlapping forms of justice which are often distinguishable lexically and which more or less correspond to periods of Indian history. Shammi Kapoor and Amitabh Bachchan, playing police officers, are official representatives of the modern legal system, referred to as '*qanoon*'. Though more or less British in form, '*qanoon*' is Mughal in vocabulary. *Insaaf* (justice), *adaalat* (court), *faisla* (decision), *mujrim* (criminal), *muqadma* (a legal case), *vakil* (lawyer), and many more legal words are of Arabic origin. Another evocative, motivating word is *farz* (duty) which, as it is most often used, transports us back through the centuries to the *Bhagvad Gita*. Amit uses the word in *Parvarish* as though to explain his relentless, even obsessive tracking of his smuggler brother Kishan (Vinod Khanna). *Sharm* (shame) carries us still further into the past, perhaps to original justice as embodied by the mother, keeper of the power to shame a misguided child away from evil and toward good.

Dramatic moments are often developed around decisions made difficult because of the conflicting 'shoulds' that rage inside, heightening tension. Amit faces such an inner clash when his mother (Indrani Mukherjee), ignoring both Krishna's lessons and the rationality and inevitability of the modern justice system, pleads with Amit to destroy the evidence that will prove her son Kishan's guilt. Her tone is that of a helpless woman full of protective love for a son who, she agrees, has gone astray but who she does not feel deserves to go to prison. Amit is torn and troubled, but his sense of love for and duty to his mother is such that he renounces his duty to his uniform in order to submit to her will, the highly internalized ultimate law before which all other allegiances disintegrate.

The binding nature of a mother's law, of course, rests on her own moral invincibility. Radha in *Mother India* was capable of killing her son to protect the honour of a village girl only because she herself had already undergone a most difficult test, yet maintained her honour. When Amit's mother pleads to him, she appears both weak and unjust. She is a changed woman, however, when she confronts Kishan. Her pitiful tone has given way to a sure and powerful voice as she lashes out at him from the fortress of her moral strength. It soon becomes clear that she has saved Kishan from the law only to better punish him herself. She shames him and curses herself for having borne him. And like Ashok's (Shammi Kapoor) mother (Lalita Pawar) in *Bluff Master*, Kishan's mother succeeds, better than any official legal body could have hoped to, in setting her son on the right path.

behind the lost-found theme

No doubt Desai's most central, most often repeated, and perhaps also his most criticized theme is that of separated family members reuniting. Manmohan Desai did not, of course, invent the theme. It is present worldwide: in the Bible, in Greek tragedies, in Shakespearean comedies, in American television serials, in European popular songs, in legends, epics, stories and films from countless cultures. And, as Desai stated, it was commonplace in Hindi cinema even before he began to make films:

> There was a film called *Kismet*. It starred Ashok Kumar and Mamta Shanti (N.B.: probably Gyan Mukherji's *Kismet*, made in 1943). To the best of my knowledge, that film had a lost-and-found theme and it ran for 120-125 weeks in Calcutta. So that was the first lost-and-found theme film that clicked in a big way. Then in 1951 Raj Kapoor made a

film called *Awaara* which I still maintain is his best film to date. He has not been able to make anything like it again. That too was a lost-and-found film, and a beautiful lost-and-found film!

Desai's point of reference is not only cinematographic. Karna, his hero from the *Mahabharata*, learns just before his death that Kunti is his long-lost mother. While Manmohan Desai did not create the theme, he nevertheless expanded it, polished it, and formalized the rules governing its use as no other filmmaker before or since. The source and the proper execution of the lost-found theme, though intriguing, are of minor interest compared with the mystery of its continued appeal. One cannot but wonder what personal experiences the spectators have had, what psychic motivations may make audiences identify with such an ancient but not outdated plot device. The most elementary answer would be that the device—used out of habit by filmmakers—is accepted almost unthinkingly by the public purely as a matter of convention. A slightly different response comes from looking at cinema in various countries and noting that each society seems to have a set of themes or centres of interest which recur with surprising regularity. Schematically speaking, the French, for example, appear to be intrigued by adultery, the Spanish during the Franco years by religion and death, Americans by the idea of an ordinary person becoming exceptional when placed in exceptional circumstances. Such recurring themes may result from imitative writing; it is equally possible that they fill the needs and address the concerns of specific audiences. Certain moments in history demand to be exorcised. The disrupting influence of wars would seem especially difficult to eliminate from the collective psyche. The violent conquering of the West and the 1860-65 Civil War (and more recently the Vietnam War) have occupied a sizeable amount of footage in the U.S. Likewise, World War II in France, England, the U.S., and the U.S.S.R., or the rise of fascism in Italy have held the attention of numerous filmmakers. In India one historical event that has surely not yet been collectively worked through is the partition of the subcontinent following Independence. The turmoil created by some ten million people being displaced in Punjab and Bengal caused both short- and long-term repercussions. Scars have been left on the national memory by this historical trauma. Many families were broken up. Though some were reunited, many others were not. A few films have approached Partition head on—M.S. Sathyu's *Garm Hawa* (1973), Deepa Mehta's *1947: Earth* (1999), or the Pakistani *Khamosh Pani* (by Sabiha Sumar, 2003). Ritwik Ghatak's films look eastward to the separation of Bengal; many are laden with nostalgia and a sense of exile. In Desai's first film *Chhalia*, Partition sets in motion the events central to the plot. A woman (Nutan) who is left behind in Pakistan is eager to meet her own family, her husband, and his family as she arrives in India six years later. The rejection she faces is total. 'You are not our daughter; our daughter is dead,' her family tell her in a scene that echoes the experience of all too many women of the period.

It is possible that in certain cases cinema functions a bit for the collectivity as the dream self works for the individual, replaying problems and traumatic moments again and again; at best, offering creative solutions, at worst, leading a person's psyche in circles, allowing sores to fester. In his film *The Prisoner* (1948) Ingrid Bergman probes the painful dreams of an abused woman whose nightmares go unheeded and whose end is tragic. On the level of a group, films centered on the lost-found theme—Desai's as well as those by other directors—might be considered a form of turning in circles: there is endless repetition and the solutions offered are not realistic. On the other hand, these films in which the family is reunited could be considered a psychological relief, a sort of moral aspirin, the happy endings counterbalancing a reality that is not always so happy.

fate

The lost-found angle in Desai's cinema depends on the ever-present, intervening hand of Fate and its cousin, Coincidence. Desai honoured fate twice in film titles (*Kismat* and *Naseeb*). And *taqdeer, muqaddar, vidhaataa*—the other words in Urdu and Hindi for fate—reappear regularly in dialogues. Manmohan Desai clearly believed personally in the power of fate. Dharam (Dharmendra) could have been speaking for the director in one line in *Dharam-Veer*, 'If it is written that I am to die, nothing can save me. If my fate is to live, nothing can harm me.' If as a human being Desai felt subject to fate, as a filmmaker he controlled it. Humans have a limited power over their own lives in reality; in fiction, within the confines of a three-hour script, for example, one can mold and determine the lives of one's characters, temporarily playing God. Fate in real life is often cruel. At times the same is true in Desai's films, but more often it is a benign presence that, say, brings saving recognition a moment before brother kills brother. The notion of fate can, of course, be a convenient excuse for refusing personal responsibility. Human beings are limited but not powerless. In *Desh Premee* the character played by Jeevan substitutes himself for fate, orders some women killed, and then hypocritically places the blame for their deaths on destiny. '*Naseeb ki baat hai*,' (It's a question of fate) he says. 'Some people's fate is to eat bread; others' is to eat bullets.'

Among Desai's films *Dharam-Veer* offers the most legendary (and mythical) look at fate. After an astrologer reveals that the villain (Jeevan) is to die at his nephew's hands, this uncle becomes obsessed with preventing the fulfillment of the prediction. Fate, though, is tricky, as Macbeth and Oedipus Rex learned when they tried to avoid their own predicted destinies. Likewise, the Pharaoh, while attempting to have no Hebrew males in the land of Egypt, came to rear one named Moses in his own palace. There is a comic quality to fate. In Woody Allen's play *God*, a modern update of a Greek tragedy, the fates are a couple of mischief-makers, Bob and Wendy, American tourists dressed in jazzy Hawaiian shirts and sporting such practical joker gadgets as hand buzzers and water-spraying lapel flowers. In Raj Kapoor's *Mera Naam Joker* (1970) Raju (Raj Kapoor) says, 'The biggest joker is above.' The irony of fate comes out, too, in a line from one of the final scenes of *Parvarish*. Mangal Singh (Amjad Khan) has gone through life thinking Kishan (Vinod Khanna) was his son; Amit (Amitabh Bachchan), his real son, sees the logic in this chance mistake, *'Insaan ko apne khel ki sazaa is hi duniyaa se mil jaati hai. Aap zindagi bhar duniyaa ko dhokaa dete rahe aur taqdeer aapko dhokaa dete rahe.'* (People get their just desserts in this world. All your life you have been tricking other people and all along fate has been tricking you.) Tales do exist such as 'The Victory of Jasvant, King of Gujarat, over the Goddess of Destiny' in which fate has, in fact, been outwitted. Generally speaking, however, destiny wins in the end. In *Dharam-Veer* the villain must succumb to the inevitable. His nephew is indeed responsible for his death. His fight against his fate merely weaves a richer story. All the plotting and scheming that pitted him against his nephew would not have been necessary had he not been told that his nephew would kill him; had he not been trying to avoid his fate, his fate would not have been his fate. It is a mental game of 'if' that both philosophers and humourists have often played. Manmohan Desai gives us an opportunity both to reflect and to enjoy.

reality

> For me, the cinema is not a slice of life, but a piece of cake.
> —*Alfred Hitchcock*[1]

how much reality does the public want or need?

The normal function of fiction is to put order where there might not be any in real life. Loose ends cannot always be tied up. While life is often messy, fiction provides a clean slate on which to draw a neat picture. Woody Allen expresses it well when, at the end of *Annie Hall*, as Alvy Singer, he shows us a play he has just written. In the play he draws upon the events we have witnessed during the 'reality' of the film. The final break-up of the couple in the film, however, has been transformed in the play into a romantic reunion with a promise of everlasting love. In a monologue with the audience afterwards, Alvy apologizes for his sentimentality, 'Tsch, whatta you want? It was my first play. You know, you know how you're always tryin' t' get things to come out perfect in art because, uh, it's real difficult in life.'

Any work of fiction, then, necessarily diverges from reality. In Hindi cinema, however, as a rule, the gap between the two is especially wide. As Desai said:

The night that you show in the films may be day; the fights may be the result of brisk cutting; the passage of time may have been created at the laboratory with a technique called dissolve. So you have illusions available to you. Why must you always create something out of them that looks like life? It can be anything, as long as it touches a chord.[2]

I don't give my audiences a chance to think. I never think seriously about a story and the much talked about logic and other such things. My only interest is to see that I present something fantastic there on the screen, something that will make the audience focus all their attention on the screen. My only concern is their everyday problems. My constant efforts are to take people into a world of fantasy where there is no worry, no serious thinking, just fun and entertainment all the way.

Who wants to see realism? People in the West! There's always some bright aspect even to a poor man's life. Take this aspect and make something rosy, like *Awaara*. See Raj Kapoor's *Awaara*. What a tramp! What did Charlie Chaplin do? A small tramp who went into fantasies. That's why his films are liked. He turned the whole thing into a comic approach. He made fun of Hitler in *The Great Dictator*. In *City Lights* he fell in love with the blind girl. But he tried to humour. I'm saying there should be humour in a film. These art filmmakers think humour is a sin: it's a cardinal sin for a person to laugh in the auditorium, according to them. What's wrong with a person having a bit of enjoyment in the theatre?

...My plots are not realistic. My characters are realistic. You see, if I make the stories real, they're not interested in seeing them. But put those characters on a trip to fantasy! When I was a kid I went to the stadium and saw Dara Singh, the famous wrestler who was in many stunt films. I imagined I was Dara Singh. I would go to the wrestling bouts full of arranged gimmicks... . There were challenges: 'Next Saturday I'll fight you!' I used to think if I were Dara Singh, if I had a body like that, I'd also hit ten people. Now, I like to make these people into what they would like to be, but aren't. What's wrong with that? They feel, '*Re*, I could've been like that chap! I could've been like Anthony!'

Given its avowed escapist nature, what is surprising about the genre is not the degree of fantasy that the films offer, but rather the extent to which reality creeps in. As every successful filmmaker knows, people must identify. Hence, even though a great part of each film may resemble a fairy tale, a dream, or even a cartoon, in certain respects a film must remain down-to-earth enough so that the spectators can project themselves onto the screen.

Obviously, identification can work at the level of wish fulfillment. It is also enhanced by realistic detail. Desai added interesting, real-life touches to his films by shooting on the streets of his town Bombay, which he often featured, at times almost personified and clearly loved. In *Bluff Master* the Govinda song sequence was shot in his own neighbourhood, in the streets of Khetwadi district. The church in *Amar Akbar Anthony*, like the Victoria School for the Blind in *Parvarish* or the Haji-Ali tomb in *Coolie* are all real Bombay institutions. Desai's street scenes, even when built on film sets, carried evocative touches: graffiti and ever-present film posters cover the walls; people live under bridges and sleep on footpaths; legless beggars hobble about, and packed, red BEST buses lumber along the streets. In film after film, too, Desai made generous use of extras; crowds in movement assured his films a life-like quality that contrasts with the theatrical sparseness typical of many other film sets. Cameo characters like the 'cigarette-paanwala' in *Parvarish* and the tea vendor in *Sachaa Jhutha* also added a flavour of authenticity. All this richness of detail and frequent identifiable touches from daily life add considerable substance to his reels of dreams and increase the power of his tales over us.

The balance between reality and fantasy is a key element in audience satisfaction. Spectators may like to dream a bit at the movies but do not necessarily want to enter never-never land. While they may want the theatre lights at the end to signal a return to the real world, they may at the same time want to carry a bit of the film with them in the week to come. And even if they go out saying, 'It's just a film,' they may also wish to believe that, like in the film, good will triumph over evil in the world around them.

illogic

A corollary to the portrayal of reality is the question of script logic. Desai and other popular Indian filmmakers have been especially criticized for weakness in this domain. In Desai's defence Rosie Thomas succinctly explained, 'Spectacular and emotional excess will invariably be privileged over linear narrative development.'[3] Indian film critics have often been unforgiving. An unnamed journalist writing for *Filmfare* wrote a typical sweeping condemnation:

> It does reflect rather badly on the tastes of our audiences, that a film like *Mard* could be a hit. But it is one of the top grossers of the year. The contempt it shows for the brains and sensibility of the viewers is to be seen to be believed…[4]

A troubling case of Desai illogic can be seen precisely in *Mard* with its disregard for language, costume and the many historic details that should form the backdrop of the film. Even if one accepts that viewer understanding is quite naturally the primary goal of the film, it is, nevertheless, disconcerting to see British rulers speaking Hindi among themselves. Of course, playing with historical fact could be understood, as Philip Lutgendorf suggests, as a subtle way of attacking the present ruling class:

> Yet given the fantasy framework, chronological and locational ambiguity, and the fact that, with the exception of Simon and a bunch of other *goras* (white folk) cast as extras, the arch villains are all played by Indian actors, one may propose that the ridiculously evil *firangis* may as easily be read as stand-ins for the 'brown sahibs'—the Indian

elite of the long-running Congress Raj—who succeeded the colonial masters.[5]

Should one continue to quibble about the apparent lack of authenticity of *Mard*, one could seek perspective by considering some of the strange things that happen in Hollywood cinema. To take but one example, much-acclaimed director John Huston, in his highly reviewed *The Man Who Would Be King* (1975) situates his film in India even though it was obviously shot in North Africa, with no attempt made for veracity in costume. Amazingly, Saeed Jaffrey speaks Hindi only to be answered in Arabic by various villagers.

The Hollywood/Bollywood comparison/contrast here is made not in the context of some ideal world of cinematic theory, but rather in response to the regular dismissal of Indian cinema by critics both in India and in Europe who in one breath praise popular Hollywood films and in the next rail against Bollywood films, even when disregard for reality in each genre is but a matter of degree. At the same time, it could be argued that to offer examples of illogic in Hollywood cinema does not bolster the case for Bollywood's lack of logic. Both could be criticized equally. Holden Caulfield in J.D. Salinger's *The Catcher in the Rye* (1951) judges Hollywood with a combination of harshness and ambivalence that might reflect many a Hindi film viewer, 'I started imitating one of those guys in the films. In one of those musicals. I hate the movies like poison, but I get a bang imitating them.'[6] Many NRIs or second-generation South Asians abroad show similar ambivalence: while avidly watching Hindi films, they caustically complain of their lack of realism and logic. Perhaps their objections betray a deeper dissatisfaction with a lack of endeavour on the part of many filmmakers. John Simpson, in *News from No Man's Land*, applies to TV journalism the criticism that screenplay writer and novelist William Goldman makes of Hollywood's tendency to lazily follow conventions:

...that when someone in a film pulls out their wallet to pay for something, they always have exactly the right amount of money in it; that when they drive to the office or the shops or the bank, there is always a parking space right outside; and that whenever a television set is switched on in the background, it will invariably start broadcasting a news item which is directly related to the subject of the film you are watching.[7]

A similar sort of laziness certainly obtains within the Indian film industry.

The effects of screen illogic are variable. Some juggling with facts or playing with common sense causes wonder only if one bothers to rethink a film in a calm moment after the lights have gone out. Other points can confuse the audience immediately or detract from a story by calling attention to themselves. How, one might ask, can a silk stocking covering an arm or a leg render a tattoo or a bullet wound invisible to inquisitive searchers? (*Raampur Ka Lakshman* and *Parvarish*) How, in *Naseeb*, could John Jani Janardhan forget his father's face even after years of separation? And why in *Suhaag* does the blinded Kishan (Shashi Kapoor) continue to wear a wristwatch? The list of such questions could go on and on.

One answer would be that Desai's speed, caricature and exaggeration make much of his illogic inconsequential. An additional response lies with the group dynamics in the theatre setting. Acceptance or rejection of any scene is often audience specific. One or two snickers can lead an entire theatre of people to take a mental step back from immersion into critical judgement.

illusion, corruption and blindness

Reality makes its entry into Desai's films in an entirely different domain—philosophically, sociologically and psychologically—when it is contrasted with deceptive appearances. Pretence and outward show confound the screen characters and the viewing public alike. What appears to be, the message reads, is not what is. *'Andar kuch aur; bahar kuch aur.'* (Literally: inside, one thing; outside, something else.) What would seem to be real is only a mirage, not to be trusted. Desai's insistence on the nebulous nature of reality and the stranglehold of the world of appearances no doubt reveals a Hindu concern. On a philosophical level, the theme of appearance in opposition to reality might well relate to *maya*, the belief that the material world is nothing more than illusion. The *Ramayana* offers the spectacle of an illusory death. Hanuman, the monkey god, is prepared to attack Ravana's palace to recapture the abducted Sita when, in order to sap the morale of Hanuman's troops, Ravana's magician makes Sita appear to die before the onlooking Hanuman. In *Roti* a policeman shoots down Mangal Singh (Rajesh Khanna), before our eyes; in the next shot we see Mangal awake sweating in his bed; the illusion in this case is caused by a nightmare. In *Desh Premee*, however, no such explanation is given as we witness one person after another die, murdered, only to see them reappear inexplicably in later scenes. Watching screen characters being fooled and misled by pretence is perhaps comforting to spectators who feel that, in a sense, all of life is a hoax in which each of us is duped from birth until death.

On a social level, pretence distorts our perception of reality. *'Log kyaa kahenge?'* (What will people say?) is an oft-heard expression both in real life and on screen. Following basic social mores includes maintaining appearances and can be seen as a necessary social skill, essential to preventing clashes and stopping wagging tongues. Where appearances are paramount, however, hypocrisy, feigning, and dissimulation are inevitable. The apparently upstanding Thakur (Amjad Khan) in *Desh Premee*, in fact, deals in smuggling and counterfeit money. For years he has maintained a good reputation not only before society but more especially in the eyes of his son (Navin Nischol), an honest police officer. When one of Thakur's collaborators (Kadar Khan) risks disclosing their illegal doings, Thakur prefers to shoot himself in the arm—no pretence here—in order to prolong his imposture as a spotless businessman. The recurrence of this theme within Manmohan Desai's cinema offers a mordant commentary on corruption parading as honesty in society at large.

Truth can be observed, but it possesses a quality of interiority that most individuals are incapable of identifying. In *Aa Gale Lag Jaa* during a skating contest, couples are formed according to their matching costumes. Preeti (Sharmila Tagore) is dressed as Laila. When Prem (Shashi Kapoor) arrives dressed as a Pathan, she protests that she is waiting for a partner dressed as Majnu. Prem stubbornly presents his case: if she looks at his heart, she will see that he is her Majnu. In *Sachaa Jhutha* Bhola (Rajesh Khanna) sings, *'Dil sachaa aur chera jhutha.'* (The heart is true; faces are false.)

Blindness, real or pretended, is found in several of Desai's films—*Budtameez, Roti, Amar Akbar Anthony, Parvarish,* and *Suhaag*. Though he denied any personal psychological motivation, one cannot but wonder if Desai's special insistence on blindness might have been, at least in part, traceable to an anxiety over his own weak eyes. Beyond such conjecture, the presence of blindness is not without philosophical implications, especially if one adds to the physically blind and the fake blind, all those characters who go about as if blind, never seeing the obvious, fooled as they are by exteriors.

A lie perpetrated by a conniving, villainous character and believed without hesitation has been central to plot development in numerous Hindi films...as well as in the *Ramayana*. Ram, in spite of his love for Sita, is willing to believe that she might not be pure after her stay in Ravana's palace. In *The Tiger and the Jackal*,[8] a story from the *Mahabharata*, a pious jackal is chosen by the king tiger to become chief minister. When conniving jackals plot to make it appear the minister has stolen the king's meal, the king immediately accepts their word and punishes the minister. So it is that in *Dharam-Veer* Raani Ma (Indrani Mukherjee) is quick to believe that Dharam's adoptive father has been responsible for her carriage driver losing his hands. The possibility of a conspiracy is ignored, as are the long years of faithful service on the part of Dharam's father. Failure to recognize innocence is paralleled by blindness to evil. Raani Ma never discerns her own brother's (Jeevan) treachery, until it is too late.

the art-entertainment dichotomy

Manmohan Desai's films did not exist in a vacuum. On the one hand, they connected positively to a tradition of popular Indian cinema whose masters Desai readily saluted. On the other hand, they stood in opposition to the modern movement of Indian art cinema which reached its peak in the eighties. Just as Desai often pointedly criticized art films and those who made them, art filmmakers often boasted of creating a much-needed alternative to the sort of cinema for which Manmohan Desai was generally seen as a prime example. A fortress atmosphere developed with each side ready to defend itself from its position of strength: to a large extent, the commercial directors had the audiences, while the art directors enjoyed critical acclaim. Serious filmmaker Saeed Mirza perceived the split between the two cinemas in these terms, 'There is a cinema of status quo and a cinema of change. That is the polarity.'[9] Manmohan Desai defended popular cinema thus:

> Why should I show them down, depressed. That's what they are undergoing every day of their lives. They're facing poverty, misery, everything. Why can't I give them an escape hatch? My films are an escape hatch.

Desai understood the function of his cinema. The escape he offered is rather like that provided by a carnival. At least once a year in nearly every culture throughout the world the need is felt to turn the rules inside out, to throw restraint to the wind, to offer an outlet for the tensions that build up because of the rigidities of society. People dress up, temporarily take on new identities, thumb their noses at rules and at those in power, and finally, fill their lives with colour, gaiety, and music.

One could reasonably object to the whole notion of the escape hatch, arguing that the time and energy that goes into the making and the consuming of such mass entertainment could more profitably be used to transform society in fact rather than in fiction, that real-life problems might be solved actively and permanently rather than vicariously and temporarily. Many new cinema directors hoped to force people out of the conscience-easing denial of surrounding misery. They may have succeeded at times; at others, their best intentions backfired. A case in point is Govind Nihalani's *Ardh Satya* (1983) in which a policeman turns senselessly violent, rotted by his own desire for self-preservation. Acclaimed by many as an accurate view of the police force and, more broadly, as a typical example of the corruption so rampant in society, the film reached a relatively wide audience and provoked much reaction. Judging from the letters to the editors of film magazines, however, the audiences seemed to interpret the film as a confirmation of the inevitability of corruption and violence. Viewers were apparently left with a sense of increased helplessness rather than with a will to change.

cross-fertilization

In spite of the chronically strained relations between art and commercial cinema in the seventies and eighties, there was nevertheless a certain amount of cross-fertilization between the two camps. Shyam Benegal and Manmohan Desai had two very different approaches to filmmaking. Benegal, a socially committed director, has often used cinema to search into reality.

The endings of his films have rarely been happy. At best, they are awakenings with his characters becoming aware or perhaps taking a stand. In spite of their differences, however, Shyam Benegal and Manmohan Desai have shared common ground. Both have looked to the epics for inspiration. Both have moralized. Both have appreciated and insisted on excellent performances from actors. And both have treated some of the same themes: the cruelty of zamindars, the separation of family members, the evil of drink, the love triangle, illegitimacy, and communal relations. The similarity of themes and the difference in treatment have sometimes made their films like *Alice In Wonderland* looking-glass images of each other. A case in point is to be found in Benegal's *Arohan* (1982) which treats only the 'lost' side of what in a Desai film would be a 'lost-found' story. Hari Mondal's (Om Puri) brother Bolai (Noni Ganguli) is forced off the family plot of land by the local zamindar (Victor Bannerjee). Leaving behind all the members of his family and also his sweetheart (Srila Mazumdar), Bolai goes to Calcutta, resolved to make an honest living in the big city. Faced with harsh realities, he soon joins a gang and spends time in and out of jail. In the meantime, Bolai's former girlfriend also comes to live in Calcutta. One day from a moving bus, she chances to see him walking along the road. She screams desperately from the window but fails to attract his attention. And then it is too late; the bus has rolled on leaving him far behind. Chance never brings them together again. Later, Hari Mondal too comes to Calcutta in what proves to be a fruitless search for his brother. After three weeks he returns to his village in despair, accompanied only by a profound sense of loss.

In a Desai film, villagers who go to the city do well. They maintain their village integrity. The separation of family members is temporary; trials and hardships are passing. In *Sachaa Jhutha* when Belu comes to Bombay looking for her brother (Rajesh Khanna), she is almost raped and barely escapes being run over. Later, she is taken hostage by the calculating criminal who is a perfect likeness of her brother. Yet in the end, the criminal is brought to justice; brother and sister are reunited, and both find love with the promise of a happy-ever-after future.

In *Sachaa Jhutha* and in *Arohan* Desai and Benegal present opposite sides of the same coin, the coin in this case being the disruption of relationships caused by rural exodus. In spite of the fact that *Sachaa Jhutha* and Desai's other lost-found stories are far-fetched, they find favour with audiences, probably in part because real life happy endings do exist. Newspapers and magazines in India have regularly held out the carrot of possible wealth and well-being in articles on inspiring personal success stories and happy reunions that take place against all odds. Desai's happy endings are not entirely false; they are only statistically improbable. *Arohan*'s sad ending probably comes closer to the experience of the majority.

Manmohan Desai regularly criticized art films and their directors; in his films, however, there is no reference to the new cinema phenomenon. The New Wave directors, on the other hand, took their stand against commercial cinema both on screen and off. Films which attempt to reflect reality are naturally forced to show the importance of commercial cinema in people's lives. Rabindra Dharmaraj's *Chakra* (1981), based on the novel by Jaywant Dalvi, is a memorable illustration of the connection between life and cinema. Looka (Naseeruddin Shah) has much in common with the Anthony character in *Amar Akbar Anthony*. Like Anthony, Looka is the *'dada'* (the big man) of his neighbourhood. Like Anthony, too, Looka strikes fear in his less assertive neighbours. Both resort to violence to insure justice. Both have their troubles with the police. Both have a certain charm. Anthony talks Bombay street Hindi. Looka does too, but his Bombaya is heavily influenced by Hindi film diction and dialogue. *'Jo dar gaya, samjho mar gaya,'* (Whoever is afraid will die), he says, quoting Gabbar Singh (Amjad Khan) from *Sholay*. Looka is the product of the cinema fantasy he has absorbed just as Anthony-Amit-Raju are inspired by real Looka types. The distinction between life and fiction is blurred as each feeds off the other. The effect is a mirror image of a mirror image. Finally though, Looka's fate and Anthony's diverge widely. Anthony enjoys precisely the happy ending that Looka fancies for himself. Anthony knows the pleasure of love with a beautiful, rich girl. He makes peace with the police. He is reunited with his long lost, loving family. He beats the true bad guys, proves his valour and gains a fair amount of respectability in the process. Importantly, he never looks the worse for the rough life he has led. He has his cake and eats it too. Looka, on the other hand, pays dearly for his fights, his illicit liquor dealings, and his attraction to women. Not surprisingly, he contracts syphilis and becomes a haggard shell of the man he was. Finally, he carries his violence to its logical conclusion and kills an innocent pharmacist to procure the medicine he needs but cannot afford to buy. The character who loses in *Chakra* is almost sure to lose sooner or later in real life. With this thought in mind, it would be interesting to know the fate of Antav, the bootlegger who once worked out of an alley opposite Manmohan Desai's office and who inspired the Anthony character in *Amar Akbar Anthony*.

Jabbar Patel's *Umbartha*, a Marathi film made in 1982 (entitled *Subah* in its Hindi version), shows women watching an outdoor projection of *Amar Akbar Anthony* during one of the peaceful moments in the centre where they live. With them, we watch a bit of the song 'Humko tumse ho gaya hai pyar'. Like the women she is responsible for, Smita Patil, playing the director, is laughing and enjoying the sight of Amitabh Bachchan and Parveen Babi speeding along in a motorboat off the Bombay coast. Yet the idyllic film scene presents a harsh contrast with the daily sadness and humiliation the women face at the centre. The inclusion of the popular cinema excerpt could be interpreted negatively as a comment on the tremendous (and unwarranted?) gap between real life and films. Or again, it could be seen positively as a moment of pleasure-bringing fantasy that temporarily brightens the lives of those with little real-life enjoyment. Certainly in post-Taliban Afghanistan cinema functions thus. Sanjeev Srivastav reporting from Kabul, on the programme 'World Update' in the BBC World Service radio, said that music and pleasure have returned, particularly in the form of Hindi popular cinema. Interviewees on the street commented, 'I like the songs and dances in Hindi films. Everything is nice. Everybody in Afghanistan loves Hindi films.'[10]

How not to regret the universal need for escape—in every culture and at all times? And how not to be thankful that artists, storytellers and filmmakers have known how to give us that escape? Ambivalence would seem an inevitable response. Maithili Rao's observations are particularly pertinent:

> We bring confused perceptions to our definition of cinema. We seek magic and metaphor in these transient images of our own distorted reflections in the movie mirror.... Distortions often seem more useful to us than drab 'realism' because they both reveal and cloak our cultural schizophrenia. Our films enthrall and exasperate us. The enthrallment comes from the desire to see ourselves as we want to be and the exasperation arises precisely because desire outstrips achievement.[11]

women

Many thought-blurring generalizations have been made concerning the negative effects of popular Hindi cinema on the status of women in India. A closer look may not reveal the negative appraisals to be unfounded but will surely show a more nuanced portrayal of the feminine screen presence than the cliché would lead us to expect. Before turning to Desai's women characters, it might be helpful to consider some of the more pronounced screen images of women in wider Hindi cinema.

Among those filmmakers who have in some way distinguished themselves are those who might be dubbed 'the patriarchs' and who tend to see women either as demure characters with little say over their destinies or as naughty children who need reprimanding. The mother figure may be conveniently absent, or if present, may herself be highly imperfect. In Hrishikesh Mukherjee's *Khubsoorat* (1980) a young woman played by Rekha flirts with rebelliousness and must atone during much of the film. The mother (Dina Pathak) in the film, meanwhile, is a tyrant to whom the entire family pays strict obedience.

A tradition of woman-centered films also exists. V. Shantaram's *Duniya Na Mane* (1937) and Mehboob Khan's

Mother India (1957) focus on the hard lives of women who struggle courageously, never succumbing to hopelessness despite the tribulations life may cast their way. Like Mehboob Khan, Bimal Roy was a filmmaker from the period often referred to as popular cinema's Golden Age. Bimal Roy confounds us, however, with films such as *Sujata* (1959) or *Bandini* (1963) in which Nutan, though front and centre and ever so beautifully lit, nevertheless projects through her dialogues the message of the long-suffering woman who glories in servility. Salim-Javed gave us macho, super-hero scripts at a time when Amitabh Bachchan was at his zenith. The result, inevitably, was less footage for women. In a series of vengeance stories, the male character captures audience attention. Yet, surprisingly, Salim-Javed screenplays—especially those made into films by Yash Chopra and Ramesh Sippy—leave room for strong women who are persons in their own right, who do not need a male for their survival, but who, through their inner force, can often tilt the male character towards a moral stance at a key moment, *e.g.,* in *Trishul* (1978), *Kaala Patthar* (1979), *Shakti* (1982), and even in *Sholay* (1975).

This he-man period also saw a flourishing of women as sexual bait. The vamp flouts the good-girl rules but pays for her lack of conformity, generally by being eliminated, as happens, for instance, to Helen in Chandra Barot's *Don* (1978). The good girl, herself, is sometimes sacrificed to serve as a catalyst to the hero's action, as when the main character's sister is raped and killed in Narendra Bedi's *Adaalat* (1977).

Some New Wave filmmakers ignored the trend of the hero-oriented seventies and eighties and drew portraits of complex heroines against a background of pointed social criticism. For example, in Shyam Benegal's *Ankur* (1974) our concern is poured on Shabana Azmi's character rather than on the cowardly young zamindar played by Anant Nag.

There are those who would add a young woman to a script as one might add a brightly coloured silk scarf to the pocket of a staid business suit, to enliven the visual effect. In T. Rama Rao's *Inquilaab* (1984), to name but one example, Sridevi plays just such a frivolous, one-dimensional character. Mukul Anand's 1991 *Hum* reflected the trend towards increasing violence in Hindi cinema in the eighties and early nineties. The strange result is a female lead who is a vamp, a playful sex object, a rape victim, and a good woman on a moral crusade, all woven into one confused character. Though Jumma (Kimi Katkar) is not physically raped, she is degraded by a virtual rape as she dances alone in male territory (a warehouse), surrounded by dozens of leering men who spray her violently with water during the distressingly memorable song 'Jumma Chumma De De'.

More recently, Sanjay Leela Bhansali's *Devdas* (2002) offers an array of women characters who, even as they remain bound by the strictures of the day, make their immense strength felt both through dialogue and body language. Whether it be Paro's wronged mother (Kiron Kher), who calls down divine retribution on her haughty neighbours, Paro herself (Aishwarya Ray) whose feelings of self-worth are never in doubt, or, above all, Chandramukhi (Madhuri Dixit), *shakti* (feminine force) is present throughout the film. Khalid Mohamed's *Fiza* (2000) offers a modern, urban, educated version of a similarly powerful heroine.

How, one might ask, do Manmohan Desai's screen women fit into this schematic view of women in Hindi cinema?

the mother

If Desai's young heroines present a certain variety, the mother figures offer solid dependability. It is important to remember Shyam Benegal's assessment of Manmohan Desai: 'He takes stereotypes and turns them into archetypes.' Many Hindi films have shown us strong central mother figures. Desai's, however, achieve the status of irreproachable super-women who appear much too good to be true. Interestingly, for Desai it was his mother characters who were drawn from reality; the young women he dismissed as merely fictional. As evidence of the claim, Desai described the women who served as his models. Of his wife Jeevanprabha he said:

> She was very god-fearing, too god-fearing. This woman was in a class all of her own.... My characters of the mother are all like her, good, solid, noble characters, strong women. She fights for her husband. In *Suhaag* she fought for her husband; when Amitabh and Shashi come to rescue her, she said, 'Leave me. Save my husband.'
>
> We may have had our spats, our quarrels, our differences, but if anybody said one word against me, she would tear that person apart. So maybe subconsciously I always brought mothers of that type in my films. I never put a bad mother in my films, or a bad woman.

Actually, this is not quite true. There is a vamp in *Raampur Ka Lakshman*, another in *Chacha Bhatija*, and there are two evil stepmothers, one in *Budtameez* and one in *Sachaa Jhutha*. Desai rightly prided himself, though, on not showing women being raped, and in fact, when the villain of the story does attempt to attack the heroine, *e.g.*, in *Dharam-Veer* or in *Suhaag*, the hero, or, more satisfyingly, the heroine herself, quickly fights the man off.

Desai listed another, unexpected source of inspiration:

> I have seen my wife's mother. Normally, the association of the mother-in-law is not good, but I respect my wife's mother. I think she is one of the greatest women I have ever encountered in my life. How she brought up her seven daughters. Then my own mother...she fought like a tiger after my father died. She never made me feel I had no father, so that's when I started respecting the mother because the mother looks after the home, looks after the kids; she gives her life for the kids. The father may not. The father goes out; he may do anything. The father will womanize, drink, he will do anything, but the mother in our country will rarely do that. That's why the mother figures are

very strong in my films, and I don't have much respect for a father figure, maybe because I have not seen my father; I was only four when he died, so I'm not able to identify much with the image of a father.

Nirupa Roy (d. 2004), who appeared in Desai's *Roti, Amar Akbar Anthony, Mard*, and, above all, *Suhaag*, was Screen Mother *par excellence*. In over 35 years in the cinema industry, Nirupa Roy acted in more than 250 films. Desai felt that her larger-than-life super-mother image came in part from the fact that early in her career she played in many mythologicals. An aura followed her as she moved into other roles:

> I feel she (Nirupa Roy) is one of the finest actresses that we have ever had in this country. Her image is that of a mother.... Believe me, every film where she has played the mother to Amitabh has clicked. There is a good rapport between the two because they are strong actors.

The Nirupa-Roy screen-mother was enriched by the actress' long experience, her professional skill and her capacity in real life to project a warmth equal to that on screen. Being in her presence, one felt blessed by her smile. Durga Khote, Indrani Mukherjee, Sharmila Tagore, Waheeda Rehman, Desai's other screen mothers, also beautifully fleshed out these characters who were models of goodness. As Rosie Thomas explains, the Mother is someone who 'largely defines (and usually concretely embodies) the field of good, that of the villain, the field of bad'.[1]

Sudhir Kakar describes the idealized mother of Hindi cinema as a 'paragon of maternal perfection'.[2] He speaks of the child's perception of, on the one hand, 'an overwhelming and overpowering "too much mother"' of early childhood, who later becomes the 'rejecting and withholding—the "too little"— mother,' and he analyses: 'The content and sequence of both these fantasies parallels the developmental fate of boys in Hindu families—great indulgence of the child in infancy followed by an abrupt separation from the mother in later childhood.'[3]

For Desai, then, the 'paragon' is real; for Kakar she is fantasy. Nirupa Roy came down in the middle, considering the screen mother to be an exaggerated reflection of reality. When a mother is so good, one naturally wants her ever close. Longing, a word for which a large body of vocabulary exists in Hindustani, has been explored and elaborated on by generations of Urdu poets and has, quite naturally been incorporated into Indian cinema-powerfully so in Mani Ratnam's *Dil Se* (1998). It normally finds its source in thwarted love, whether on the physical or the metaphysical plane; the Laila-Majnu story is its most memorable illustration. Longing exists in Desai's films, but it tends to be reserved for a son who feels the pain of separation from his mother (the pain of 'too little mother' that Kakar describes?). That pain can even be a driving force for a Desai hero, (significantly *not* for the heroines). In *Coolie* Iqbal has no more than a picture to remind him of his lost mother Salma (Waheeda Rehman). Like an icon, she watches over him from inside her frame year in, year out. Desai was convinced of the appeal of the missing mother. One cannot but wonder if the filmgoers do (or did?), in fact, respond to this theme as strongly as Desai believed, and if so, whether viewers could be fantasizing the horror of losing their own good mothers or could be identifying with the screen hero, either because their real-life mothers have likewise disappeared or because the women who bore them fall painfully short of the ideal. With this thought in mind, it is interesting to note that wholly fallible—but not wicked—mothers have begun to appear on screen in recent years, particularly in Shyam Benegal's *Zubeida* (2001) and Khalid Mohamed's *Tehzeeb* (2003).

If Desai mothers represent warmth and abundant love, they are also the binding link to morality. In *Suhaag*, little Kishan is forced to drink whiskey. Amit, the street waif, accompanies the boy home. His mother, seeing her son drunk, slaps him—and then gives him a forgiving hug. Later, as an adult, Amit apologizes to this same woman for his own addiction to liquour, 'If only I had had a mother to slap me, I wouldn't have kept drinking till now.' And only a mother will do. In *Desh Premee* the leper woman (Sharmila Tagore) who helps Raju (Amitabh Bachchan) escape from the police is actually his long-lost, but unrecognizable mother. He apologizes to the kind woman, 'If I'd had a mother to watch after me, maybe I wouldn't be in trouble with the law today.'

She replies, 'But you had your father, didn't you?'

'Yes,' he answers, 'but a mother is always a mother, right?' to which she readily agrees.

One wonders about the reactions of women spectators to such mother figures. For those who are mothers, the role model—and adulation that accompanies it—could be attractive. Then again, it could be annoying. In the western world motherhood is a tarnished state. Since the advent of Freudian psychology, the image of the 'mother' has been irretrievably undermined. One psychologist appeased (in a matter of speaking) the readers of a popular U.S. women's magazine by telling them not to worry about their roles as mothers. No matter what they did, they would be wrong, so they might as well relax! Hindi cinema as a general rule, and a Manmohan Desai film in particular, gives quite a different (and comforting?) message: So long as one is a mother—and not a stepmother—one can do no wrong.

If mothers are invariably good, their husbands are often weak, even bad. In *Suhaag* Vikram Singh (Amjad Khan) refuses to acknowledge his family, drives them from his palace, and later becomes a notorious criminal. Kishanlal (Pran) in *Amar Akbar Anthony* does not hesitate to gain wealth through smuggling when destiny offers the opportunity. The men in *Chhalia* (Rehman) and in *Dharam-Veer* (Pran) meanly doubt the fidelity of their wives whose faithfulness is beyond reproach. Desai's preference for the goddesses and his disdain for Rama who sent his good wife Sita into exile, or for the womanizing Krishna, found expression in his regular portrayal of strong, good women on the one hand and far from perfect men on the other. He said:

> ...In my films I always talk about *'Ma, sherovali.'* ...I'm not a devotee in the sense I'm...I'm a sinner, but I'm a great believer in the devi—Durga, Amba, Lakshmi. We have many gods and goddesses in our religion. I'm more for the goddesses than the gods. I feel a woman is a supreme creation. It is she who conceives, she who bears the child after nine months, she who takes care through hardship. She brings into the world a new life. That's why you rarely find a bad woman in my films. I rate them very high. I respect them more than I would a man.

If men can neither be as good as women nor as fundamentally creative, they can participate vicariously in the uplifting state of motherhood. Prem (Shashi Kapoor) in *Aa Gale Lag Jaa* is as self-sacrificing and ever-present in his son's life as any mother. In *Amar Akbar Anthony* the three dispersed children are adopted by men, not by couples. And in *Dharam-Veer* the hunter Joala (Pran) is injured immediately after the consummation of his marriage to the princess (Indrani Mukherjee); he goes into a coma for exactly nine months, waking precisely when his wife gives birth. His magic falcon catches his newborn son in mid-air and delivers it to the kind couple who have been caring for Joala. His 'pregnancy' over, however, Joala goes on his way, leaving the son he does not know is his, in the hands of the generous couple. Women have often conjectured that men envy their power to bear children. Here would seem to be proof of that envy, generously and unselfconsciously expressed.

the wife

Desai's women could well be criticized from a feminist standpoint, at least in their roles as wives. Grammar is used to express submission, *i.e.*, a wife is addressed with the informal *'tum'* while she addresses her husband with the respectful *'aap'* form for 'you.' Some mindful Indian women were enraged at the film *Suhaag*, particularly when Durga (Nirupa Roy) not only accepts her scoundrel husband back after years of absence but even refuses to allow him to apologize to her. Yet Durga is active and maintains her dignity throughout the film. After she is thrown out on the street where she must fend for herself, she is strong and capable of providing for herself and her son. Also, when she is first forced to leave her husband, she does not shrink silently out. She invokes heavenly justice, calling down a curse on him, 'You're sending me and the children out of here today, but one day destiny will be on the side of these children (twin boys), and you will come begging to them,' a prophecy that we see fulfilled.

More offensive than Durga's attitude is the doormat behaviour of the wife (Indrani Mukherjee) in *Bhai Ho To Aisa*. The bad husband in *Suhaag* sends his wife away, but in so doing, leaves her free to live her life in peace. In *Bhai Ho To Aisa* Thakur (Shatrughan Sinha) keeps his wife by his side and causes her daily anguish. He forces her to give him her jewels, even her *mangal sutra* (a necklace, the symbol of marriage), to pay for his dancing girl. When Thakur resorts to physical violence on his wife, his younger brother (Jeetendra) jumps to her defense and strikes Thakur back. Rather than thanking her brother-in-law, however, she slaps him for raising a hand against her husband, a singular response that is, fortunately, not repeated in another Desai film. If the audience is made to understand what a bad example Thakur is setting, they are not led to believe that the wife's response is less than ideal. Roopa (Hema Malini), the younger brother's spunky girlfriend, serves to offset this image of total self-effacement a bit, but her gumption is not sufficient to subvert the message given by the wife who, despite the ill-treatment she has suffered, nevertheless, prays, Savitri-like, that a poisonous snake might kill her and spare her husband. Concerning Savitri, Desai said:

> She was very good; I like her. My characters of the mother are based on her—pure, good, would fight for her husband. Savitri is the embodiment of the good woman who, they say, pleaded even with the God of Death to spare her husband's life.

Such a vision of womanhood is probably partially a reflection of a present reality and a persistent myth, partially unconscious propaganda to female viewers, and partially plain and simple wishful thinking. It is this last motivating factor that would seem to unite the majority of male filmmakers worldwide and that is the only plausible explanation for their tendency to show aging men playing love interests to women 20 to 40 years their juniors, unaware of, or unconcerned by the reactions of many women spectators.

screen time

Generally, woman viewers feel as offended by the absence of women on screen as by their ill treatment there. Women rarely frequent pornographic films, nor do they tend to patronize womanless fight films. Being made to feel non-existent is demoralizing. Screen time counts. Hindi cinema is typical of a trend around the world to give men more visibility than woman. On American television, for which 1980s figures exist, men occupied, on average, three times as much air space as women. The 21st century has not improved matters; in Rosanna Arquette's 2002 documentary *Searching for Debra Winger*, no-longer-young American actresses bemoan a lack of good scripts and long for 1930s and 40s when actresses like Barbara Stanwyck wielded real power in the industry.

Within Desai's work the amount of footage for women varies. In the early films like *Chhalia* and *Budtameez*, both essentially love stories, Nutan and Sadhana share a reasonable portion of the limelight with Raj Kapoor and Shammi Kapoor respectively. In keeping with trends, later films saw reduced space for women. One gauge of the degree of woman orientation in any film could be the extent to which women characters are developed outside a romantic angle. Among Desai's Amitabh starrers, *Parvarish* and *Suhaag* merit consideration in this respect. In *Parvarish* Shabana Azmi and Neetu Singh have several excellent scenes all to themselves. They are introduced to the audience not as objects of male desire, or even interest, but rather as professionals, as financially independent and highly competent pickpockets. And they interact not only with the heroes but also, on their own terms, with many other characters. In contrast, Rati Agnihotri in *Coolie* has very few scenes in which she is not in playing opposite Amitabh Bachchan; this female dependence on the male lead is but one negative result of the increasing reliance on Bachchan in the later years of Desai's career.

In *Suhaag* Anu (Parveen Babi), a medical student—who apparently spends little time actually studying—arrives at Kishan's (Shashi Kapoor) mother's house, offering to do some small jobs in exchange for money to donate to a worthy cause. Ma (Nirupa Roy) at first says she has no work to be done. When Anu spots Kishan's photo inside the house, however, and lets out an exclamation of recognition, the mother cleverly surmises that this must be the '*sandalwali*,' the girl whose sandal Ma found in Kishan's pocket the night before. In mock severity, to the sound track of light and teasing music, the mother grabs the now-reluctant girl, pulls her in, and brings out the 'incriminating' sandal. Anu tries to deny it is hers, but it is impossible to lie to Ma. Still harsh, Ma, moving into the traditional mother-in-law role, gives Anu housework to do. Kishan discovers Anu's presence when she serves him his breakfast. His only thought is to have her disappear quickly from his life. But Ma sternly insists that he pay the girl while Ma gives her a coconut as a good omen and a sign of welcome. Suddenly assured that Ma is now on her side, that Kishan will soon be her husband, Anu lowers her eyes demurely as any good daughter-in-law should and, being unable to cover up with a sari—she is in a sun dress—she uses her hair to hide part of her face. In the outside world Kishan is strong; he is a policeman whose valour is beyond reproach. Inside the house, once his mother has given her blessing and has joined forces with this pretty, but independence-threatening young woman, he is utterly defenseless. These scenes are interesting for several reasons. The young woman is and is not in her traditional soon-to-be-wedded role. She and the future mother-in-law are assumed to be responsible for all cooking and cleaning. The mother-in-law's authority remains unchallenged as she orders the daughter-in-law about. Yet the complicity that develops between them as they use their combined, if different, wiles to override Kishan's wishes is a delightful subversion of male power. A top actress is rarely, if ever, paid as much as a correspondingly high-ranking actor. (Aishwarya Rai or Julia Roberts might be exceptions to the rule.) In this well-written sequence in *Suhaag*, though, we witness two actresses so in command and so perfectly attuned to each other that a highly paid male star, when he enters the scene, momentarily becomes the accessory.

Shashi Kapoor, however, was categorical, 'The female is exploited in his (Desai's) films. Like in *Suhaag* she is a silent sufferer. His films are hero-oriented. I think that is also one of his hidden fantasies, from childhood maybe, the man who can win!'

Or at least he can win in the outside world. In Satyajit Ray's 1984 *Ghaire Baire* (*The Home and the World*), based on Tagore's 1916 novel, we observe the contrasting female and male use of space. Though subtle, a similar spatial differentiation applies in Desai's films. Desai's magic—perhaps macho—time is occasionally suspended, particularly in interior scenes, for example in *Chhalia* when Shaanti (Nutan) sits in Chhalia's hut mending clothes. In the romantic *Aa Gale Lag Jaa* Prem (Shashi Kapoor) is the care-giver who raises his child and thus, to some extent, moves into 'woman time.' Nurturing and domesticity involve a slowing of time. Setting the table or washing dishes become meaningful acts, during which emotions can be explored.

active heroines

Desai also shows women who win. An array of spunky heroines push men around, fight with them, make fools of them, combat alongside them, and defend themselves against them. Neetu Singh in *Dharam-Veer* has the perfect physique for her role as the gypsy girl. She is tough, and she knows how to look after her own interests. At the palace door she bluffs, exuding an air of confidence while demanding that the guard announce her presence to the prince inside. The guard, unconvinced, bars her passage. When the prince's cousin (Ranjeet) arrives and insists that she be let in, she struts flauntingly past the guard, expressing with her whole body the attitude that Parveen Babi, as Anu, conveys by thumbing her nose at Kishan during the song '*Kahin Bhi Le Chalo*' in *Suhaag*.

In a country in which feminists regularly rail against the status of women, one might wonder about these active heroines. The women who cannot be kept down are, after all, not uncommon in Hindi cinema. A recent example is the striking seeker of justice played by Raveena Tandon in Madhur Bhandarkar's *Satta* (2002). Manmohan Desai gave us especially active heroines. He was not a passive person, and he was not interested in passivity in the characters he brought to screen or even, for that matter, in characters from the epics. Sita, the one to whom things happen, held little attraction for Desai. Likewise, Draupadi had no special merit. 'She's no heroine!" he said. 'She did nothing. She was stripped by the Kauravas and, Lord Krishna, who supports her, gave her a sari from the air.' Savitri, he appreciated not only for her fidelity to her husband and her penchant for placing her husband's needs before her own but also for her fighting spirit. Other precedents for these active women role models exist in Indian history, myth, legend, and literature. As Desai said:

> Good and courageous mother figures are ever present; yes, we respect women in our country. Our ex-prime minister has been a woman, and a great prime minister, Mrs. Indira Gandhi. And you see from our scriptures, the great Shivaji warrior, he had a mother Jigabai; she encouraged him, taught him to become a warrior. The same thing: we have Rani Padmini of Chittore. She, along with other Rajput women, they committed sati rather than fall in the hands of the invaders, the Mughal invaders.

To Desai's list might be added the fighting queens, Razia Sultana, Rani Durgavati, Rani of Jhansi, Noor Jahan, and Chand Bibi, who courageously protected their subjects and territories. The limelight in which Phoolan Devi, the late notorious/famous woman dacoit-cum-politician, found herself can perhaps be attributed to the resonance she gave to the battling heroines of the past. Cinema history gives us another model. The Greco-Welsh, Australian-born Fearless Nadia, was greatly appreciated for her physical daring in her stunt films at Wadia Movietone (*e.g. Hunterwali* in 1935, *Diamond Queen* in 1940). It is possible that courage in any form exercises a consistently strong appeal and that it is gender blind. At the end of Mahesh Bhatt's *Arth* (1983), Pooja (Shabana Azmi), earlier the victim of her husband's philandering, takes a bold stand by refusing to accept him back when he returns, humbled and repentant. 'If I had done the same thing,' she asks him, 'would you have taken me back?' Her words hit him like a sword fighter's *'Touché!'* and the audience in Bombay, particularly the male members, responded with wild applause. The line works again in a more recent film *Kuch Naa Kaho* (by Rohan Sippy, 2003) in which Namrata (Aishwarya Rai) finally stands up to her bullying husband.

Manmohan Desai's young women are not only courageous. They are also feisty, often showing the sort of anarchic spirit that is the essence of Desai's comedy. A nice heroine would not trap a man into marrying her, but Anu (Parveen Babi) in *Suhaag* and the gypsy girl (Neetu Singh) in *Dharam-Veer* do precisely that. And in *Parvarish* the heroines flout society's rules by going brazenly to the hero's parents to ask for their sons' hands in marriage. 'That's just a spoof,' Desai said. 'Normally, it's the boys who are supposed to go to the girls' parents and ask the parents. I just had a little change, just a little bit of variation, so that I don't get bogged down with the same angle in every film.' A surprising source of inspiration for his tomboy heroines was a comic strip character:

> The heroine, I'd rather fashion on this one: Modesty Blaise. I'm very fascinated by Modesty Blaise and Willy Garvin. Every day you get their comic strip in the paper. She's a terrific character. I'm dying to make a film. It's action based. She and Willy Garvin are partners, but the best thing is they are so much together, but they don't sleep with each other. He has a lot of affairs with other women. She sleeps with other men. But they are like a team. They work together to solve all the cases. They fight all the bad men. She's a great fighter, a great expert in karate, in everything. So is Willy Garvin, and they're always together, but they never make love together. They're friends. A fabulous character. I believe, I'm not sure, in the West somebody did make a film on Modesty Blaise and Willy Garvin.[4] But I would like to make it in India, if I could just find a good angle, an emotional angle to that character. But the only thing is that in our films we can't have a hero and heroine not in love with each other and sleeping around with others. That's where the image of Savitri comes in. She's not supposed to touch any other man.

Interestingly, just as women can act tough like men and men can 'mother' like women, so the Savitri model can be espoused by a male character. In *Aa Gale Lag Jaa* Prem (Shashi Kapoor), ever faithful to Preeti (Sharmila Tagore), says to the young woman with a crush on him, 'Don't you know that once an

Indian man has loved one woman, he cannot even think of another?' Desai's subconscious would seem to have been in command, expressing the wish that he, the notorious womanizer, could be so faithful.

physical desire

Femininity also encompasses another quite different dimension in Desai's films. Women may be respected for being Savitri-like, but they are desired for other reasons. From the outset, a certain sexual undercurrent—rarely lewd or overplayed—is present in Desai's work. In *Chhalia,* the hero (Raj Kapoor) invites the homeless Shaanti (Nutan) to stay in his humble dwelling. Before he can actually allow her in, however, he must scurry about, to jazzy background music, taking down the girlie pictures that decorate his walls. In *Budtameez* the undercurrent is strengthened by crosscurrents. The animated cartoon of the lady chaser during the titles sets the pace of this film made at the height of Shammi Kapoor's reign. Titillation is the rule. Shots from behind feature Sadhana in a bathing suit and clinging pants. When Shyam (Shammi Kapoor) and Shanta (Sadhana) are caught in the forest in the rain, their only shelter is the still-standing doorway of an ancient ruin. If they remain face-to-face below this arch, and *if* he does not breathe, the two will not touch. The sudden appearance of a cobra, poised to strike, adds an unmistakable phallic image to the already charged scene. In *Coolie* Rati Agnihotri's hips have replaced Sadhana's. The song *'Jawani Ki Railway'* is introduced with Iqbal (Amitabh) fingering the railway crossing barrier racily as he says, 'Shaadi ke liye uparvaale ne javaani ke sirf chaar din rakhe. Yeh char din men nikal gae na, to samajh lo ki signal down aur apni gaari gai.' (Youth lasts only a fleeting moment, and it was given by the One Above for the sake of marriage. When that moment is over, you understand, the signal goes down, and my train is gone.)

The barrier then lowers in time with his falling intonation. The syncopated, hip-swaying music that follows is picturized with an easily read symbol, a broken water jug.

Yet the atmosphere is light, not lurid. Desai's films do not centre on passion or stunted desire. It is significant that in both *Budtameez* and *Aa Gale Lag Jaa* jokes are made about Majnu, the legendary, forlorn lover driven mad by his passion for Laila. Male-female relationships in Desai's films regularly exude not passion—a heavy, generally thwarted, and often violent desire—but rather, either a soft and sentimental feeling of romance or a lighthearted sense of fun, neither of which conveys the sense of tragedy that accompanies most of the world's great tales of love. In *Amar Akbar Anthony* three beautiful shapely girls are central in the heroes' motivations. Yet we have our laughs even during a declaration of love. Jenny (Parveen Babi) is confessing in church and mentions Anthony's (Amitabh Bachchan) name, 'I think I, I...' And out pops Anthony's head from the booth where we supposed the priest to be, 'Do you love me?' The humour of the situation is compounded by his unlikely explanation for his presence in the box: he was cleaning!

The undercurrent that was always present in Desai's films, in *Mard* turned into a small tidal wave, perhaps in translation of Desai's own moods or interests, but more likely simply in keeping with the times. The sex angle in *Mard* was not unique or isolated. Films made as the eighties progressed, generally, gave clear proof that the Indian film industry had become convinced of the selling power of sex. In Rahul Rawail's *Betaab* (1983), for instance, when heroine (Amrita Singh) is bitten by a snake, the hero (Sunny Deol) sucks venom from her leg while she writhes and moans suggestively on the ground to affect a lightly disguised bedroom scene. The same sort of allusions to sexual relations are found even in the serious world of art cinema. At the end of Gautum Ghose's *Paar* (1984), Naseeruddin Shah, playing a poor harijan, listens anxiously, with his ear against Shabana Azmi's abdomen, for the faint heartbeat of the baby in his wife's womb. An apparently deliberate confusion is created in the scene between a deep concern for the living fruit of a couple's union and the thrill of the union itself. Some films from South India, made with no artistic or intellectual pretensions, regularly offered more blatant sexuality, much to the chagrin of many writers of letters to editors of film magazines. At one time only the vamp could bare and seduce on the Hindi film screen. In the eighties, the major stars did the same. Mores were changing. At least in urban India, the country was undergoing something of a sexual revolution. Aparna Sen's *Paroma* (1985), with its story of a middle class housewife guiltlessly involved in an extramarital affair, may have been a cinematic hint of a wider social phenomenon that continued to grow, perhaps reaching something of an apex with Deepa Mehta's *Fire* (1996) in which two frustrated middle class sisters-in-law turn to each other for sexual satisfaction; the taboo of homosexuality was lifted.

Mard, then, with its couple who set a haystack in motion with their pulsations, was a departure from Manmohan Desai's earlier relative reserve, but it was not unlike other films of the eighties. Likewise, the racy song *'Hum to tambu men bambu lagaaye baithe'* (I put my bamboo in the tent) exhibits an open lustiness that carries Desai's imprint, neither passionate nor lascivious, but rather, fast, lively, and witty.

Subhash K. Jha's analysis of the Freudian implications in *Mard* is worth noting, especially for his perception that the sexuality in *Mard* is not limited to the dialogues or to the girl-boy relationship.

> A strong current of sexuality runs through the very structure and style of this tale of masculinity. Each of the 'action' sequences (which are the highlights of Desai's films) builds the sense of injustice within the situation to a climactic peak, with almost sexual frenzy. The release comes in an orgasmic explosion when the tangewallah rides into the scene. The 'coming' is captured in long shots in which Raju 'comes'

hurling, shattering mirrored partitions and the likes, with a passionate urgency.⁵

If Savitri represents traditional modesty and fidelity, Radha, another mythic figure, represents desirability. Radha and Krishna's love has been elevated to spiritual heights. It is the very physical nature of their relationship, however, that has largely set the norms for the behaviour of screen couples. To varying degrees, the majority of unmarried heroines exemplify Radha, and most screen couples play out their romance in the Radha-Krishna fashion. (A recent, unmistakable example of this lineage is the splendid song sequence of *'Morey Piya'* in Sanjay Leela Bhansali's *Devdas*.) The *Gita Govinda* describes the couple's relationship as one of agony alternating with bliss. They first suffer each other's absence, then take joy in each other's presence. But union and harmony are fleeting, soon followed by jealousy and anger. Many romantic song picturizations have maintained this condensation and stylisation, so common in traditional dance. Often, though, the entire development of hero-heroine relations, though less emphatic, adheres to this pattern of vacillation between who needs and who is needed, who cares and who is indifferent, who searches for and who is sought after, who provokes and who is provoked.

Judging the distribution of power between the sexes in this context becomes extremely complex. If power could be made visible, it might resemble a ball, first captured forcibly by one, then thrown willingly to the other, back and forth, back and forth. Part of *Desh Premee* exemplifies this shifting power. Dancing in a gambling casino, Asha (Hema Malini) appears free and spirited until we see two strong men who would bar her escape. She seems twice a victim, then, when Raju (Amitabh Bachchan), to protect his flight from the police, takes her hostage. 'Coward!' the inspector yells, 'Hiding behind a woman!' In the ensuing fight, Asha appears no more than a pawn. Raju's control is broken, though, when, after they flee, Asha inexplicably thanks him.

'For what?' he asks perplexed.

'You saved me,' she answers, 'from my step brothers who forced me dance at the club.' He is nonplussed. On the run, the two become part of a group wedding. The ceremony ended and the danger seemingly passed, Raju throws off his wedding turban and starts to walk away. Noticing his former hostage following him, he asks what she is doing. Casting her eyes down, she answers, 'In India wives walk behind their husbands, not in front.' Certain of her morally indisputable case, she counters his every argument. Yet when he defiantly walks away, she again heaves the victim's sigh...until the sight of patrolling policemen sends Raju scurrying back to her protection. Asha mockingly sings and dances around him and claps her hands tauntingly in his face, *'Jaao, ji jaao, par itna sunlo, tori churiyon pehen lo, ek gajra silvaalo.'* (Go on, dear, go away, but listen to this: if you want to be a woman, then put on a bracelet.)[6] Her song barely ended, her stepbrothers arrive, apparently to Raju's relief. Yet when they attempt to carry her off, he valiantly fights to free her. Once again she tries to follow him; once again he protests, and once again she begins her song. He surrenders, and they enter a nearby hotel. The next morning her 'husband' has gone, leaving no name or address. Violins underscore her pitiful state. Raju disappears from Asha's life, but the final word is hers. Much later, he chances to see her being harassed, comes to her defense, and at last publicly recognizes her as his wife. Such power fluctuation, common throughout Desai's cinema, is not only an unending re-enactment of the pain and frivolity of youthful love; it is also a comment on the nature of power within a couple and perhaps on the transitory nature of power itself.

the manmohan desai legacy

'The only thing worse than not being taken seriously enough is being taken too seriously.' Manmohan Desai did not say this. Billy Wilder did. Yet one could easily imagine Desai echoing Wilder's words. Having a book written about his work seemed to leave Manmohan Desai with mixed feelings. Pride was quickly tempered with caution and accompanied by a reaffirmation of his central and unchanging priorities:

> In the West people may read meanings into my films which I hadn't consciously intended. But they may be right. At least they're taking an academic interest in me while I'm still alive. What matters, above all, is that my audiences have never let me down. They've always given me a hero's welcome. Finally what counts is pleasing not the critics, but the public.[1]

In recent years the Bombay film world, or 'Bollywood,' as it has come to be known, has been forced to evolve. For a period of time, television, video and satellite TV offered ever greater choices in entertainment to Indian spectators, draining many theatres in the process. Hindi cinema then began to revive by the mid-nineties, as it has at various times in the past. Mani Ratnam's films from the South brought a breath of fresh air, and 'family cinema' made a popular comeback. Bombay 'yuppie' films like Farhaan Akhtar's *Dil Chahta Hai* (2001) and the 'desi' films made by ethnic Indians in the U.S., *e.g., American Chai* (by Anurag Mehta, 2002), are changing the configuration of Hindi popular cinema and its extensions abroad. At present, in spite of the fact that box office figures show the majority of films to be failures, the industry has never had a greater following. Thanks to the video revolution, Hindi cinema has been able to maintain the allegiance of generations of ethnic Indians residing abroad. DVD technology has overcome the problems of poor quality in videos, and has, in addition, facilitated subtitling and permitted non-Hindi speakers—whether non-Indian or ethnic Indian who have lost the language but not the inclination to see Indian films—to keep abreast of a world that was once largely closed because of language barriers. Middle class disdain has generally given way to acceptance inside India and outside; Hindi cinema has even become a major welding force and source of identity for the Indian disaspora. Ph.D. students of physics and mathematics chat online across the U.S. or around the world about arcane minutia gleaned from decades of Hindi film productions. Mira Nair's *Monsoon Wedding* and Gurinder Chadha's *Bend It Like Beckham*, though arguably not Hindi films as such, have nevertheless given a broad spectrum of spectators in the West a taste of India on screen along with a desire to see more. Some spectacular productions such as *Lagaan, Kabhie Khushi Kabhie Gham, Hum Dil De Chuke Sanam, Dil Se*, and, particularly, *Devdas*, which was shown in Cannes in 2002 and then released in France by the largest of French distributors, have attracted wide audiences. Nasreen Munni Kabir's series of documentaries and well-chosen Indian films shown on Channel 4 and BBC television in Britain and on the Turner Movie Channel in the U.S. have made Hindi cinema available to viewers living outside the areas of traditional distribution for Indian films abroad. Aishwarya Rai was among *Time* magazine's top 100, 'The A-list of the world's most influential people.'[2] Globalization has become a fact of life. People, ideas, information and films move across the planet with ever increasing speed and in multiple directions. Bolivian television has shown Hindi films, and Spanish cinema websites list Indian films matter-of-factly along with films from across the world. Reflection on Indian cinema, too, has increased. Books are being published, and papers on various aspects of Indian popular cinema are being presented at university conferences.

And where, one might ask, do Manmohan Desai's films fit in this newly emerging picture of Indian cinema? The answers are complex. His cinema has not been forgotten. A google search of his name reveals page upon page devoted to his work: reviews of his films, his filmography, lines of dialogue from *Amar Akbar Anthony*, DVDs for sale, transcribed or Devanagari versions of his film songs, and downloadable songs that can be listened to by computer. At the British Film Institute's website devoted to South Asian cinema[3], *Amar Akbar Anthony* is listed in the nineteenth position among the all-time favourite Hindi films, *Sholay* being number one. Yet when the Pompidou Center in Paris had an Indian film retrospective from February to April 2004, no Manmohan Desai film was selected for showing. And many young second generation Asians living abroad speak of his cinema as dated, something they vaguely remember having seen on video as children. A wider American public has an appreciation for his style of cinema but finds the length of the films an insurmountable barrier. Nevertheless, Desai has gone from being often maligned to something of an icon. In its opening shots, Mukul Anand's *Khuda Gawah* shows a tribute to Manmohan Desai. Though his paternity is not regularly acknowledged, one can assume Desai's influence in the way younger directors bring the city of Bombay/Mumbai lovingly to the screen. Critic, screenwriter and director Khalid Mohamed, for example, in his *Fiza* (2000) shows simple residential Bombay streets, crowded thoroughfares, parks, the coastline, or landmarks like the Haji Ali Shrine. Asked about Desai, Khalid Mohamed replied, 'I personally cherish his generosity as a person to me and love some of his films with undiminished zeal.'[4]

A much more troubling reference to Manmohan Desai comes during the opening credits of *Yeh Hai Jalwa* (2002), directed by David Dhawan and produced by Ketan Desai. Manmohan Desai himself regularly introduced his own productions with dedications. In the case of *Mard* the Censor Board Certificate is followed by a single shot in simple yellow lettering against a red background: 'Dedicated to the loving memory of.' There is no background sound for the successive shots of four individual, framed and garlanded photos, each with a name below: Late Shri Kikubhai C. Desai, Late Smt. Jeevanprabha M. Desai, Late Shri Subhash Desai, Late Shri Mohammed Rafi. These are respectively: 1. Manmohan Desai's father 2. his wife 3. his brother 4. the famous singer. These dedication shots are followed by more acknowledgments to several people who facilitated the making of the film. The case of *Yeh Hai Jalwa* is markedly different in that even though Manmohan Desai died in 1994, the film is introduced as 'Manmohan Desai Productions: *Yeh Hai Jalwa*.' The next shot shows the titles of Desai's big hits in the background while in the foreground we read: 'This film is a live dedication to Shri Manmohan Desai.' Manmohan Desai himself is next shown in a back shot in his director's chair; he stands, turns, and, framed by the neon-lit names of his top films, he points to the right, gives a big smile and says, 'Action!' In the following shot we see the beginning of the pre-film credits, which again underscore his name: 'Manmohan Desai presents.' Unfortunately, despite the fact that David Dhawan is considered a money-spinning director, the film that follows has none of the verve, none of the wit, none of the spirit of invention that characterized Desai's films. The question will not go away: What would Manmohan Desai think if he could see his image and his name used thus? While he was alive, many accused Manmohan Desai's cinema of being formulaic. The 'formula,' however, apparently carried the director's own trademark because no one has been able to replace him.

Quite by chance on a spring day in 2002, one small piece of evidence of Manmohan Desai's enduring appeal popped up unexpectedly as I walked along rue Faubourg St. Denis in Paris. At one end of this street is a massive, late seventeenth- century classic arch, adorned with Latin inscriptions. The monument is a reminder that here once stood one of the medieval gateways into the old heart of the city. Today Faubourg St. Denis is a thriving, cosmopolitan neighbourhood, attracting people from every continent. It is an active, even vibrant, area where people scurry to make a living, meet compatriots, shop for traditional French pastries or finely ground fresh coffee, eat Turkish kebabs or Pakistani sweets, buy phone cards to connect to the world at a reasonable price...and buy or rent Indian videos and DVDs. The smells of Indian spices from one shop combine with Gitane cigarette smoke wafting from a proletarian Parisian café across the street. Here it was, then, that one afternoon a drunken man, wine bottle in hand, was weaving down the sidewalk, singing a song from *Dharam Veer*: 'Main galiyon kaa raajaa, tum mahalon ki raani' (I'm the king of the streets; you're the queen of the palaces). Now Paris is rich in charm and overflowing with culture, but its inhabitants rarely sing. When they do, passers-by take note. One could suppose, because the man was drunk, that he was sad, and yet he was singing a happy song and spreading cheer. It seemed appropriate. Years later and far from his Bombay home, Manmohan Desai, who had also known both sadness and joy, was still pleasing a member of his public.

endnotes

1 the filmmaker: the man

1. The majority of the quotes from the director were gathered in a series of interviews I had with Manmohan Desai in January 1984. Other unaccredited quotes date either from an April 1987 audio interview Manmohan Desai did for me or from a filmed interview conducted by Khalid Mohamed the same month, the edited version of which became Nasreen Munni Kabir's 'The Miracle Man: Manmohan Desai,' a programme in Channel 4's *Movie Mahal* series. In order to maintain the flavour and flow of Manmohan Desai's speaking style, I have made only minor cuts in his speech. For the sake of clarity, there has been occasional rewording.
2. Kikubhai Desai was then a film producer and the owner of Paramount Studios in Bombay, later known as Filmalaya. His productions included *Circus Queen, Golden Gang, Amazon, Akela, Bansari Bala, Thief Of Baghdad, Sheikh Chilli* and *Sneh Bandhan*.
3. After those words were spoken in January, 1984, Desai played a larger role in the leadership of the industry. In 1986 he headed the United Group which won the elections for the control of the IMPPA (Indian Motion Picture Producers' Association).
4. *India Today*, 31 May 1984.

5. *India Today*, 31 May 1984.
6. *Filmfare*, 1-15 May 1984.
7. *The Illustrated Weekly Of India*, 24 November 1985.
8. *Filmfare*, February 1-15 1986.

2 amar akbar anthony

1. *Filmfare*, 1-15 July 1984.

3 coolie

1. http://www.indiaemb.org.eg/section%203/sec%203%20eng/MUSLIM%20ETHOS%20IN%20INDIAN%20CINEMA.html (retrieved 15 March 2004)

4 kaleidoscope

1. *Chhalia*, like *Aa Gale Lag Jaa*, is full of close and medium shots that make it work particularly well on a television screen, in contrast to Desai's later big budget spectacles.

5 kinetics

1. http://www.artsandopinion.com/2003_v2_n2/kingwell.htm (retrieved 12 May 2004)

6 technical choices

1. Jacobs, Lewis (1970).
2. *Bobby* by Raj Kapoor, 1973.
3. Interviewed by Ram Mohan for *Cinema Vision India*, vol 1. No. 4, p. 33.
4. Mohammed Rafi, b. 1924, d. 1980.
5. From Feroz Khan's *Qurbani*, 1980.
6. One wonders to what extent Kadar Khan learned the colloquial idiom from the 'roadside' and to what extent those along the roadside have learned from his dialogues. The attempt to

disentangle the loop between the language of the media and the language popularly spoken has so far left linguists perplexed.
7. For a description and photos of Mistry's 1965 *Mahabharat*, visit: http://www.uiowa.edu/~incinema/Mahabharat.html

7 the players

1. http://www.bfi.org.uk/showing/nft/interviews/azmi/paycheque.html (retrieved March 7, 2004).

8 the child

1. Kakar (1983), p. 97.

9 comedy

1. Mast, Gerald (1973), p. 270.
2. Translation by Connie Haham.

10 serious undertones

1. *Filmfare*, 1-15 April 1983
2. http://www.bitscape.info/research/screen_3p.htm (retrieved 23 February 2004).
3. http://news.bbc.co.uk/2/hi/south_asia/2770437.stm (20 June 2003).
4. Rangacharya, Adya (1980), p. 102.
5. For an interesting discussion on the negative role of the mother's brother in the family, see Kakar (1983).

11 reality

1. http://www.brainyquote.com/quotes/a/alfredhite142022.html
2. From an interview with Sumit Mitra for *India Today*, 31 May 1984.
3. Thomas, Rosie (1985), p. 124.
4. *Filmfare*, 16-31 December 1985.
5. http://www.uiowa.edu/~incinema/Mard. (retrieved 29 April 2004).

6. Salinger, J.D. (1951), p. 33.
7. Simpson, John (2002) p. 125.
8. From *Amar Chitra Katha*, 'Tales of the *Mahabharata*'.
9. From an interview with Iqbal Masud, *Indian Cinema* 1980-1985, p. 40.
10. BBC World Service, 2 September 2003.
11. *Film Comment*, May 2002, p. 37.

12 women

1. Thomas, Rosie (1995) p. 160.
2. Kakir, Sudhir (1983) p. 92.
3. *ibid.* p. 94-95.
4. Joseph Losey made *Modesty Blaise* in 1969 with Monica Vitti and Terence Stamp.
5. *Filmfare*, 1-15 February 1986.
6. Interestingly, this music was chosen to introduce a Scandinavian-based radio production devoted to a discussion on feminism.

13 the manmohan desai legacy

1. In an interview with Lens Eye of *The Times Of India*, 20 October 1985.
2. *Time*, 26 April 2004.
3. http://imagineasia.bfi.org.uk/poll/index.html

Filmography

chhalia

Year:	1960 (Black and white)
Producer:	Subhash Desai
Story and Dialogue:	Inder Raj Anand
Lyrics:	Qamar Jalalabadi
Music:	Kalyanji Anandji
Camera:	N. Satyan
Cast:	Raj Kapoor, Nutan, Pran, Rehman, Shobhana Samarth, Ramlal, Master Mopet, Gul, Shyamlal, Jagdish Kamal

Shaanti (Nutan) marries a man of a good family (Rehman); Partition separates them. When Shaanti returns from Pakistan with her six-year-old son, her family disown her, and her husband refuses to accept that the child Anwar is his. Shaanti is ready to throw herself from a tower when Chhalia (Raj Kapoor), a local pickpocket, saves her. She moves into his modest home. He soon falls in love with her though he is too timid to admit it. Shaanti, her son and husband must be reunited, and Chhalia must bow out.

bluff master

Year:	1963 (Black and white)

Producer:	Subhash Desai
Story:	Madhusudan Kalelkar
Lyrics and dialogue:	Rajinder Krishen
Music:	Kalyanji Anandji
Camera:	N. Satyan
Cast:	Shammi Kapoor, Saira Banu, Pran, Lalita Pawar, Mohan Choti, Tun Tun, Rashid Khan, Niranjan Sharma

Ashok (Shammi Kapoor), an educated but unemployed young man, bluffs his way through life, selling fake lottery tickets, fake muscle cream, etc. The rich Seema (Saira Banu) has a conniving guardian who, in order to maintain control of her money, would like to marry her off to Ram Kumar (Pran), a humourless, constantly sniffing, import-export dealer. Ashok becomes an honest man and overcomes multiple obstacles before he and Seema can be united.

budtameez

Year:	1966 (Black and white)
Producer:	Jagdish Varma
Story:	Jwala Mukhi
Screenplay:	Jagdish Kanwal, Jwala Mukhi
Dialogue:	Jagdish Kanwal
Lyrics:	Hasrat Jaipuri, Shailendra
Music:	Shankar-Jaikishan
Dances:	P.L. Raj
Camera:	Mohan Keswani
Cast:	Shammi Kapoor, Sadhana, Laxmi Chhaya, Kamal Mehra, Purnima, Brahm Bharadwaj, Manorma, Jagdish Raj, Dilip Dutt, Poonam, Anil Nagrath

Shyam's (Shammi Kapoor) half-sister is very fond of him, but his stepmother wants him out of their house. He goes to Bombay to make his fortune and meets Shanta (Sadhana), a spoilt rich girl. Her grandfather gives him a job as manager of their home. He manages to drive away Devdas, her clownish suitor (Kamal Mehra), and melts the heart of the man-hating Shanta.

kismat

Year:	1968 (Colour)
Producer:	Kamal Mehra
Story:	Manmohan Desai
Dialogue:	Brij Katyal
Lyrics:	S.H. Bihari, Noor Devasi
Music:	O.P. Nayyar
Camera:	Keki Mistry
Cast:	Biswajeet, Babita, Helen, Shetty, Kamal Mehra, Jagdish Raj

Vicki (Biswajeet), a singer, buys a guitar in which microfilmed government secrets has been placed by Scorpio, mastermind enemy agent. Pursued by the villains, he escapes onto a freight train, where he meets Roma (Babita) who is running away from home. Johnny (Kamal Mehra), a mad scientist and crazy detective, tries to help the couple, but they are taken to Scorpio's island den. Scorpio proves to be Roma's father in disguise. He repents and saves the couple before a battle to the finish with his gang.

sachaa jhutha

Year:	1970 (Colour)
Producer:	Vinod Doshi, Rajni Desai
Story & screenplay:	J.M. Desai
Dialogue:	Prayag Raj
Lyrics:	Indivar, Gulshan Bawra, Qamar Jalalabadi
Music:	Kalyanji Anandji
Camera:	Peter Pereira
Cast:	Rajesh Khanna (double role), Mumtaz, Vinod Khanna, Faryal, Prayag Raj, Kamal Kapoor, Jagdish Raj, Ratanmala, Pravin Paul, Viju Khote, Santosh, Jullian Billa, Dog Rexy, Naaz

Bhola (Rajesh Khanna) migrates to the city to make money for his crippled sister Belu's (Faryal) dowry. There he is mistaken for Ranjeet (Rajesh Khanna), a notorious jewel thief, who decides to groom his look-alike to be able to take his place, thus giving himself a perfect alibi during his burglaries. Policewoman Rita (Mumtaz) is assigned to gather proof of Ranjeet's guilt; she unwittingly falls in love with the innocent Bhola.

shararat

Year:	1971 (Colour)
Producer:	Ratan Mohan
Story & screenplay:	K.B. Pathak
Dialogue:	Prayag Raj
Lyrics:	Hasrat Jaipuri, Indivar
Music:	Ganesh
Camera:	D.K. Dhuri
Cast:	Biswajeet, Mumtaz, Shatrughan Sinha, Junior Mehmood, Sujit Kumar, Faryal, Raj Mehra, Durga Khote, Madhumati, Lata Sinha, Kamal Mehra, Ram Avtar, Tun Tun, Anil Dutt, Neelam, Kirti Kumar

Radha, a village tanga driver (Mumtaz) saves the rich and pregnant Meeta (Faryal) from suicide. As a favour, Radha agrees to pretend to be Meeta and to visit the relatives Meeta has not seen since childhood. Meanwhile, Meeta goes in search of her missing husband Vinod Kumar (Sujit Kumar). Ma (Durga Khote) is impressed that 'Meeta' has remained so Indian in spite of her ten years of study abroad. Her own son Hari (Biswajeet) who lived abroad suffers from alcoholism and shows a disdain for overseeing the family's tea factory. Under Radha's influence he reforms, and the two fall in love.

raampur ka lakshman

Year:	1972 (Colour)
Producer:	A.A. Nadiadwala
Story & Screenplay:	K.A. Narayan
Script Supervision:	Prayag Raj
Dialogue:	K.B. Pathak
Lyrics:	Majrooh Sultanpuri
Music:	R.D. Burman
Camera:	Sudhin Mazumdar
Cast:	Randhir Kapoor, Rekha, Shatrughan Sinha, Padma Khanna, Sulochana, Faryal, Roopesh

Kumar, Manmohan Krishna, Randhir, Raj Mehra, Tiwari, Keshav Rana, Ranjeet, Shyam Kumar, Viju Khote, Rajan Kapoor, Kirti Kumar, Master Ratan, Master Chickko, Ramesh Deo

A train accident separates a family. The eldest son is caught by a thief and taught to steal. The mother is believed dead. The father and second son Lakshman begin a new life in Raampur. Years later, Lakshman's friend Prakash takes a job in the city where he is framed for murder. Lakshman (Randhir Kapoor) goes to his aid. There Lakshman falls in love with Rekha (Rekha), who is already being courted by Kumar (Shatrughan Sinha), Lakshman's lost brother, in appearance, a rich and respectable businessman.

bhai ho to aisa

Year: 1972 (Colour)
Producer: A.K. Nadiadwala
Story & Screenplay: K.B. Pathak
Dialogues: Prayag Raj
Lyrics: Sahir Ludhianvi
Music: Sonik-Omi
Camera: N.V. Srinivas
Special Effects: Babubhai Mistry
Cast: Jeetendra, Hema Malini, Shatrughan Sinha, Indrani Mukherjee, Jeevan, Jayshree T., Bipin Gupta, Ranjeet, Sapru, Pravin Paul, Bela Bose, Jankidas, Tiwari, Viju Khote, Bobby, Jagdeep

Thakur Ram Singh (Shatrughan Sinha), the corrupt older brother of a land-owning family, spends his time drinking in a courtesan's palace while his wife (Indrani Mukherjee), his younger brother Bharat (Jeetendra) and his father pray in the family temple. At the father's death, Ram hopes to force the submissive Bharat to sign over the property to him. Roopa (Hema Malini), the priest's daughter, refuses to marry Bharat if he cannot stand up to tyranny. Bharat then fakes his own death and pretends to be the dacoit Mangal Singh in order to gain the upper hand over his brother.

aa gale lag jaa

Year:	1973 (Colour)
Producer:	A.K. Nadiadwala
Story:	J.M. Desai
Screenplay:	Prayag Raj
Dialogues:	K.B. Pathak
Lyrics:	Sahir Ludhianvi
Music:	R.D. Burman
Choreography:	Kamal
Fights:	Ravi Khanna
Camera:	Peter Pereira
Cast:	Shashi Kapoor, Sharmila Tagore, Shatrughan Sinha, Master Tito, Om Prakash, Shobha Khote, Jagdeep, Shaantaanu, Jagirdar, Sulochana, Ruhee, Jilani, Usha Chowdhery,

Prem (Shashi Kapoor), a poor romantic skating champion, falls hopelessly in love with Preeti (Sharmila Tagore), a beautiful, rich medical student. Prem wins Preeti's heart— and her body—but the couple are soon separated by Preeti's class-conscious father (Om Prakash). Preeti is then hurriedly engaged to Amar (Shatrughan Sinha), a medical student about to begin his studies abroad. In his absence, she gives birth to a boy who she is told was stillborn. Prem convinces Preeti's father to allow him to adopt the child. Six years later, Dr. Amar, now returned and soon to be married to Preeti, will treat the polio-stricken child Rahul (Master Tito).

roti

Year:	1974 (Colour)
Producer:	Rajni Desai
Associate Producer:	K.K. Talwar
Story:	J.M. Desai
Screenplay:	Prayag Raj, K.B. Pathak
Dialogue:	Akhtar Ul Iman, Kadar Khan
Lyrics:	Anand Bakshi
Music:	Laxmikant Pyarelal
Camera:	K. Vaikunth
Special Effects:	Babubhai Mistry

Cast:	Rajesh Khanna, Mumtaz, Nirupa Roy, Sujit Kumar, Jeevan, Jagdeep, Om Prakash, Pinchoo Kapoor, Jagdish Raj, Paintal, Praveen Paul, Master Ripple, Viju Khote, Madhu Mandhare, Master Ravi, Avinash, Shyam Kumar, Master Tito, Dogs: Hero and Frankie, special appearances: Vijay Arora, Jeetendra, Asrani

Little Mangal (Master Tito) is orphaned and then adopted by a rich gangster (Pinchoo Kapoor) who raises the boy to be a daring smuggler (Rajesh Khanna). After a prison break, Mangal is believed dead. Chance leads him to a Kashmiri village where a blind old couple (Nirupa Roy and Om Prakash) take him in. Bijli (Mumtaz), a tough, loud, bidi-smoking girl soon gives him her heart. Mangal dreams of making a new life for them both, but Bijli dies at the hands of the gangster boss while Mangal dies by her side, shot by the police.

chacha bhatija

Year:	1977 (Colour)
Producer:	Baldev Pushkarna, M.M. Malhotra
Story:	Prayag Raj
Screenplay & Dialogue:	Salim-Javed
Lyrics:	Anand Bakshi
Music:	Laxmikant Pyarelal
Camera:	V. Durga Prasad
Dance:	Kamal, P.L. Raj, Robert
Cast:	Dharmendra, Hema Malini, Randhir Kapoor, Yogita Bali, Rehman, Anwar Hussain, Indrani Mukherjee, Jeevan, Roopesh Kumar, Sonia Sahani, Dev Kumar, Durga Khote, Satyajit, Tun Tun, Sunder, Bhagwan, Hercules, Kesto Mukherjee

In seeming answer to Seeta's (Indrani Mukherjee) prayers for a baby, Sonia (Sonia Sahani) gives her her illegitimate child, then blackmails Seeta, makes Seeta's husband disown her, marries the husband in order to raise her own child, and chases the husband's younger brother Shankar from the house. Seeta learns that she is pregnant. Her grown son Sundar (Randhir Kapoor) falls in love with Pinky (Yogita Bali) whose affections are disputed by Sonia's son. The grown Shankar (Dharmendra) is a black market cinema ticket dealer in love with Mala, a local barmaid (Hema Malini). Shankar befriends Sundar and then realizes when he sees his *bhabhi* (sister-in-law) that he and Sundar are uncle and nephew. Together they mount a plot to oust the usurping Sonia and her son and to reunite the family.

parvarish

Year:	1977 (Colour)
Producer:	A.A. Nadiadwala
Story idea:	Mrs. J.M. Desai
Scenario:	K.K. Shukla
Screenplay:	Prayag Raj
Dialogue:	Kadar Khan
Lyrics:	Majrooh Sultanpuri
Music:	Laxmikant Pyarelal
Camera:	Sudhin Mazumdar
Dance:	Kamal
Cast:	Shammi Kapoor, Amitabh Bachchan, Vinod Khanna, Neetu Singh, Shabana Azmi, Kadar Khan, Amjad Khan, Dev Kumar, Indrani Mukherjee, Heena Kauser, Master Ratan, Master Tito, Chand Usmani, Shaikh, Bhushan Tiwari, Viju Khote, Tom Alter, Yusaf, Meena, Baby Deepa, Baby Shalu, Dilip, Mulchand, Ekram Kashmiri, Shyam Varma

Police officer (Shammi Kapoor) sends Mangal Singh (Amjad Khan) to prison. Mangal's dying wife begs the officer to take her newborn son with him, that the child may never fall under her evil husband's influence. The officer and his wife (Indrani Mukherjee) accept the infant Amit (later Amitabh Bachchan) and raise him as a brother to their own son Kishan (later Vinod Khanna). Amit, the dacoit's son, grows into an upright police officer while Kishan, the police officer's son, turns to a life of crime. Two pickpocketing sisters (Neetu Singh and Shabana Azmi) steal their way into the brothers' family. A glimpse of Mangal Singh rekindles the sisters' desire for revenge against the man who killed their parents years before. Amit, meanwhile, discovers

Kishan's ties with the underworld. Amit refuses to allow love for his brother to deter him from duty. Not a moment too early, Kishan realizes his mistake, repents, and joins his true father and adopted brother to track down Mangal.

dharam-veer

Year:	1977 (Colour)
Producer:	Subhash Desai
Story ideas:	Mrs. J.M. Desai, Mrs. Pushpa Sharma
Screenplay:	Prayag Raj
Script:	K.B. Pathak
Dialogue:	Kadar Khan
Lyrics:	Anand Bakshi, Vithalbhai Patel
Music:	Laxmikant Pyarelal
Camera:	N.V. Srinivas
Dance:	Kamal
Cast:	Dharmendra, Jeetendra, Zeenat Aman, Neetu Singh, Indrani Mukherjee, Pran, Jeevan, Ranjeet, Sujit Kumar, Dev Kumar, Chand Usmani, Azad, Hercules, Sapru, B.M. Vyas, Neelam, Wonder Bird Sheroo, Pradeep Kumar

The poor but valorous hunter Joala (Pran) marries the princess Meenakshi (Indrani Mukherjee) alone and before God; the couple spend only one night together. The twin sons of that union, Dharam (Dharmendra) and Veer (Jeetendra), though separated at birth, grow up as best friends. Meenakshi's scheming brother (Jeevan) wants to eliminate his sister and to put his own son (Ranjeet) on the throne. Twenty years later, Dharam falls in love with the haughty princess Pahlavi (Zeenat Aman). Veer wins the heart of a gypsy girl named Roopa (Neetu Singh). The two friends are made into bitter enemies before they learn they are brothers and join forces against their plotting uncle and his company of sailing brigands. Meenakshi, now queen mother, is wounded. Joala dies saving her. The wicked uncle, too, dies, as predicted by an astrologer, at the hands of his nephew.

amar akbar anthony

Year:	1977 (Colour)

Producer:	Manmohan Desai
Story:	Mrs. J.M. Desai
Screenplay:	Prayag Raj
Scenario:	K.K. Shukla
Dialogue:	Kadar Khan
Lyrics:	Anand Bakshi
Music:	Laxmikant Pyarelal
Camera:	Peter Pereira
Dance:	Kamal
Cast:	Vinod Khanna, Rishi Kapoor, Amitabh Bachchan, Neetu Singh, Shabana Azmi, Parveen Babi, Nirupa Roy, Jeevan, Pran, Mukri, Yusuf, Hercules, Nasir Hussain, Protima Devi, Master Ravi, Master Bittu, Baby Shabia, Madhumati, Nadira, Helen, Ranjeet

See Chapter 2 devoted to the film.

suhaag

Year:	1979 (Colour)
Producer:	Prakash Trehan and Subhash Sharma
Story idea:	Late Mrs. J.M. Desai
Story:	Prayag Raj
Screenplay:	K.K. Shukla
Dialogue:	Kadar Khan
Lyrics:	Anand Bakshi
Music:	Laxmikant Pyarelal
Camera:	V. Durga Prashad
Dance:	Kamal and Suresh Bhatt
Cast:	Shashi Kapoor, Amitabh Bachchan, Rekha, Parveen Babi, Nirupa Roy, Amjad Khan, Ranjeet, Kadar Khan, Jeevan, Jagdish Raj, Hercules, Komila Wirk, Krishan Dhawan

At the opening of *Suhaag* Durga (Nirupa Roy) bears twin sons, but the corrupt Vikram Singh (Amjad Khan) refuses to acknowledge his children and banishes all three. In the city one of Durga's sons is stolen, sold to a beggar chief (Jeevan). As an adult Amit (Amitabh Bachchan) loves alcohol, the goddess Durga and Basanti (Rekha), a dancing girl in a nearby courtesan parlour. The other son, Kishan, fed on milk and his mother's love, becomes a respectable policeman (Shashi Kapoor). In the course of his duty, Kishan meets Anu (Parveen Babi). The two young women, Anu and Basanti, it soon transpires, are sisters. Kishan and Amit become friends and when Kishan is blinded by the now notorious gangster Vikram Singh, Amit follows Kishan's advice and joins the police force in order to give chase to the man he cannot guess is his own father. After learning that they are brothers, Amit and Kishan bravely save their father's life. He in turn finally recognizes his wife and sons and gives his eyes to the blinded Kishan.

naseeb

Year: 1981 (Colour)
Producer: Manmohan Desai
Story idea: Late Smt. J.M. Desai
Story: Prayag Raj
Screenplay: K.K. Shukla
Scenario: K.B. Pathak
Dialogue: Kadar Khan
Lyrics: Anand Bakshi
Music: Laxmikant Pyarelal
Camera: Jal Mistry
Dance: Kamal
Cast: Amitabh Bachchan, Rishi Kapoor, Shatrughan Sinha, Hema Malini, Kim, Reena Roy, Amjad Khan, Prem Chopra, Kadar Khan, Shakti Kapoor, Pran, Jeevan, Shobha Khote, Amrish Puri, Mukri, Yusuf Khan, Lalita Pawar, Dulari, Jagdish Raj, Meena Rai, Ekram, Abbas Muntajir

A winning lottery ticket leads to deadly enmity among four friends. Namdev (Pran) is framed for murder and then apparently killed. Ms. Gomes (Lalita Pawar) raises his two sons John and Sunny along with her daughter Julie. The adult John Jani Janardhan (Amitabh Bachchan) becomes a waiter at the 5-star restaurant that Raghu (Kadar Khan) and Damu (Amjad Khan) have opened with the lottery money. John boxes after hours to put his brother Sunny (Rishi Kapoor) through school. Damu's son Vicki (Shatrughan Sinha) has remained John's best friend. After many trials, John, Sunny and Vicki find love with Miss Asha (Hema Malini) Kim (Kim) and Julie (Reena Roy). Namdev returns to India, where he joins his sons and Vicki in a final fight, defeating the treacherous Raghu and international criminal Don (Amrish Puri) in a burning revolving restaurant.

desh premee

Year:	1982 (Colour)
Producer:	Subhash Desai
Story:	Prayag Raj
Screenplay:	K.B. Pathak
Dialogue:	Kadar Khan
Lyrics:	Anand Bakshi
Music:	Laxmikant Pyarelal
Camera:	Peter Pereira
Dance:	Kamal, P. L. Raj
Cast:	Amitabh Bachchan (in a double role), Hema Malini, Sharmila Tagore, Navin Nischol, Parveen Babi, Shammi Kapoor, Uttam Kumar, Premnath, Parikshat Sahani, Kadar Khan, Prem Chopra, Amjad Khan, Jeevan

See Chapter 10: Serious Undertones
Self Sacrificing or Self-Seeking

coolie

Year:	1983 (Colour)
Producer:	Ketan M. Desai Desai
Executive Producer:	Manmohan Desai
Director:	Prayag Raj and Manmohan Desai
Story:	Prayag Raj
Additional Story:	Pushpa Raj Sharma
Screenplay:	K.K. Shukla
Dialogue:	Kadar Khan
Lyrics:	Anand Bakshi
Music:	Laxmikant Pyarelal
Camera:	Peter Pereira
Dance:	Kamal

Cast: Amitabh Bachchan, Waheeda Rehman, Rishi Kapoor, Rati Agnihotri, Shoma Anand, Suresh Oberoi, Kadar Khan, Om Shivpuri, Satyan Kappu, Nilu Phule, Goga, Puneet Issar, Mukri, Shobha Khote, Kishan Dhawan, Ashalata, Tun Tun, Sajjan, Sheik, Vilas Rakte, C.S. Dubey, Sulochana Monkar, Prem Sagar, Sunil Dhawan, Master Ravi, Master Nadeem, Baby Shabana, Baby Sadia, Amrish Puri, Chandrashekhar

See Chapter 3 devoted to the film.

mard

Year:	1985 (Colour)
Producer:	Manmohan Desai
Executive Producer:	Ketan M. Desai
Director:	Manmohan Desai
Co-directors:	Anil Nagrath and Pammy Varma
Story:	Prayag Raj
Additional Story:	Pushpa Raj Sharma
Screenplay:	K.K. Shukla
Dialogue:	Inder Raj Anand
Additional Dialogue:	Anil Nagrath and Sohel Don
Lyrics:	Rajinder Krishen, Prayag Raj, Indivar
Music:	Anu Malik
Camera:	Peter Pereira
Dance:	Kamal
Cast:	Amitabh Bachchan, Amrita Singh, Nirupa Roy, Dara Singh, Prem Chopra, Goga Kapoor, Kamal Kapoor, Bob Christo, Manek, Satyan Kappu, Seema Deo, Helena, Dan Dhanoa, Kirti Kumar, Christopher, Joginder, Wonder Dog Moti

India is under the British yoke. When the people protest General Dyer's (Kamal Kapoor) looting of the country's treasures, they are massacred. Raja Azaad Singh (Dara Singh) heroically impedes the British theft. Azaad Singh's wife Durga (Nirupa Roy) bears a son; Azaad Singh carves the name *Mard* (man) on the baby's chest. The

Anglo-Indian doctor Hari (Prem Chopra) helps the British to capture Azaad Singh and to dispossess him of his kingdom. In the resulting turmoil, Durga is separated from her baby and finds herself mute. The child is adopted by a kindly couple. Azaad Singh is sentenced to life in prison. The British award Doctor Hari a castle and a lucrative position in return for his services.

Twenty years later the doctor's spoiled daughter Ruby (Amrita Singh) and Raju 'tangewala'—Mard—(Amitabh Bachchan) fall in love, thus angering Ruby's father's, whose choice for her is Danny (Dan Dhanoa), General Dyer's son. In Danny's slave labour camp Durga and her husband are reunited. Raju and his father must battle the villains in order to liberate all from the camp.

gangaa jamunaa saraswathi

Year: 1988 (Colour)
Producer: S. Raamanathan
Director: Manmohan Desai
Screenplay: K.K. Shukla
Dialogue: Kadar Khan
Lyrics: Prayag Raj, Indivar
Music: Anu Malik
Cast: Amitabh Bachchan, Mithun Chakraborty, Jaya Pradha, Meenakshi Seshadri, Nirupa Roy, Amrish Puri

Thakur Hansraj (Amrish Puri) is a jealous brother and uncle who renders his sister (Nirupa Roy) a widow and takes control of her property. Young Gangaa vows revenge. An adult, Gangaa (Amitabh Bachchan) rides his red truck to the rescue of the dancing girl Saraswathi (Jaya Pradha), who falls in love with Gangaa, who, in turn, falls in love with Jamunaa (Meenakshi Seshadri). Meanwhile, Shankar Qawal (Mithun Chakraborty) is smitten by Jamunaa, not realizing that she is the same woman that his friend Gangaa loves. Jamunaa, pregnant with Gangaa's child, is rejected by her community but befriended by Saraswathi who delivers the baby. Gangaa, Jamunaa and baby Munna are briefly reunited before a bomb planted on a bridge sends the family into the river below. Gangaa saves Munna but believes his wife dead. Shankar finds Jamunaa as she washes ashore, amnesiac.

Just as she is ready to marry Shankar, her memory returns. A final showdown with Thakur sees Gangaa suspended above a pit of crocodiles. The cobra that Gangaa has earlier protected comes to his rescue. Shankar and Saraswathi die sacrificing their lives for Jamunaa and Gangaa who are reunited.

bibliography

The Actor's Book of Movie Monologues, (edited by Smith, Marisa and Schewel, Amy), Penguin Books, New York, 1986.

Aihara, Byron, Hindi popular 'Bollywood' cinema. http://bollywood501.com

Allen, Woody, *Four Films of Woody Allen: Annie Hall, Interiors, Manhattan, Stardust Memories*, Random House, New York, 1977.

Amar Chitra Katha (series), published by Mirchandani, H.G., for India Book House Education Trust, Bombay.

A Treasury of Asian Literature, (edited by Yohannan, John D.), Mentor Books, New York, 1961.

L'avventurose storie del cinema indiano (2 volumes), (Collana diretta da Lino Micciché, Cinemasia 85/Pesaro), Marsilio Editori, Venice, 1985.

Bahadur, Satish, 'Aesthetics: From Traditional Iconography to Contemporary Kitsch,' *Indian Cinema Superbazaar*, (edited by Vasudev, Aruna and Lenglet, Philippe), Vikas Publishing House Pvt. Ltd.., New Delhi, 1983.

Banerjee, Shampa, *Profiles: Five Film-makers from India: V. Shantaram, Raj Kapoor, Mrinal Sen, Guru Dutt, Ritwik Ghatak*, Festival of India U.S.A., Directorate of Film Festivals, National Film Development Corporation Limited, New Delhi, 1985-1986.

Barnouw, Erik and Krishnaswamy, S., *Indian Film*, Oxford University Press, New York, 1980.

Bhatia, Vanraj, interviewed by Ram Mohan, 'The Rise of the Indian Film Song,' *Cinema Vision India*, Vol. 1, No. 4, Bombay, 1980.

Chopra, Anupama, *Sholay, The Making of a Classic*, Penguin Books, New Delhi, 2000.

Chopra, Anupama, *Dilwale Dulhania Le Jayenge*, British Film Institute, London, 2002.

Chute, David, 'The Road to Bollywood,' *Film Comment Magazine (The Film Society of Lincoln Center)*, New York, May-June, 2002, p. 38.

Chute, David, 'The Family Business: No Matter Where You Look in Hindi Cinema, the Clan's the Thing,' *Film Comment*, New York, May 2002, pp. 45-47.

Cinema in India, (quarterly), Karanjia, B. K. (Founding Editor) and Chandran, Mangala, (Managing Editor), National Film Development Corporation Limited, Bombay, 1987-1990.

Cinema India-International, (quarterly), Ramachandran, T.M., (editor and publisher), Bombay, 1984-1988.

Cinema Vision, published by Siddharth Kak, Bombay, Vol. 1/4, Vol. 2/1.

Clarens, Carlos, *Crime Movies, from Griffith to the Godfather and Beyond*, W.W. Norton & Company, New York, 1980.

Coolie ke Dialogue (Hindi), Bombay, 1984.

Crawford, Travis, 'Bullets Over Bombay,' *Film Comment*, New York, May 2002, pp. 53-55.

Das Gupta, Chidananda, *The Painted Face, Studies in India's Popular Cinema*, Roli Books Pvt. Ltd., New Delhi, 1991.

———, *Talking about Films*, Orient Longman Limited, New Delhi, 1981.

Deleury, Guy, *Le modèle indou*, Hachette, Paris, 1979.

Derné, Steve, *Movies, Masculinity, and Modernity, An Ethnography of Men's Filmgoing in India*, Greenwood Press, Westport, Connecticut, 2000.

Dwyer, Rachel, *Yash Chopra*, BFI Publishing, London, 2002.

Esslin, Martin, *An Anatomy of Drama*, Temple Smith, London, 1976.

Haham, Connie, 'Salim-Javed's Special Contribution to Cinema,' *Screen* (India), 6 April 1984.

———, 'In Quest of Heroism,' *Screen* (India), December 6, 1986.

Haun, Harry, *The Movie Quote Book*, Omnibus Press, London, 1981.

Indian Cinema 1980-1985, Film Utsav India, Festival of India, U.S.A., Directorate of Film Festivals, National Film Development Corporation Limited, New Delhi, 1985.

Le cinéma indien, (under the direction of Jean-Loup Passek, textes de Raphaël Bassan, Nasreen Munni Kabir, Henri Micciollo, Phillippe Parrain, Jean-Loup Passek, Henri Stern, et Paul Willerman), Centre Georges Pompidou, L'Equerre, Paris, 1983.

L'Inde, séduction et tumulte, (directed by Cruse, Denys), Autrement, Paris, 1985.

Jacobs, Lewis, *Movies as Medium,* Farrar, Strauss and Giroux, New York, 1970

Kabir, Nasreen Munni, *Bollywood: The Indian Cinema Story,* Channel 4 / Pan MacMillan, London, 2001.

———, *Guru Dutt, A Life in Cinema,* Oxford University Press, Delhi, 1996.

———, (director) 'The Miracle Man: Manmohan Desai,' one programme in Channel 4's *Movie Mahal* series, Hyphen Films,1987.

———, 'Playback Time, A Brief History of Bollywood Film Songs,' *Film Comment,* New York, May 2002, pp. 41-43.

———, *Talking Films: Conversations on Hindi Cinema with Javed Akhtar,* Oxford University Press, New Delhi, 1999.

Kakar, Sudhir, 'The Cinema as Collective Fantasy' *Indian Cinema Superbazaar,* (edited by Vasudev, Aruna and Lenglet, Philippe), Vikas Publishing House PVT LTD., New Delhi, 1983.

Kazmi, Nikhat, *Ire in the Soul, Bollywood's Angry Years,* Harper Collins Publishers India, 1996.

Kingwell, Mark http://www.artsandopinion.com/2003_v2_n2/kingwell.htm (retrieved May 12, 2004)

Kumar, Kanti, 'The Trend of Violence on the Indian Screen & Its Influence on Children,' September1999, http://www.bitscape.info/research/screen_3p.htm (retrieved February 23, 2004)

Lutgendorf, Philip, 'Philip's Fil-ums Notes on Indian Popular Cinema,' http://www.uiowa.edu/~incinema/

Mast, Gerald, *The Comic Mind: Comedy and the Movies,* Bobbs-Merrill, New York, 1973.

Manushi, A Journal about Women and Society, New Delhi, 1983-1984.

Medved, Michael, *Hollywood vs. America, Popular Culture and the War on Traditional Values,* Harper Collins Publishers, New York, 1992.

Mohan, Ram, 'Looking for the Special Effects Man in the Small Type,' *Cinema in India,* January-March 1989.

Naseeb ke Dialogue aur Geet (Hindi) (condensed), Bharat Prakashan, Bombay.

Nizami, (translated and edited by Dr. Gelpke in collaboration with Mattin, E. & Hill, G.), *The Story of Layla and Majnun*, Shambhala, Boulder, Colorado, 1978.

Parrain, P., *Regards sur le cinéma indien*, Editions du cerf, Paris, 1969.

Rangacharya, Adya, *The Indian Theatre*, National Book Trust, India, New Delhi, 1980.

Rao, Maithili, 'How to Read a Hindi Film and Why,' *Film Comment*, New York, May 2002, pp. 37-40.

Salinger, J.D., *The Catcher in the Rye*, Penguin Books Ltd., Harmondsworth, Middlesex, England, 1951.

The Secret Politics of Our Desires: Innocence, Culpability and Indian Popular Cinema, edited by Ashis Nandy, Oxford University Press, Delhi, 1998.

Shaw, Idries, *The Exploits of the Incomparable Mulla Nasrudin*, Picador, London, 1973.

Simpson, John, *News from No Man's Land: Reporting the World*, Pan Macmillan Ltd., London, 2002.

Les stars du cinéma indien, Kabir, Nasreen Munni (editor), Centre Georges Pompidou et le Centre National de la Cinématographie, Paris, 1985.

Suhaag Sachitr, Geet aur Dialogue (Hindi), Narayan and Co. Booksellers, Patna.

Thomas, Rosie, 'Melodrama and the Negotiation of Morality in Mainstream Hindi Film,' *Consuming Modernity*, ed. Carol A. Breckenridge, University of Minnesota Press, Minneapolis,1995, pp. 157-182.

———, 'Indian Cinema: Pleasures and Popularity,' *Screen* 26:3-4 Fall/Winter 1985, pp. 116-131.

Tully, Mark and Masani, Zareer, *From Raj to Rajiv, 40 Years of Indian Independence*, BBC Books, London, 1988.

Valicha, Kishore, 'Why are popular films popular?' *Cinema in India* - Vol. 3, No. 2, April - June 1989. (extracted from the chapter 'The Indian Scenario' from the book *The Moving Image: A Study of Indian Cinema* , Orient Longman Limited, New Delhi, 1988.

Villain, Dominique, *L'oeil à la caméra*, Cahiers du cinéma/Editions de l'Etoile, Paris, 1984.